DEMOCRATIC TRANSITIONS IN EAST AFRICA

Democratic Transitions in East Africa

Edited by

PAUL J. KAISER
University of Pennsylvania

F. WAFULA OKUMU
African Union

ASHGATE

© Paul J. Kaiser and F. Wafula Okumu 2004

All rights reserved. No part of this publication may be reproduced, stored in a retrieval system, or transmitted in any form or by any means, electronic, mechanical, photocopying, recording or otherwise without the prior permission of the publisher.

Paul J. Kaiser and F. Wafula Okumu hereby assert their moral right to be identified as the editors of the work in accordance with the Copyright, Designs and Patents Act, 1988.

Published by
Ashgate Publishing Limited
Gower House
Croft Road
Aldershot
Hants GU11 3HR
England

Ashgate Publishing Company
Suite 420
101 Cherry Street
Burlington, VT 05401-4405
USA

Ashgate website: http://www.ashgate.com

British Library Cataloguing in Publication Data
Democratic transitions in East Africa
1. Democracy - Kenya 2. Democracy - Tanzania 3. Democracy - Uganda 4. Kenya - Politics and government - 1978-2002
5. Kenya - Politics and government - 2002- 6. Tanzania - Politics and government - 1964- 7. Uganda - Politics and government - 1979-
I. Kaiser, Paul J. II. Okumu, F. Wafula
320.9'676

Library of Congress Cataloging-in-Publication Data
Democratic transitions in East Africa / by Paul J. Kaiser and F. Wafula Okumu.
p. cm.
Includes bibliographical references and index.
ISBN 0-7546-4278-X
1. Democratization--Africa, East. 2. Africa, East--Politics and government. I. Kaiser, Paul J. II. Okumu, F. Wafula.

JQ2945.A58D46 2004
320.9676--dc22 2004020005

ISBN 0 7546 4278 X

Printed and bound by Athenaeum Press, Ltd.,
Gateshead, Tyne & Wear.

Contents

List of Charts and Tables

List of Contributors

Stephen F. Burgess is Deputy Chair and Professor in the Department of Strategy and International Security, U.S. Air War College, and an Associate of the U.S. Air Force Counter-Proliferation Center (CPC). Since 1999, he has taught international security studies, international organizations and peace operations, and African politics and security. His three books are *Smallholders and Political Voice in Zimbabwe, The United Nations under Boutros Boutros-Ghali, 1992-97,* and *South Africa's Weapons of Mass Destruction* (forthcoming with Helen Purkitt). Burgess and Purkitt produced a monograph, *The Rollback of the South African Chemical and Biological Warfare Program,* which has been featured on *60 Minutes,* in *The New York Times,* and *The Washington Post.* Besides his work on African political economy and security, Burgess is also conducting research on South Asian security. Before 1999, Dr. Burgess was a faculty member at Vanderbilt University, the University of Zambia, and Hofstra University. He completed his Ph.D. at Michigan State University and was a Fulbright-Hays fellow at the University of Zimbabwe.

Thomas Burgess is Assistant Professor of History at Hampton University. His research focuses on the history of the Zanzibari Revolution. Dr. Burgess is presently preparing two book-length manuscripts for publication: *Imagined Generations: Youth, Discipline and Revolution in Zanzibar, 1950-80*, and *Walk on Two Legs: A Memoir of the Zanzibari Revolution* (editor). His articles have appeared in several edited volumes, as well as *Africa Today* and *International Journal of African Historical Studies.*

Earl Conteh-Morgan is Professor of International Studies at the University of South Florida. Among other books, he is the author of *Democratization in Africa: The Theory and Dynamics of Political Transitions*, and most recently *Collective Political Violence: An Introduction to the Theories and Cases of Violent Conflicts.* He has also published articles in *Armed Forces & Society, Journal of Social Philosophy, Journal of African Policy Studies,* and *International Journal of Peace Studies.* Dr. Conteh-Morgan is currently working on a project that explores the interface between globalization and human security from a constructivist perspective.

Bruce Heilman is Lecturer in the Department of Political Science and Public Administration at the University of Dar es Salaam. He has extensive experience with elections, working for the International Foundation for Electoral Systems to observe the 1995 elections in Zanzibar and the Union of Tanzania. For the 2000 Tanzanian general elections, he served as TEMCO's Political Analyst and he also worked with TEMCO on the 2003 by-elections. He has published articles on mainland Tanzania and Zanzibar electoral politics in *Africa Today* and *Third World Quarterly*, among others.

Paul J. Kaiser is Associate Director of the African Studies Center and Adjunct Associate Professor of Political Science at the University of Pennsylvania. In addition to co-editing special issues of *Africa Today* ("Citizenship in Africa") and the *Journal of Asian and African Studies* ("Phases of Conflict in Africa"), he has also published a wide array of articles on politics in East and Central Africa in the *Journal of Modern African Studies*, the *African Studies Review*, *Africa Today*, and *Third World Quarterly*, among others. He is currently working on a book-length biography on Julius Nyerere.

Ryan E. Letourneau is a 2002 graduate of the Thomas Jefferson Program in Public Policy at The College of William and Mary. He completed his undergraduate degree at Florida State University and presently works for the U.S. government.

Dean E. McHenry, Jr. is Professor of Political Science in the Department of Politics and Policy at Claremont Graduate University. After completing his undergraduate work at Oberlin College (1961), he went to East Africa to participate in the Teachers for East Africa Program. He attended Makerere University to earn a Diploma in Education, prior to being posted to Mpwapwa Secondary School in Tanzania. On return to the U.S., he received his M.A. (1966) and Ph.D. (1971) from Indiana University. He taught at the University of Dar es Salaam in 1970/71, 1974/76, and 1986, the latter as a Fulbright Lecturer. In addition to many articles on Tanzania, he has published *Tanzania's Ujamaa Villages, The Implementation of a Rural Development Strategy* (Berkeley: Institute of International Studies, University of California, 1979), and *Limited Choices, The Political Struggle for Socialism in Tanzania* (Boulder: Lynne Rienner, 1994). In the U.S., he has taught at the University of Illinois, Brown University and Claremont Graduate University. He was the first president of the Tanzania Studies Association.

Stephen N. Ndegwa is Associate Professor of Government at The College of William and Mary and a Public Sector Governance Specialist at The World Bank. He is the author of *The Two Faces of Civil Society* and several publications on African politics, democracy, citizenship, and ethnicity that have appeared in journals such as the *American Political Science Review*, *African Studies Review* and *Africa Today*. His edited works include *The Uncertain Promise of Southern Africa* (with York Bradshaw) and *A Decade of Democracy in Africa*.

Laurean Ndumbaro is a Senior Lecturer in the Department of Political Science and Public Administration at the University of Dar es Salaam where he teaches courses on politics and public administration. He was the leader of TEMCO's observer delegation to Zanzibar for the 2000 general elections. His scholarly writings include a number of articles on Tanzanian political parties, electoral politics, democratic transitions, civil society, and corruption.

Samuel A. Nyanchoga obtained his Ph.D. in History from Kenyatta University in 2000 where he taught courses on World History, Southern, Eastern, and West African History. He also served as the National Vice Chair of the Kenyan-American Studies Association from 2000-2001. In 2001, he was a Fulbright Scholar at Boston University, focusing on American history. Dr. Nyanchoga has published a wide array of book chapters on Kenya, specifically focusing on political parties and the democratization process, the Asian question, and the history of agriculture in the western region of the country. He is currently conducting research on local African perspectives on colonialism and a comparison of the Kenyatta and Moi regimes.

F. Wafula Okumu is an Analyst at the Conflict Management Centre of the African Union. Before joining the A.U., he was an Academic Programme Associate in the Peace and Governance Programme at the United Nations University, and he held teaching posts at Chapman University, Mississippi University for Women and Prescott College. He has contributed to edited volumes on a variety of topics, including child soldiers in Africa, ethnic politics in Kenya, conflict in Africa, the African Union, and environmental challenges on the continent.

Joshua B. Rubongoya is Professor of Political Science at Roanoke College. A former journalist in Uganda, he has conducted research on democratic transitions, the women's movement, and ethnicity in Uganda. Dr. Rubongoya has published numerous book reviews and is currently working on a manuscript on political legitimacy and democratic transition in Uganda.

Acknowledgements

This collaborative effort began in the summer of 1998, when we were teaching at neighboring universities in rural Mississippi. Dissatisfied with existing research on the democratic transition processes in sub-Saharan Africa at the time, we decided to work together on this project. Given our particular experiences in East Africa, and recognizing the need to examine transitions in regional context, we decided to identify scholars interested in focusing on Kenya, Tanzania and Uganda. Each author was asked to examine a particular theme relevant to the transition process comparatively, providing a regional perspective on the democratic project in East Africa.

We would like to extend our thanks to all of the contributors to this volume, who remained committed to the project during our own personal transitions to new professional challenges beyond the confines of the "deep South". In lieu of listing everyone who assisted us in bringing closure to this endeavor, we would like to mention some of the institutions along the way that provided us with the physical space and intellectual environment to work: the Mississippi University for Women, Mississippi State University, Chapman University, the United Nations University, and the University of Pennsylvania. At Penn, we would like to offer our special thanks to Andrea Seligman for carefully (and repeatedly!) editing of the final manuscript, and Jay Sy for preparing the manuscript for the production process. Thanks also to our colleagues at Ashgate, who were supportive of the idea and agreed to publish the volume.

Paul J. Kaiser, Philadelphia, Pennsylvania
F. Wafula Okumu, Addis Ababa, Ethiopia

List of Abbreviations

4 Cs	Citizens' Coalition for Constitutional Change
ACFODE	Action for Development
ACK	Anglican Church of Kenya
AIDS	Acquired Immune Deficiency Syndrome
ANC	African National Congress
ASP	Afro-Shirazi Party
ASPYL	ASP Youth League
CCM	*Chama cha Mapinduzi*
CEC	Catholic Episcopal Conference
CHADEMA	*Chama cha Demokrasia na Maendeleo*
CMB	Coffee Marketing Board
CNU	Coalition for National Unity
COTU	Central Organization of Trade Unions
CRC	Constitutional Review Commission
CUF	Civic United Front (*Chama cha Wananchi*)
DANIDA	Danish International Development Agency
DP	Democratic Party
DRC	Democratic Republic of the Congo (formerly Zaire)
EAC	East African Community
ECA	Economic Commission for Africa
ERP	Economic Recovery Program
ESAF	Enhanced Structural Adjustment Facility
ESAP	Economic and Social Action Program
FAD	Foundation for African Development
FIDA	Federation for Women Lawyers
FORD	Forum for the Restoration of Democracy
FORD-A	Forum for the Restoration of Democracy-Asili
FORD-K	Forum for the Restoration of Democracy-Kenya
FORD-People	Forum for the Restoration of Democracy-People
FOWODE	Forum for Women in Democracy
FRELIMO	*Frente de Libertação de Moçambique*
GDP	Gross Domestic Product
GEMA	Gikuyu Embu Meru Association
GNP	Gross National Product
GNU	Government of National Unity
HIPC	Highly Indebted Poor Country
HRW	Human Rights Watch
IFES	International Foundation for Election Systems
IMF	International Monetary Fund
IPFC	Inter-Political Forces Committee

IPK	Islamic Party of Kenya
IPPG	Inter-Parliamentary Parties Group
KACA	Kenya Anti-Corruption Authority
KADU	Kenya African Democratic Union
KANU	Kenya African National Union
KCA	Kikuyu Central Association
KCGA	Kenya Coffee Growers Association
KMA	Kenya Manufacturers Association
KNC	Kenya National Congress
KNUT	Kenya National Union of Teachers
KPU	Kenya People's Union
KSC	Kenya Social Congress
KY	Kabaka Yekka Party
LDP	Liberal Democratic Party
LSK	Law Society of Kenya
MOU	Memorandum of Understanding
MP	Member of Parliament
NAC	National Alliance for Change
NAK	National Alliance [Party] of Kenya
NARC	National Rainbow Coalition
NAWOU	National Association of Women of Uganda
NCA	National Convention Assembly
NCCK	National Council of Churches of Kenya
NCCR	National Convention for Construction and Reform
NCCR-M	National Convention for Construction and Reform-Mageuzi
NCEC	National Convention Executive Committee
NCIM	National Council of Independent Monitors
NDP	National Democratic Party
NEC	National Elections Commission
NGO	Non-Governmental Organization
NLD	National League for Democracy
NLP	National Labor Party
NOCEM	National Organization for Civic Education and Elections Monitoring
NPK	National Party of Kenya
NRA	National Resistance Army
NRC	National Resistance Council
NRM	National Resistance Movement
NRM-O	National Resistance Movement Organization
OAU	Organization of African Unity
ODA	Official Development Assistance
OECD	Organization of Economic Cooperation and Development
OIC	Organization of Islamic Conference
PAC	Pan African Congress
PCEA	Presbyterian Church of East Africa
PICK	Party of Independent Candidates of Kenya

PJC	Peace and Justice Commission
POB	Political Organizations Bill
PONA	Popular National Party
PRGF	Poverty Reduction and Growth Facility
RC	Resistance Council
SAP	Structural Adjustment Program
SDP	Social Democratic Party
SIDA	Swedish International Development Cooperative Agency
SPLA	Sudan Peoples Liberation Army
TAA	Tanganyika African Association
TADEA	Tanzania Democratic Alliance Party
TAMWA	Tanzania Media Women Association
TANU	Tanganyika African National Union
TAZARA	Tanzania-Zambia Railway
TEMCO	Tanzania Elections Monitoring Committee
TGNP	Tanzania Gender Networking Program
TLP	Tanzania Labor Party
TLS	Tanganyika Law Society
TPP	Tanzania People's Party
TUFW	Tanzanian Union Federation of Workers
UAWL	Uganda Association of Women Lawyers
UDI	Unilateral Declaration of Independence
UDM	United Development Movement
UDP	United Democratic Party
UJCC	Uganda Joint Christian Council
UK	United Kingdom
UMD	Union for Multi-party Democracy in Tanzania
UMDF	Uganda Multilateral Debt Fund
UN	United Nations
UNDP	United Nations Development Program
UPC	Uganda Peoples Congress
UPDP	United People's Democratic Party
US	United States
USAID	United States Agency for International Development
USSR	Union of Soviet Socialist Republics
UTP	United Tanganyika Party
UWEONET	Uganda Women's Organization Network
UYD	Uganda Young Democrats
WB	World Bank
ZANLA	Zimbabwe African National Liberation Army
ZEC	Zanzibar Elections Commission
ZLSC	Zanzibar Legal Services Centre
ZNP	Zanzibar National Party
ZPPP	Zanzibar Pemba and People's Party

Chapter 1

The Challenges of Democratic Transition in East Africa

Paul J. Kaiser and F. Wafula Okumu

Genocide in Rwanda, massive floods of refugees and displaced people in the Horn of Africa, and violent civil wars in the West African countries of Sierra Leone and Liberia are testimonies to the tremendous cost to grassroots communities when the authority and legitimacy of national political systems and leaders are called into question. The transition to and consolidation of democracy represents one tangible strategy to restore authority and legitimacy of political rule, providing the peace and security necessary for political enfranchisement and economic opportunity. The essays in this volume represent an attempt to explore the factors that are crucial to the emergence of democratic political systems on the African continent, specifically focusing on the East African countries of Kenya, Tanzania, and Uganda.

The past decade has been a period of political transition for these East African countries. This transition has been influenced by local, national, and international factors that include the historical legacy of colonialism, the establishment of political parties/party systems, political leadership, constitutionalism, civil society, the economic reform process (with particular emphasis on the role of international financial institutions), the international community (particularly donor countries), and regime legitimacy. These factors have played different, yet instrumental roles in establishing and/or subverting an enabling environment for democracy to flourish, and they also serve as explanatory variables for understanding how and why there is sub-regional differentiation in the transition process. This edited volume highlights the political challenges facing Kenya, Tanzania, and Uganda during this crucial transition period, and it also provides insights that are applicable to other countries engaged in this process in Africa and beyond.

The Case of Kenya

For more than three decades, Kenya was heralded as a success story in a region rife with political instability and chaos. After over twenty years of authoritarian rule by the country's first President, Jomo Kenyatta, Vice President Daniel arap Moi assumed the presidency and he remained in power until December 2002. The country experienced relative stability until 1992, when multi-partyism was introduced. The Kenyan government eventually accepted the multi-party system after much prodding from local opposition forces and Western donors. President Moi's Kenya African National Union (KANU) government successfully manipulated this transition for a decade, with the incumbent president remaining in power for two consecutive elected terms despite pre-election, government-orchestrated regional violence, and opposition claims of repeated and systematic registration and electoral irregularities. The December 2002 election of National Rainbow Coalition (NARC) presidential candidate Mwai Kibaki heralds a new chapter in Kenya's protracted transition. However, it remains to be seen if this alternation of power will ultimately lead to a stable and predictable democratic environment.

The Case of Tanzania

After Tanganyika achieved its independence in 1961 (and subsequently merged with Zanzibar in 1964 to form Tanzania), President Julius Nyerere soon became disenchanted with the system that he inherited from the British. This led to the establishment of a political and economic order based on his personal vision of African socialism, or *ujamaa,* that was articulated in the 1967 Arusha Declaration. After approximately twenty years of Nyerere's African socialism, economic and political stagnation led elected successor President Ali Hassan Mwinyi to cautiously steer the country toward economic and political reform. Tightly managed by the ruling *Chama cha Mapinduzi* (CCM) party, Tanzania mainland and Zanzibar islands CCM presidential candidates won the relatively peaceful 1995 and 2000 elections amidst accusations by local organizations, opposition political parties, and a wide array of international observers, that the electoral processes were marred by a combination of coercion, organizational ineptitude, and planned electoral fraud. Contention was especially pronounced in Zanzibar, where the opposition Civic United Front (CUF) was defeated by CCM in 1995 and 2000 amidst heightened controversy and subsequent violence. With a tenuous political détente holding in Zanzibar, and unsuccessful attempts by opposition parties to form a coalition to contest against the CCM presidential nominee in 2005, it remains to be seen if the country can continue the gradual process of political liberalization.

The Case of Uganda

In January 1986, Yoweri Museveni and his National Resistance Army assumed control of Uganda's capital of Kampala after years of violent civil war. Shortly thereafter, Museveni declared himself president and then proceeded to develop a functioning political system from the carnage left behind by the corrupt and violent leaders Idi Amin, Milton Obote, and Tito Okello. In lieu of advocating multi-partyism, the National Resistance Movement (NRM) was created to carefully enfranchise urban and rural dwellers without fomenting ethnic divisions that were the hallmark of past administrations. The 1994 Constituent Assembly elections demonstrated local support for Museveni's plan, with NRM supporters capturing approximately two thirds of the seats. A new constitution was established shortly thereafter, with Museveni subsequently winning two consecutive "no-party" presidential elections and a referendum that controversially legitimized the "movement" system of government in the land-locked country. With the political landscape quickly changing in the country, the future of the movement experiment is in doubt, along with the relative political calm that the NRM has provided.

Definitions, Transitions and Endpoints

> We live in a democratic age. Through much of human history the danger to an individual's life, liberty and happiness came from the absolutism of monarchies, the dogma of churches, the terror of dictatorships, and the iron grip of totalitarianism. Dictators and a few straggling totalitarian regimes still persist, but increasingly they are anachronisms in a world of global markets, information, and media. There are no longer respectable alternatives to democracy, it is part of the fashionable attire of modernity. Thus the problem is *within* democracy [italics in original]. This makes them more difficult to handle, wrapped as they are in the mantle of legitimacy.[1]

The increasingly global demand that authoritarian governments initiate sustained transitions to multi-party democracy has tested the will and creativity of many incumbent African leaders wishing to remain in power. Across the continent, variations on the democratic ideal have proliferated. Democratic experiments have been labeled "pseudo,"[2] "virtual,"[3] "illiberal,"[4] "semi,"[5] and "embryonic,"[6] to name just a few. Regardless of the label created or normative assumptions employed, a transition is underway that is fundamentally altering the authoritarian structures developed by the first generation(s) of African leadership. After a brief discussion of the characteristics of this democratic transition process, we will provide an overview of the structure and content of this edited volume.

A political transition requires an "interval between one political regime and another ... delimited, on one side, by the launching of the process of dissolution of an authoritarian regime and, on the other, by the installation of some form of democracy (or) the return to some form of authoritarian rule."[7] This transition takes place when there is a genuine change in a political system and "not just in the individuals holding positions of political power." Change has to occur also "in the assumptions and methods of the political system, in how the system legislates, formulates, and implements policies, and in the ways in which individuals gain access to power."[8] Such a transition can be influenced by a number of factors. Among these are the duration and the methods of the incumbent authoritarian regime.[9]

A transition process "begins with an opening whereby the authoritarian regime is weakened and the possibility emerges for political change." An opening can be created by factors such as "protests, strikes, the death of the leader, conflict in the ruling bloc, economic crises, and international events." However, the progress of transition, once it is launched, is determined by "the strength and preferences of both the authoritarian incumbents and the opposition." The authoritarian regime can either support the transition process after getting "guarantees of protection or influence under the new government" or it "may refuse to exit." In the later scenario, the transition can only "succeed if the opposition is able to gain enough support" to obtain power through an electoral defeat or mass action.[10]

Since authoritarian incumbents have little interest in introducing political changes that undermine their dominance in the political system, they often initiate reform only "when they perceive that they have little choice but to attempt to channel social movement opposition into political parties … [or they] try to use the electoral arena as a means to manipulate the opposition." Authoritarian incumbents often prefer graduated reforms to single iterations; the aim is to "make only the minimum number of concessions necessary to ensure the opposition's continued participation without conceding anything more." Incumbent rulers also "divide and conquer the opposition" by "supporting artificial 'window dressing' opposition parties." Finally, they attempt to get "strikers, students, and other potentially disruptive trouble makers 'off the regime's back,' and out of the unpredictable realm of street demonstrations and picket lines and into the highly regulated realm of campaigns and elections."[11]

The initial stages of a democratic transition are deemed successful when a government "meets the minimal definition of democracy,"[12] in which the political system "supplies regular constitutional opportunities for changing the governing officials, and a social mechanism which permits the largest possible part of the population to influence major decisions by choosing among contenders for political office."[13] The democratic transition process is subsequently consolidated when democratic norms and institutions are strengthened and the new regime "does not have the perverse elements undermining (democracy's) basic characteristics."[14] This process should also provide "all the relevant political forces a chance to win from time to time," and make "even losing under democracy more attractive than losing under non-democratic alternatives."[15] Consolidation is further enhanced after a period "leading to a truly competitive and 'free and fair' election in which there is a genuine possibility of an alternation of government from an authoritarian incumbent regime, or remnants of such, to the opposition."[16] There needs to be a broad consensus representing a cross-section of society that democratic practice is the only acceptable type of rule, or "the only game in town."[17]

But how long does it take to complete a transition? Some have argued that the transition "from legalization of opposition parties to the holding of free and fair, direct elections for president or the national congress could last over 30 years,"[18] while others caution that transitions will fail if an incumbent authoritarian regime controls the liberalization process or strengthens its support coalition.[19]

The contributors to this volume have carefully charted this transition in East Africa by comparatively addressing key themes that have emerged in contemporary research on democracy on the continent.

Key Themes Under Investigation

Historical Context

There are a number of studies that have highlighted the democratic values and practices that characterized the pre-colonial period. Studies have been conducted on the mechanisms of traditional debate and consultation, systems of checks and balances, accountability, and popular inclusion in political decision-making.[20] In Thomas Burgess' chapter on the historical context of current democratic transitions underway in East Africa, he points out that although there were few parallels between traditional and Western models of popular democracy in the region, authority during the pre-colonial period was wielded with a degree of social responsibility and respect for the rule of law. There were also adequate mechanisms to check and balance power, even in so-called stateless and acephalous societies. Colonial rulers, however, profoundly altered these indigenous political institutions and practices.

The colonial states that were established in the region were inherently undemocratic since they restricted the practice of democratic values to the European community. Africans were subject to repressive and arbitrary rule that was deliberately practiced to assure that colonial control was efficient and cost-effective. Diamond, Lipset, and Linz note that the character of colonial rule "gravely disadvantaged" the development of democracy in Africa since competitive politics and popular participation among Africans was not allowed until the twilight of colonial rule.[21] Consequently, the democratic transitions in East Africa are reflective of the region's colonial experiences.

Political Parties

After a long period of single-party rule, the three East African countries under investigation are experimenting with various party systems. However, this effort is being complicated by a range of factors elucidated by Dean McHenry in his chapter on the relationship between political parties/party systems and democracy in East Africa. According to McHenry, unfolding events in Kenya, Tanzania and Uganda challenge many widely held assumptions about political parties, party systems, and democracy in general. The lack of any identifiable, "consistent relationship" between political parties/party systems and the level of democracy in East Africa offer valuable insights into the nature of democracy in the region and the factors that facilitate its successful consolidation.

National Leadership

As Joshua Rubongoya demonstrates in his chapter, the enthusiasm of East African political elites for political reform has often not been matched by a commitment to establishing full-fledged democracies. This national elite, which Shaw calls "state-centric factions,"[22] is mainly composed of high-ranking bureaucrats, a *comprador bourgeoisie* class, and military personnel, who have acquired immense wealth and political power through control of the state. Bratton points out that "the absence of a true *bourgeoisie* has blocked the emergence, not only of capitalism in Africa, but also of democracy." Due to the national elites' dependence "on the state for economic survival, they attach an inestimably high premium to capturing and maintaining state power."[23] Consequently, these elites have had a vested interest in limiting rather than promoting political changes that will usher in democratic practices. Rubongoya carefully examines how political leaders in East Africa have attempted to control and/or subvert the political transition process in order to remain in power.

Constitutionalism

Stephen Ndegwa and Ryan Letourneau argue for the importance of constitutional development to the democratic transition process in East Africa. Their chapter demonstrates that constitutions play an important role in establishing democracy since they proscribe the use of power for personal ends, and they prescribe procedures to safeguard against this possibility. In order to adopt a new (or revised) constitution based on these assumptions, there needs to be a national consensus on common national interests and goals, the need for constitutional reforms, and the procedures necessary to achieve these reforms. Without this understanding, constitutions lose their relevance and efficacy. Ndegwa and Letourneau contend that great strides have been made in the constitutional reform process, even if it is still a work in progress subject to the legacy of authoritarianism and exclusion documented by Thomas Burgess in chapter two.

Civil Society

Samuel Nyanchoga contends that even though there was a vibrant associational urban life during the period leading to independence, the voluntary associations that were formed to promote cultural identity and membership welfare were soon absorbed into the state. Some of these associations later transformed themselves or merged into political parties. Since the advent of multi-partyism in the 1990s, a second wave of civil society organizations emerged to promote political liberty, constitutional reform, human rights, and development.

Since the early 1990s, a large number of diverse and outspoken organizations, including church, women's, and human rights groups, have proliferated in East Africa. Their power has been enhanced by the financial support of foreign donors, which have chosen to invest in civil society in lieu of undependable governments. It is this sector that, due to weak opposition political parties, has assumed a leadership role in demanding political reform. Nyanchoga critically examines the impact of these organizations on the democratization process in East Africa by specifically addressing why civil society organizations have emerged as an important alternative to weak opposition political parties. While there is sub-regional differentiation among the three counties under investigation, Nyanchoga identifies the positive and negative roles that civil society organizations have played in East Africa's transition process.

The Donor Community

The chapters by Bruce Heilman/Lauren Ndumbaro and Stephen Burgess focus on two aspects of donor involvement in the region. For Heilman/Ndumbaro, North/South bilateral relations have impacted the political reform process, but these efforts have not been sustained or consistent. The authors conclude that while the donors have been able to strengthen pro-democratic forces through financial assistance and programs, there have also been unintended results, with many activists in opposition political parties and progressive civil society organizations viewing donors, and not the people of the region, as the guardians of the transition process.

Stephen Burgess' study specifically examines the impact of international financial institutions on the transition process. The author demonstrates that the divergent donor-recipient relations across the region, combined with the different perspectives on the relationship between the political and economic reform processes, defies generalizability and simplistic depictions of the relationship between structural economic reform and democracy.

Political Legitimacy

In the volume's final chapter, Earl Conteh-Morgan argues that the maintenance of state hegemony, the personalization of power, and the centralization of the executive branch have greatly handicapped the transition to democratic rule, thus calling into question the sustainability of the democratic project in all three countries. In order to facilitate democratic consolidation and sustainability in the region, he contends that responsible and progressive leadership, combined with an active and responsible civil society, are essential.

The Regional and Comparative Context

How Kenya, Tanzania, and Uganda succeed in further transforming themselves into democracies will have far-reaching implications for regional integration and development. To date, the transition from single-party to multi-party rule has proven to be difficult, contentious, and violent at times. Many East African advocates for change have been killed, jailed, or exiled for their pursuit of democracy in their respective countries, with others suffering from human and civil rights abuses. Despite these setbacks, the hope for a democratic future is now widespread throughout the region, and the few gains that have been achieved will not be easily reversed.

All three countries are seriously attempting to develop a regional common market that facilitates the free flow of goods and services, and some are advocating for greater political harmonization in the region. The hard lessons these countries learned from the collapsed East African Community have remained vivid throughout this recent regional integration process. During the first incarnation of the East African Community, success was hampered by differences in leadership personality, political ideology, and economic system. Even though pervasive corruption has hampered current regional economic liberalization efforts, Kenyan, Tanzanian, and Ugandan leaders have all indicated their desire to further integrate their economies based on free market ideals.

The regional integration process is also pressuring each country to engage in political reform efforts. When one country successfully moves forward in the political reform process, citizens of neighboring countries use this success as a reference point for their own quest for a more democratic order. This level of political interdependence is not new to the region. The instabilities that engulfed Uganda in the 1970s resulted in a 1978 Tanzanian invasion, while Kenya was turned into a haven for Ugandan refugees. After the December 1997 election of President Moi in Kenya, some opposition leaders protested the flawed elections and threatened to use violence if the results were not overturned. Uganda's President Museveni, who violently protested the 1981 election of Milton Obote of Uganda, flew to Kenya and warned the opposition leaders against the resort to violence. As these examples demonstrate, the three countries under investigation have a vested interest in the political and economic changes taking place in the region, since each country is affected by the actions of its neighbors.

The reliance of Kenya, Tanzania and Uganda on foreign aid, combined with the donor community's vested interest in the region, have exposed these countries to external pressure to adopt externally imposed or prescribed political and economic solutions to development woes. These donor countries, through their embassies and the financial organizations that they control, have demanded specific political and economic reforms as conditions for aid disbursement. The political changes associated with this "structural adjustment" perspective include the holding of multi-party elections in Kenya and Tanzania. Uganda has been exempt from this donor demand, instead receiving accolades for its recovery from protracted civil war and sustained economic growth. International actors are working, albeit inconsistently, to ensure that Kenya, Tanzania, and Uganda do not revert back to the statist tendencies of the 1970s and 1980s.

The chapters in this volume elucidate the protracted and uneven democratic transition process in the region. While there is no guarantee that this process will inevitably result in consolidated democracies in East Africa, the foundation has been laid for a more democratic future. This edited volume represents an attempt to explore the factors that have subverted or facilitated this transition process, while building on existing research.

A number of single-country case studies have focused on the politics of Kenya, Tanzania and Uganda. Some of these studies directly address the political transition currently underway, while others identify and examine particular elements of this multifaceted process.[24] However, there are some notable exceptions to this claim. The 1979 edited volume by Barkan and Okumu, and subsequently updated by Barkan in 1994, offer useful comparative and regional insights into political developments in Kenya and Tanzania, but Uganda is not included in the analyses. Books by Pinkney, Berg-Schlosser and Siegler, and Assensoh, have also explored political dynamics in East Africa comparatively, and the contributions to this volume seek to build on, and complement these studies.[25]

There is also an array of interesting books that address the democratic transition process in sub-Saharan Africa more generally,[26] with some studies identifying representative cases across the continent,[27] and other cross-national studies that identify, code, and statistically analyze key factors as a way to move to the level of generalizability.[28] Finally, there are studies that are organized specifically by themes addressed by volume contributors, looking at these issues at the country-specific and cross-national levels of analysis.[29]

The contributors to this volume have addressed thematic issues relevant to the African experience and informed by many of the studies mentioned above. They have attempted to balance empirical specificity with conceptual perspective in order to reach a broad audience inclusive of newcomers to the study of African politics and those with more advanced empirical and/or conceptual foundations. Taken as a whole, this book will be of interest to students of African politics and history given the wealth of information provided on each country, as well as the articulation of the key challenges that characterize the democratic transition process in East Africa specifically. In addition to the well-documented chapter contributions, readers will also benefit from the selective list of monographs, newspapers/magazines from the region, and key scholarly journals that were repeatedly cited by the authors. The authors also collaboratively developed a chronology of key events that provides historical context for the chapter contributions.

While the contributors have attempted to avoid excessive repetition of historical events, this was occasionally unavoidable since the chapters focus on the democratic transition process during the same time period. The contributors do, however, provide different perspectives and they occasionally come to divergent conclusions about similar historical events, informed by their unique thematic approach. This potential liability emerged as one of the volume's strengths, highlighting the utility of the comparative, regional approach.

How can a sustained transition be implemented that ultimately results in the consolidation of democracy in East Africa? The various contributors to this volume have analyzed the common trends and problems that the three East African countries are facing as they attempt to establish democratic societies. The transition has been a protracted one because of the historical experiences, the nature of the political institutions (including the constitution, government and political parties), the efficacy of civil society organizations, and the impact of international financial institutions and bilateral relations, on the East African countries under investigation. In order for the transition to move forward and for democracy to be consolidated, there needs to be enlightened political leadership, institutional legitimacy, a vibrant civil society, and a shared vision and partnership with international actors. In short, an enabling political and economic environment at the local, national, and international levels needs to be established and sustained.

Notes

1. Fareed Zakaria, "The Rise of Illiberal Democracy," *Foreign Affairs* vol. 76, no. 6 (1997), p. 42.
2. Larry Diamond, *Prospects for Democratic Development in Africa*, *Essays in Public Policy* (Hoover Institution, Stanford University, 1997).
3. Richard Joseph, *State, Conflict and Democracy in Africa* (Boulder: Lynne Rienner, 1999).
4. Zakaria, "The Rise of Illiberal Democracy," 1997.

[5] Crawford Young, "The Third Wave of Democratization in Africa: Ambiguities and Contradictions," in Richard Joseph, ed., *State, Conflict and Democracy in Africa* (Boulder, CO: Lynne Rienner, 1999), p. 35.

[6] John Harbeson, "Rethinking Democratic Transitions: Lessons from Eastern and Southern Africa" in Richard Joseph, ed., *State, Conflict and Democracy in Africa* (Boulder, CO: Lynne Rienner, 1999), p. 53.

[7] Guillermo O'Donnell and Philippe C. Schmitter, *Transitions from Authoritarian Rule: Tentative Conclusions About Uncertain Democracies* (Baltimore, MD: John Hopkins University Press, 1986), p. 6.

[8] Mary Ellen Fischer, "Introduction," in Mary Ellen Fischer, ed., *Establishing Democracies* (Boulder, CO: Westview Press, 1996), p. 5.

[9] O'Donnell and Schmitter, *Transitions from Authoritarian Rule*, 1986.

[10] Gretchen Casper, "The Benefits of Difficult Transitions," *Democratization* vol. 7, no. 3 (Autumn 2000), p. 47.; see also Michael Bratton, and Nicolas Van de Walle, "Popular Protest and Political Reform in Africa," *Comparative Politics* vol. 24 (1992), pp. 419-442; and Juan Linz and Alfred Stepan, *Problems of Democratic Transition and Consolidation* (Baltimore, MD: John Hopkins University Press, 1996).

[11] Todd Eisenstadt, "Eddies in the Third Wave: Protracted Transitions and Theories of Democratization," *Democratization* vol. 7, no. 3 (Autumn 2000), pp. 14-15.

[12] Casper, "The Benefits of Difficult Transitions," p. 47.

[13] S.M. Lipset, *The Political Man* (Garden City, NY: Anchor Books, 1963), p. 26.

[14] Samuel J. Valenzuela, "Democratic Consolidation in Post-Transitional Settings: Notion, Process, and Facilitating Conditions," in Scott Mainwaring, Guillermo O'Donnell, and J. Samuel Valenzuela, eds., *Issues in Democratic Consolidation* (Notre Dame, IN: University of Notre Dame Press, 1992).

[15] Adam Przeworski, *Democracy and the Market* (Cambridge: Cambridge University Press, 1991).

[16] Joel Barkan, "Protracted Transitions Among Africa's New Democracies," *Democratization* vol. 7, no. 3 (Autumn 2000), p. 232.

[17] Juan Linz and Alfred Stepan, *Problems of Democratic Transition and Consolidation* (Baltimore, MD: John Hopkins University Press, 1996), p. 5.

[18] Eisenstadt, "Eddies in the Third Wave," p. 18.

[19] Casper, "The Benefits of Difficult Transitions," p. 48; see also Douglas A. Chalmers and Craig H. Robinson, "Why Power Contenders Choose Liberalization," *International Studies Quarterly* vol. 26 (1982), pp. 3-36.

[20] Such studies are, for example, Naomi Chazan, "Between Liberalism and Statism: African Political Cultures and Democracy," in Larry Diamond, ed., *Political Culture and Democracy in Developing Countries* (Boulder, CO: Lynne Rienner, 1994); Robert Smith, *Kingdoms of the Yoruba* (London: Methuen, 1976); and I. Schapera, *A Handbook of Tswana Law and Custom* (London: Frank Cass, 1970). See also V. G. Simiyu, " The Democratic Myth in the African Traditional Societies," in Walter Oyugi et al., eds., *Democratic Theory and Practice in Africa* (Portsmouth, NH: Heinemann, 1988).

[21] Larry Diamond, Seymour Martin, and Juan Linz, "Building and Sustaining Democratic Government in Developing Countries: Some Tentative Findings," *World Affairs* no. 150 (Summer 1987), p. 6.

[22] Timothy M. Shaw, "Popular Participation in Nongovernmental Structures in Africa: Implications for Democratic Development," *Africa Today* vol. 37, no. 3 (1990), p. 16.

[23] Michael Bratton, "The Politics of Government-NGO Relations in Africa, *World Development* vol. 17, no. 4 (April 1989), p. 425.

[24] *For studies on Kenya, see*: Gibson Kamau Kuria, *Majimboism, Ethnic Cleansing and Constitutionalism in Kenya* (Nairobi: Kenya Human Rights Commission, 1994); David Throup and Charles Hornsby, *Multi-party Politics in Kenya* (Oxford: James Currey, 1998); Ann Watson, ed., *Modern Kenya* (Lanham: University Press of America, 2000); and Jennifer Widner, *The Rise of a Party State in Kenya: From "Harambee!" to "Nyayo!"* (Berkeley: University of California Press, 1992).
For studies on Tanzania, see: Dean McHenry, *Limited Choices, The Political Struggle for Socialism in Tanzania* (Boulder, CO: Lynne Rienner, 1994); Samuel S. Mushi and Rwekaza S. Mukandala, eds., *Multi-party Democracy in Transition, Tanzania's 1995 General Elections* (Dar es Salaam: Tanzania Election Monitoring Committee [TEMCO], Department of Political Science and Public Administration, University of Dar es Salaam, 1997); and Geir Sundet, ed., *Democracy in Transition, The 1995 Elections in Tanzania* (Oslo: Norwegian Institute of Human Rights, Human Rights Report No. 8, June 1996).
For studies on Uganda, see: Justus Mugaju, and J. Oloka-Onyango, eds., *No-Party Democracy in Uganda: Myths and Realities* (Kampala: Fountain Publishers, 2000); Phares Mutibwa, *Uganda Since Independence: A Story of Unfulfilled Hope* (Trenton, NJ: Africa World Press, 1992); Thomas R. Ofcansky, *Uganda: Tarnished Pearl of Africa* (Boulder, CO: Westview Press, 1996).

[25] A.B. Assenoh, *African Political Leadership: Jomo Kenyatta, Kwame Nkrumah and Julius K. Nyerere* (Malabar, FL.: Krieger Publishing Co., 1998); Robert Pinckney, *The International Politics of East Africa* (Manchester: Manchester University Press, 2001); Joel D. Barkan, ed. *Beyond Capitalism vs. Socialism in Kenya and Tanzania* (Boulder: Lynne Reinner, 1994); Joel D. Barkan with John J. Okumu, *Politics and Public Policy in Kenya and Tanzania* (Westport: Praeger, 1979); Dirk Berg-Schlosser and Rainer Siegler, *Political Stability and Development: A Comparative Analysis of Kenya, Tanzania, and Uganda* (Boulder, CO: Lynne Rienner, 1990).

[26] See Larry Diamond, and Marc F. Plattner, eds., *Democratization in Africa* (Baltimore: The John Hopkins University Press, 1999); Jean Germain Gros, ed., *Democratization in Late Twentieth-Century Africa: Coping with Uncertainty* (Westport: Greenwood Press, 1998); Richard Joseph, ed., *State, Conflict, and Democracy in Africa* (Boulder, CO: Lynne Rienner, 1999); John Mukum Mbaku, *Multi-party Democracy and Political Change: Constraints to Democratization in Africa* (Brookfield: Ashgate, 1998); Kidane Mengisteab and Cyril Daddieh, *State Building and Democratization in Africa, Faith, Hope, and Realities* (Westport: Praeger, 1999); Emeka Nwokedi, *Politics of Democratization, Changing Authoritarian Regimes in Sub-Saharan Africa* (Munster: LIT Verlag, 1995); Dov Ronen, *Democracy and Pluralism in Africa* (Boulder: Lynne Rienner, 1986); John A. Wiseman, *Democracy in Black Africa: Survival and Revival* (New York: Paragon House Publishers, 1990); John A. Wiseman, *The New Struggle for Democracy in Africa* (Aldershot: Avebury, 1996); John A. Wiseman, ed., *Democracy and Political Change in Sub-Saharan Africa* (London: Routledge, 1995).

[27] See Julius E. Nyang'oro, *Discourses on Democracy: Africa in Comparative Perspective* (Dar es Salaam: Dar es Saalam University Press, 1996); Bamidele A. Ojo, ed., *Contemporary African Politics, A Comparative Study of Political Transition to Democratic Legitimacy* (Lanham, NJ: University Press of America, 1999); Robert Pinkney, *Democracy and Dictatorship in Ghana and Tanzania* (New York: St. Martin's Press, 1997); Gary D. Wekkin, *Building Democracy in One-Party Systems: Theoretical Problems and Cross-Nation Experiences* (Westport: Praeger Publishers, 1993).

[28] The major work in this area is by Michael Bratton and Nicolas Van de Walle, *Democratic Experiments in Africa: Regime Transitions in Comparative Perspective* (Cambridge: Cambridge University Press, 1997).

[29] Below you will find some key books that address chapter contribution themes:
Historical Context: Mahmood Mamdani, *Citizen and Subject: Contemporary Africa and the Legacy of Late Colonialism* (Princeton, NJ: Princeton University Press, 1996); Crawford Young, *The Colonial State in Comparative Perspective* (New Haven, CT: Yale University Press, 1994).
Leadership: Patrick Chabal, *Political Domination in Africa: Reflections on the Limits of Power* (Cambridge: Cambridge University Press, 1986); Samauel Decalo, *Pyschoses of Power: African Personal Dictatorships* (Boulder: Westview Press, 1989); Robert H. Jackson and Carl G. Rosberg, *Personal Rule in Black Africa* (Berkeley: University of California Press, 1982).
Political Parties: Max Mmuya and Amon Chaligha, *Political Parties and Democracy in Tanzania* (Dar es Salaam: Dar es Salaam University Press, 1994); Dieter Nohlen, Michael Krennerich, and Bernhard Thibaut, eds., *Elections in Africa, A Data Handbook* (Oxford: Oxford University Press, 1999).
Constitutionalism: Holger Hansen, Bernt, and Michael Twaddle, *From Chaos to Order: The Politics of Constitution-Making in Uganda* (Kampala: Fountain Publishers, 1995); Kenneth W. Thompson, ed., *The U.S. Constitution and Constitutionalism in Africa* (Lanham: University Press America, 1990).
Civil Society: Susan Dicklitch, *Elusive Promise of NGOs in Africa: Lessons from Uganda* (New York: St. Martin's Press, 1998); Stephen N. Ndegwa, *The Two Faces of Civil Society: NGOs and Politics in Africa* (West Hartford: Kumarian Press, 1996); Apolo Nsibambi, ed., *Decentralization and Civil Society in Uganda: The Quest for Good Governance* (Kampala: Fountain Publishers, 1998).
Economic Reform: Arne Bergsten, Arne and Steve Kayizzi-Mugerwa, *Crisis, Adjustment, and Growth in Uganda* (New York: St. Martin's, 1999); Ishrat Husain and Rashid Faruqee, eds., *Adjustment in Africa: Lessons from Country Case Studies* (Washington, D.C.: World Bank, 1994); J.M. Nelson, and S.J. Eglinton, *Encouraging Democracy: What Role for Conditioned Aid?* (Washington D.C.: Overseas Development Council, 1992); David Sahn, Paul A. Dorosh, and Stephen D. Younger, eds., *Structural Adjustment Reconsidered: Economic Policy and Poverty in Africa* (Cambridge: Cambridge University Press, 1997); Jennifer Widner, ed., *Economic Change and Political Liberalization in Sub-Saharan Africa* (Baltimore: Johns Hopkins University, 1994).
International Context: Jean Grugel, ed., *Democracy without Borders: Transnationalism and Conditionalities in New Democracies* (London: Routledge, 1999); Goran Hyden and Rwekaza Mukandala, *Agencies in Foreign Aid: Comparing China, Sweden, and the United States in Tanzania* (London: Macmillan Press, 1999).
Legitimacy and Authority: Adebayo O. Olukoshi and Liisa Laakso, eds., *Challenges to the Nation-State in Africa* (Upsala; Nordic Institute of African Studies, 1996); James S. Wunsch and Dele Olowu, eds., *The Failure of the Centralized State: Institutions and Self-Governance in Africa* (Boulder, CO: Westview Press, 1990).

Chapter 2

The History of an Ideal

Thomas Burgess

In the history of ideas and institutions in East Africa, liberal multi-party democracy is of recent origins, almost as new to the region as the establishment of independent African states. The British introduced democratic reforms only in the terminal years of colonialism, in order to "prepare" Africans to rule themselves. Such reforms departed dramatically from colonial ruling practices in place since the 1890s. They were not inspired by pre-colonial African political traditions, but were borrowed directly from Western concepts of goverance developed throughout the 19th and 20th centuries. This must be remembered when assessing East African democratic experiments of the past forty years.

The first generation of African political leaders rose to power through the establishment of political coalitions with proven competitiveness in the multi-party elections of the 1950s and early 1960s. They inherited constitutional governments that, at least in theory, guaranteed fundamental democratic rights, such as due process, freedom of association, religion, and the press. Each East African state respected the separation of powers between legislative, executive and judicial branches. Public accountability through regular multi-party elections, in which each adult citizen had equal voting rights, was also a component of post-war colonial democratic experiments. That independent East African nations have not consistently adhered to all of these principles is a function of the fragility of national communities invented during colonial rule and the very recent history of democracy in the region.

In the development of independent states, African leaders have sometimes abandoned democratic ideals out of expediency, ambition, or conviction. Ongoing political instability has, of course, played a major role in the failure of democratic experiments. During civil war and ethnic tension, democratic ideals have been shelved. Multi-party democracy has in fact been blamed for exacerbating social conflicts. Fragile democratic institutions have not proven to be an effective deterrent to the personal ambitions of national political figures. African leaders have chosen, finally, to adapt democratic principles inherited from the British to local realities.

Repeated attempts to reconcile "tradition" with "modernity" characterized the political histories of the region's more stable nations during the first two decades of independence. In general, these experiments placed more value on the maintenance of social and political unity than on the toleration of dissent. Institutions of political pluralism were sacrificed in order to sustain at least the appearance of national consensus. African nationalists justified these measures through appeals to socialist principles or pre-colonial African ruling traditions. They argued that this approach to governance was necessary in order to achieve national development objectives and to succeed in the oft-cited war against poverty, ignorance, and disease. Such experiments, once regarded by many international observers as boldly innovative and remarkably appropriate to local needs and conditions, came under increasing criticism by the end of the Cold War. A decade later, scholars assert there are few justifications, if any, for political systems that do not adhere to fundamental democratic principles as originally conceived in the West. Ironically, African traditions have been invoked on behalf of democracy, as they once were in the suspension of the same principles associated with this political ideal.

The purpose of this chapter is to describe the historical background to contemporary conflicts over democracy in East Africa. I will focus in particular on the recent origins of democratic principles in the region, so closely related to the process of establishing modern nation states in the wake of colonialism. With independence, Africans initially relied upon foreign democratic models that were only adopted after considerable debate and open political conflict since they departed so obviously from colonial and pre-colonial traditions. Democracy undermined colonialism's previously unquestioned ruling strategies. Democratic principles did not emerge organically over decades of trial and error, but were hammered out at various constitutional conferences held in London in the early-1960s, where a certain degree of compromise was permitted in order to obtain consensus, and to satisfy what appeared to be the more pressing necessity of rapid colonial withdrawal from the region. The tentative and last minute approach of the British to democratic reforms was reflected in Africans' limited loyalty to institutions the West regarded as sacred after independence.

Pre-Colonial East Africa

Despite the presence of widely varying methods of political organization in pre-colonial East Africa, few parallels exist between these and 19th and 20th century Western models of popular democracy. In general, rulers wielded authority on behalf of corporate entities such as clans or ethnic groups rather than on behalf of private individuals or nations that transcended ethnic identities. The prevailing wisdom was that all members of a community shared the same interests, religious beliefs, and codes of conduct, since everyone was believed to be related according to ties of blood kinship. Personal relationships and the principle of reciprocity were more important than the protection of pluralism, or abstract notions of democracy, in which individual rights and responsibilities are well defined.[1]

This meant that local leaders wielded their authority with the same kind of social responsibility they exercised over their own families. Political legitimacy was defined according to age, gender, and wealth. Sometimes power was invested in individuals distinguished according to birth or reputed ritual expertise. Among the Kalenjin of Kenya, Olumwullah observes that in the selection of village elders, "knowledge of custom, discretion, and substance coupled with wealth stood as the basic criteria."[2] While power could not be claimed or exercised without a certain degree of popular consensus, general agreement in the community was not an expression of democratic principles but rather adherence to patriarchal, gerontocratic, or monarchical ruling assumptions. The political contracts of the pre-colonial period did not recognize the right of all adults to have an equal say in community affairs, or to choose their leaders and representatives from among all elements of the community. Instead, ordinary people respected the authority of fathers, elders, and chiefs as an extension of their religious beliefs and their concepts of the natural and ancestral means by which to order society. Political legitimacy was closely related to ritual authority. Elders ruled in the name of the ancestors, and were entrusted to carry out the will of the community at large. Popular ideas of citizenship were so closely related to religious beliefs that opposition to legal or political decisions or decrees was far less common than disputes between members of corporate ruling elites, whose limited numbers usually permitted the recovery of consensus after debate or discussion.

Most societies conducted their affairs without chiefs or ruling bureaucracies. In these circumstances, power was decentralized, permitting male elders to participate in councils on the village level. Formal political institutions were deliberately maintained with a minimum of complexity and hierarchy. Those political systems that concentrated power in village assemblies of elders most closely approximated the 20th century definition of democracy. On this small scale, social contracts operated effectively when societies recognized the necessity for those entrusted with power to remain worthy of that public trust. Although decisions were commonly made according to consensus achieved often through long debate, power was still exercised by an exclusive age set or council of village notables. Junior males simply waited until they graduated into power, while women sought to exercise influence through informal means.[3] Although pre-colonial societies did not develop political systems comparable to Western democracy, that does not suggest Africans lived under unmitigated tyranny. On the contrary, it can be argued that pre-colonial systems of local rule were as effective in maintaining public order and cohesion as any system introduced since.[4]

Chiefs ruled far less commonly than councils of elders. Sometimes, as in the case of the Kimbu of western Tanzania, chiefs were elected by councils of elders. They exercised a ritual role in society, and were often heavily dependent on elders who retained the right to depose the chief for poor conduct.[5] They were also dependent on the apparent goodwill of the ancestors. It was also possible for a range of political systems to coexist within the same locality, and for a society to experiment with different political systems in response to war, immigration, or drought. Kimambo demonstrates this for the Pare in the early-1800s, who organized themselves into lineage systems as well as states.[6] Iliffe has argued that high rainfall, permanent agriculture and dense population tended in East Africa to encourage more "articulated" political systems, where power was exercised on a larger scale and in a more formal way.[7] Kingdoms differed from chiefdoms in that paramount chiefs or kings exercised authority over multiple clans, and depended upon a loyal cadre of sub-chiefs or administrators to enforce their decrees. Monarchs tended to seek to centralize power in their own hands at the expense of sub-chiefs of individual clans. The kings of Shambaa in the Usambara Mountains of north-eastern Tanzania had a council of commoners, and exercised powers limited by what his subjects were willing to endure: "He alone had power over life and death. He could seize property without compensation and women without bridewealth. He levied tribute and redistributed it to his agents. He alone controlled rain medicine."[8] Upon the accession of a new king the people shouted, "Give us rain. Give us bananas. Give us sugar cane ... Give us food. You are our king, but if you do not feed us properly we will get rid of you. The country is yours; the people must have their stomachs filled."[9]

The power of the kings of Shambaa thus depended on the principle of reciprocity. What the king appropriated in the form of tribute he was supposed to return in the form of rain or redistribute to his followers. Through centuries of development, Buganda emerged as the most centralized state in the region of Lake Victoria. Buganda's steady expansion in the 17th and 18th centuries permitted the kings or Kabaka to dispense gifts of cattle, women, and lands to loyal subordinates, and thereby to concentrate unprecedented power in their own hands.[10] Gradually local chiefs owed their positions not through hereditary claims, but by the favor of the king, which was based on loyalty and merit rather than birth. By the 19th century, this system encouraged complete devotion to the sacred person of the Kabaka, who was chief judge, high priest, and head of state. Such a system could extract taxes and mobilize for war on a level unmatched by any of Buganda's neighboring kingdoms.[11]

Another emerging state of the 19th century was the Sultanate of Zanzibar, encompassing the islands and coastal areas of East Africa. The Sultans were personally responsible for reshaping the demographic profile of the coast, encouraging sustained Arab and Asian immigration, as well as the importation of thousands of African slaves each year through most of the 19th century.[12] The Sultanate was also instrumental in the incorporation of East Africa into systems of world trade that exchanged African ivory and slaves for guns, cloth, and iron. The new economy of the 19th century, in which Zanzibar town enjoyed a commanding commercial position, brought about a dramatic escalation of violence and disorder in East Africa. Poor, weak, and scattered societies were unable to defend themselves from the raids of their neighbors and caravans from the coast. The collection of slaves and ivory upset customary political relations, with some becoming rich from the long distance trade of accumulated guns in the region. Military prowess became a competitive alternative to ritual power. According to Iliffe, "trade and guns had destroyed the interdependence of rulers and subjects. Chiefs no longer relied on tribute and spearmen but on gunmen who collected slaves to pay for firearms."[13]

Colonial Politics to 1945

According to the terms of the 1890 Treaty of Heligoland, Germany and Great Britain divided East Africa between them, with German East Africa bordered on the north and east by the British protectorates of Zanzibar, Kenya, and Uganda. Both Britain and Germany experimented in the early-1890s with indirect rule through imperial chartered companies. By 1896 chartered companies proved unable to accomplish a minimum of colonial objectives. Subsequently, all four territories were administered by London or Berlin. Colonial governments commanded sufficient resources to eliminate African military opposition and establish a basic economic infrastructure to defray the costs of local administration. No major revisions to the border agreements of 1890 were necessary until World War I, when the Treaty of Versailles required the Germans to relinquish all of their African colonial possessions. The British assumed a League of Nations mandate over what became Tanganyika in 1920. After World War II, Tanganyika became a United Nations Trust Territory, still under British administration.

The Germans and British had no intention of extending their own representative systems of government to their new colonial possessions. Colonialism was an inherently authoritarian enterprise. Democracy was not the message colonial administrators, missionaries and merchants sought to bring to the continent. Rather, Christianity, work discipline, education, and obedience were the virtues more publicized by the colonials. Europeans came, they thought, to reform savage societies proven unable to govern themselves without violence and oppression, or to "protect" them from less scrupulous foreign powers than themselves. Colonials sought African acquiescence and cooperation rather than representation.

When African resistance to colonial rule was eventually crushed, the Germans and British chose to rule indirectly through local chiefs. Some of these chiefs were already in power, while others were appointed by colonial authorities. Chiefs were imbued with local political legitimacy, but they ultimately served colonial interests. Karugire questions the fundamental assumption of indirect rule, as a system established to encourage "native" development through the preservation of local systems of political authority. He regards this as sheer fantasy since in most societies indirect rule bore little comparison to pre-colonial political arrangements. Councils of elders played no role in the new order. Indirect rule was a "mass of contradictions incapable of reconciliation ... These new-style chiefs, who were created by the colonial government, both in centralized and segmentary societies, could not, by any stretch of imagination and English grammar, be said to be furthering the evolution, less still the preservation of traditional institutions."[14]

Iliffe asserts that indirect rule, initially intended to be both inexpensive and reformist, eventually came to be strongly conservative and increasingly the object of African protest.[15] Ibingira faults indirect rule for preserving ethnic divisions at a time when the British should have been more concerned with encouraging national identities.[16]

Indirect rule was not applied to growing immigrant communities from Europe and Asia that were already considered to be "civilized" by colonial authorities. For non-Africans, the British provided limited and sometimes purely symbolic representation on colonial Legislative Councils (Legcos). These bodies at first tended to be consultative, and were controlled by appointed majorities of salaried employees of the colonial state. Nevertheless they potentially served as forums for minority communities to press for concessions from the colonial government. Over the years, these parallel systems provoked a debate over the content and form of territory-wide ruling institutions. Could the Legcos become actual parliaments with broadly defined lawmaking capabilities and elected by an ever widening franchise? Or should indirect rule be adapted to national politics and administration, with the creation of a federation of districts and regions drawn according to ethnic boundaries, and administered by local chiefs and "tribal" councils? Since the former of these two options was, after varying degrees of conflict, eventually the ideal in all four East African colonies, the following discussion will locate the genesis of the idea of national democracy within the Legcos, rather than in institutions of indirect rule.

Kenya

Prior to 1945, Kenya experienced the most profound disputes in East Africa over the nature of democracy. These conflicts were closely related to decades of struggle between European and Asian immigrant communities for access to power and land in the colony. Excluded through World War II from the competition over political representation, Africans waited until the 1950s and early 1960s to win a succession of reforms leading ultimately to the institution of African majority rule, followed closely thereafter by independence. African majority rule was the culmination of a 60-year debate in Nairobi, London, Bombay, and Johannesburg regarding the future of a land that appeared to early European visitors as a vast terrain open for European racial expansion. The European settler community in Kenya called for the presence of large, settler-elected legislative majorities. Asians also demanded elections that excluded Africans. However, they contended that elections should be organized on a common-roll basis in order to guarantee their dominance over the less populous European community. The language of democracy in Kenya was employed to assert the interests of tiny immigrant communities rather than to demand equal representation for all subjects of the British crown.

The debate began as early as 1901, when Sir Harry Johnston's report on East Africa recommended to parliament in London that the central highlands of Kenya were suitable to become "white man's country," with the region of East Africa becoming an "America of the Hindu."[17] London encouraged both European and Asian immigration in order to help pay the costs of the recently completed railroad from Mombasa to Kisumu. White settlers arrived from South Africa, Australia and Canada, territories in which white racial expansion had been long underway, and which were rapidly achieving local white self-rule. As early as 1902, the miniscule settler community began to demand strict limitations on Asian immigration, greater white control over African labor, and the formation of a Legco in which only Europeans would enjoy representation. In 1906, London permitted the formation of a Legco, despite the presence then of less than 2,000 European settlers. Winston Churchill remarked the following year that "never before in colonial experience has a council been granted where the number of settlers is so few."[18]

The conflicting demands of Asians and Europeans were supposed to be resolved by the "White Paper" issued in 1923 by the Colonial Office. The document preserved the all-white land policies in the "White Highlands," and rejected Asian demands for common-roll elections. The official document offered Asians five elected seats in the Legco, which was not enough to upset the settler majority, and it also rejected settlers' demands for restrictions on Asian immigration. Most importantly, the White Paper for the first time clearly asserted London's felt obligation to develop the colony on behalf of the African majority rather than either of its politically mobilized immigrant communities. The White Paper made no provisions, however, for African representation of any kind, leaving local governance to Asians and Europeans. During the inter-war years, East Africa's first effective African nationalist organization emerged, the Kikuyu Central Association (KCA). After years of articulating African demands for the protection of their land, labor and village customs, the organization was banned in 1930, and African nationalist organizations did not permanently resurface until after World War II.

Uganda

In Uganda, colonial agents chose to make treaty agreements with the pre-colonial kingdoms of Buganda, Ankole, Toro, and Bunyoro. The British agreed to respect the rights of kings and their subordinate chiefs to exercise limited administrative authority over territories that roughly corresponded to their pre-colonial boundaries. While such arrangements were loosely defined as indirect rule, differences between ruling practices in Uganda and other East African colonies had emerged by 1900. Bagandan kings won the right to appoint twenty local chiefs and to supervise a legislative assembly, or Great Lukiiko. This body had responsibility over "native" administration, and was empowered to submit proposals to the king that could be enacted into law with the approval of the colonial government. The British extended comparable privileges to no other society in East Africa. The Bagandan elite were rewarded for their cooperation with the British during the 1890s, "pacifying" and establishing colonial administrative structures in Buganda's neighboring territories. Buganda obtained unusual political autonomy as well as jurisdiction over territories they conquered from their neighbors during the process of "pacification", most notably over Bunyoro's "Lost Counties."[19]

At least one British observer commented on the incompatibility of indirect rule and the continued existence of "native" states.[20] But until World War II, this did not arouse serious concern. Because local districts exercised wide-ranging administrative duties and were drawn according to ethnic boundaries, Africans with talent and education aspired to local government positions, rather than to have a voice in Legco deliberations. The "tribe" remained the focus of debate and group loyalties. This meant that although Uganda's Legco first met in 1921, it remained for Africans an "exotic" institution until after World War II,[21] with little relevance to local issues.

Tanganyika

The colonial government of Tanganyika also established a Legco to give representation to Asians and Europeans, while excluding Africans. However, the European community in Tanganyika was smaller in number and more divided linguistically and geographically than settlers of the White Highlands. They held out no hopes that Tanganyika, as a League of Nations mandate, would become another white settler community such as Southern Rhodesia. Furthermore, many of the issues that divided Asians and Europeans in Kenya simply did not apply south of the border. European settlers were not actively interested in either restricting Asian immigration or designating a particular region of the territory as a "whites only" preserve. Although when the Legco first convened in the 1920s Europeans unofficially outnumbered Asians, this did not result in serious ongoing confrontation. Africans for their part did not obtain representation on the Legco until 1945.

In Zanzibar, the British gradually extended their administration, despite continuing to rule theoretically on behalf of the Sultans. It was not until the 1950s that they abandoned legislation that favored Arab political and economic position in the islands. Despite the abolition of slavery, the overall effect of British rule was to freeze relations in Zanzibar according to what they were at the outset of colonial rule.[22] The Legco that was established in 1926 gave membership to Arabs and Asians. Africans waited until 1946 to obtain a seat on the council. Here, as in Kenya, the British demonstrated a conservative approach to colonial governance, favoring of the local (Arab) agricultural elite threatened by the expansion of Asian economic power and the aspirations of the African majority.

Colonial Democratic Reforms and Post-colonial Nation Building (1945-1980)

After World War II, the British became convinced of the necessity of constitutional reform and the development of political institutions in their East African colonies. African nationalism, the precedent of Indian independence, the anti-colonial principles of the United Nations Charter, and the spread of western education in Africa, all played a role in encouraging democratic reforms in this region of the British Empire. Colonial authorities now believed that Africans were "ready" to gain entrance to territory-wide Legcos, and that the emerging numbers of educated African elites should be given at least some political experience and voice in Legco debates. The colonial doctrine of "multi-racialism" – rather unique to East Africa – emerged in the 1950s as a way for the British to retain control, encourage racial cooperation, and promote economic development in the colonies as a precursor to self-rule in the distant future. Limited African political representation was permitted for the first time, but colonial authorities did not adhere to the principle of one person, one vote. Instead, multi-racialism was a careful, unequal balancing of the demands of competing racial communities, with favored minority communities still retaining dominance. By 1960, the British realized multi-racialism in East Africa was untenable. Acceding to the principle of African majority rule, they decided to withdraw from all of their East African territories as soon as local circumstances permitted.

Although all four colonies experienced limited political reforms immediately before independence, British commitment to the idea of democracy in East Africa was gradual, uneven, and conflicted. As the British gradually conceded African majority rule, the privileges of minority communities such as European settlers, Arab planters, or the Baganda, could not be sustained. In implementing constitutional reforms, the British ultimately surrendered their own authority in East Africa and severed their working relationships with favored ruling partners of the past. The British resisted all attempts by their former allies to either maintain their positions of political preeminence or to demand separate statehood. Facing almost certain political eclipse, these communities led the way in criticizing colonialism, which secured communal privileges for many years.

Nationalism in East Africa assumed multiple forms. For some, it was a defense of colonial prerogatives in the face of constitutional reform. For many educated African elites, it was an organized rebuke of British imperialism and an assertion of African readiness for independence and majority rule. By the end of the 1950s, the inadequacy of indirect rule as a system of national governance was apparent. A cohort of nationalist elites emerged as a result of post-war constitutional reforms and the expansion of the powers of the Legcos. These elites called for dismantling the structure of colonial ruling coalitions comprised of minority communities, the British, and local chiefs. They argued that power should be placed in the hands of elected African officials rather than local chiefs or kings. Most African nationalists thus supported the emergence of new systems of national governance that claimed few structural references to pre-colonial political institutions.

During the transition to independence, new spaces opened up for contests in which local communities would inherit the most power, patronage, and autonomy. The vehemence of these contests during the final moments of colonialism suggested that popular commitment to democracy was, in many cases, both instrumental and contingent. Democracy remained as abstract as the concept of a multi-ethnic nation-state. Post-war political reforms were not effective in erasing long standing authoritarian political practices. However, these reforms remained an important precedent and historical memory for the first generation of independent African leaders.

Kenya

After World War II, Kenyan Governor Sir Philip Mitchell developed plans for self-government along multi-racial lines. Mitchell considered multi-racialism a viable alternative to an African, European, or Asian dominated state. The goal was to provide all racial communities in the colony a political voice, while still recognizing British imperial tutelage, and "the great spiritual and moral force and the long social and political experience of the people of Great Britain" living in the colony.[23] Mitchell increased African-appointed representation in the Legco while remaining hostile to the efforts of Eliud Mathu and other African members of Legco to combat settler domination of that assembly.[24]

The fundamental partnership between settlers and London-appointed officials remained largely unchanged until the beginning of the Mau Mau Emergency in late 1952. Principally a Kikuyu revolt against land alienation in the "White Highlands" and ongoing political and economic discrimination against Africans, Mau Mau complicated the regime's plans to implement gradual and limited constitutional reforms towards the creation of a multi-racial society. The rebellion compelled London to exert pressure on Mitchell's successor to implement accelerated and wider ranging reforms. Colonial agents believed they could contain and defeat the rebellion by military means, and by addressing at least some of the grievances that fueled African resistance in order to gain the cooperation of "responsible" Africans who did not agree with the Mau Mau rebellion. Sir Evelyn Baring adopted a strategy that included land redistribution, villagization, and the establishment of a "Home Guard" comprised of 25,000 loyal Kikuyu. African workers now freely organized labor unions; peasants could now grow coffee and other cash crops, secure bank loans, and obtain private ownership of their lands. These measures seriously eroded the dual economy comprised primarily of African subsistence agriculture and European commercial production. Multi-racialism remained the official policy of the colonial regime, however. The Lyttleton Constitution of 1954 was another attempt to devise a system of unequal racial power sharing that would enable the British to maintain colonial authority until after 1975.[25]

Multi-racialism proved an unsustainable philosophy in the face of determined African resistance. The 1957 elections, conducted according to a franchise strictly limited by income and education, resulted in nationalists capturing the majority of seats reserved for Africans. Prominent African moderates lost their seats to a new generation of politicians, including Tom Mboya and Oginga Odinga, who were unified in their opposition to the defense of settler political influence. They continually demanded further constitutional concessions on the path towards majority rule. By 1959, it became clear to colonial officials that the ambiguous balance between African nationalism and settler influence in the colony could no longer be maintained. For the suppression of Mau Mau, the government depended heavily on the services of loyalist Kikuyu, whose allegiance depended on access to employment and continuing economic expansion. Embarrassing outbreaks of violence such as the Hola Incident,[26] convinced the British to accept the demands of African nationalists and dramatically shorten the timetable for independence.

Through negotiations at the Lancaster House Conference in London in 1960, a new constitution gave Africans a majority of Legco seats for the first time. In these circumstances, two nationalist parties emerged, the Kenya African Democratic Union (KADU) and the Kenya African National Union (KANU). Divided primarily along ethnic lines, KANU represented Luo and Kikuyu interests, and KADU was an alliance of smaller ethnic groups. In 1961, KANU won 19 seats, and they sustained their dominance among African voters until independence.

In further constitutional conferences, KADU representatives wanted a federal constitution that gave regions wide ranging powers, control over local government services, and taxing authority. They also wanted a bicameral legislature, with an upper house, or senate, equal in authority to a lower house. Regional assemblies would elect senators, with each region given equal representation in that body. KADU favored political decentralization in order to avoid domination by numerically and economically powerful ethnic groups. KANU called for a strong national government, an independent judiciary, a unicameral legislature, and a Bill of Rights that stipulated freedom of religion, the right to property, a fair trial, and cultural and educational rights.[27] The most important point of debate, however, was over the issue of federalism versus centralization. The British favored federalism as a means of preserving some political influence for Kenya's racial minorities, and in order to limit the capacity of African nationalists to impose radical changes on colonial institutions.

However, KANU electoral triumphs over-shadowed the federalist idea, with the party gaining 68 out of 112 contested Legco seats in the May 1963 elections. By this time Jomo Kenyatta, imprisoned at the beginning of the Mau Mau Emergency for his alleged role in the rebellion, was released and had assumed a leadership in KANU. Kenyatta emerged as a relative moderate, despite his demonization by the British in previous years. He made clear his desires for national reconciliation and his lack of sympathy for many of Mau Mau's tactics. Kenyatta became prime minister in June 1963 in preparation for full independence in December of that year. KADU subsequently dissolved and the majority of its leadership joined KANU.

Kenyatta and his colleagues were strengthened in their efforts to establish a strong unitary state with a powerful executive branch. By amendment to the constitution in 1966, the senate was officially abolished.[28] Kenyatta's executive power increased as a result of the passage of several constitutional amendments.[29] The president, for example, could declare a state of emergency and detain anyone without trial considered an enemy of the people.[30] The constitution was amended in 1964 and again in 1968 to exclude from automatic succession to the presidency first Oginga Odinga and then Tom Mboya, whose politics, popularity or ethnicity were unacceptable to the largely Kikuyu-dominated ruling oligarchy.[31] Such measures did not limit all dissent.

In May 1966, the Kenya People's Union (KPU) was founded by KANU politicians like Oginga Odinga, who were disillusioned with government policies they felt were creating a new privileged African capitalist elite and ignoring the aspirations of average citizens. KPU demanded that the regime implement more land reform, provide more health and educational services, and accelerate the Africanization of the economy and civil service underway since independence. KPU found its greatest support among the Luos in western Kenya, and among workers and students.[32] KPU opposition was inspired by a far more doctrinaire form of socialism than Tom Mboya's version of "African Socialism" and by the frustration felt by many who had participated in the Mau Mau struggle, who felt that they were marginalized despite their nationalist efforts. The KPU was declared illegal in October 1969, quickly ending its attempt to contest KANU policies and authority. The mysterious, violent deaths of Tom Mboya in 1969 and J.M. Kariuki in 1975, and the continued detention in the 1970s of prominent radical politicians, members of parliament (MPs), and academics made it clear that the government would not tolerate determined and organized political opposition. Despite widespread fears of a bloody succession dispute, when Kenyatta died in 1978, Vice President Daniel arap Moi assumed the presidency in a smooth and constitutional transition.[33]

During the Kenyatta years local and parliamentary elections were held on a regular basis. Despite institutional similarities, parliamentary proceedings in Kenya in the 1960s and 1970s in many ways diverged from Western democratic traditions:

> The process of competition, mutual criticism, and bargaining between government and opposition parties that characterize political life in the West was never established. For the same reason, the legislature never became an important arena for the deliberation and making of public policy. Nor did the electoral process provide voters with a choice of policy alternatives, or a choice between competing governing elites.[34]

Despite these limitations under Kenyatta, parliament evolved as a significant representative institution in national political life. Barkan comments that "backbenchers" in parliament actively debated government budgets and policy initiatives and established commissions of inquiry into government policies. MPs made efforts to encourage transparency and accountability within government, despite being severely limited in their ability to propose their own legislative agendas.[35] They also served as "entrepreneurial agents" of the periphery, actively representing their constituents by gaining access to government grants and matching aid for local self-help projects in their home areas. In the 1969 elections, 54 percent of incumbents were voted out of office for their failure to obtain government resources for their home areas. Such efforts received unofficial endorsement in a post-colonial state that repressed party identities and national debates about national policies, but which assumed a commanding and fostering role in the dispensation of patronage. Barkan asserts that "though the distribution of rewards resulting from this system is rarely equitable, such distribution as does occur generates support for the regime among local elites and the population as a whole."[36]

Kenyatta thus maintained a system that continued to possess institutional similarities with the constitutional reforms implemented during the last years of colonialism, and which still depended primarily upon civil servants for policy implementation. Colonial era laws and courts survived, but were sometimes ignored or manipulated to serve the interests of the ruling elite. The dominant nation building ethos of the Kenyatta years grafted neo-patrimonialism onto the Westminster model. While clientalism in the Kenyatta years encouraged the proliferation of forms of civil society such as peasant *harambee* unions that did not question the ruling oligarchy's monopoly on power, it also encouraged corruption. The economic inequality and underdevelopment fostered by patronage politics resulted in growing popular discontent in the 1980s and 1990s, provoking growing ethnic conflict and demands for multi-party elections.

Uganda

In Uganda, there was never any serious talk of multi-racialism. In pursuing democratic reforms, Uganda faced altogether different issues than other East African territories. When the Legco emerged as a representative, authoritative national assembly in the 1950s, it was not considered a threat to the interests of European and Asian minorities. However, the Baganda elite regarded constitutional reform as a breach of contracts made at the outset of colonial rule that awarded Buganda a uniquely autonomous position within the colony. Bugandan separatism became a major force in Ugandan politics and was inspired by memories of pre-colonial state formation, and by the colonial preservation and codification of their pre-colonial political institutions.

In the late-1940s, Governor Sir John Hall opened the territory's Legco to African representation, seating eight Africans on the council. The Great Lukiiko expressed serious reservations about any Bugandan representation on the Legco, considering it a rival institution that threatened Bugandan prerogatives. Despite this opposition, Hall's replacement, Sir Andrew Cohen, rapidly expanded African membership in the council. Cohen also convinced Kabaka Mutesa II to accept the partial democratization of the Lukiiko; sixty out of 89 members of that body would now be elected. Kabaka's government would also be given responsibility over primary education, health and agricultural services within Buganda. At the time, such initiatives did not appear to Cohen as fundamentally contradictory.

Bugandan separatism was further provoked by fears in the early 1950s that the British were planning a federation of all of their East African territories. To prevent such an outcome, the Kabaka and the Lukiiko demanded Buganda be given independence separate from the rest of Uganda. Cohen decided in 1953 to send the Kabaka into exile due to his lack of cooperation with British policies. All sectors of Baganda society called for the Kabaka's immediate return, and made normal government operations impossible to carry out. After months of negotiation, the Buganda Agreement of 1955 attempted to resolve the "Kabaka Crisis." In exchange for the Kabaka's return, the Baganda elite agreed to send representatives to the Legco, to remain part of Uganda, and to abide by provisions that reduced the power of the Kabaka to that of a constitutional monarch, with his ministers appointed by and responsible to the Lukiiko. While Governor Cohen achieved compliance to his demands, the Kabaka's triumphant return transformed him into a popular hero and further encouraged Bugandan separatism.[37]

Despite the 1955 agreement, Buganda withdrew its representatives from the Legco in 1958, and refused to take part in territory-wide elections the same year. Despite a franchise which permitted three-quarters of all adult males to vote, the formation of national political parties was seriously handicapped by the Bugandan boycott. It was also handicapped by Uganda's own peculiar version of indirect rule, which drew district boundaries according to ethnic divisions and the frontiers of pre-colonial states, and gave district councils wide-ranging powers over local government. The colony's first elections, not surprisingly, demonstrated the inability of political parties to develop mass followings or nation-wide appeal. For most Baganda, as well as among a large majority of those living in the other kingdoms within Uganda, such as Bunyoro, Toro, Busoga and Ankole, the expectation was that independence would bring a return to pre-colonial political relationships.[38]

Buganda represented by far the most serious threat to the emergence of a unified post-colonial state. Buganda demanded federal status, the right to form its own army and police force, negotiate international treaties, and to establish a judicial system independent of the state.[39] The British refused to consider these demands and scheduled further elections in 1961, according to a universal adult franchise. The Lukiiko prohibited all Baganda from registering to vote, and unilaterally declared Bugandan independence for January 1961. Nothing came of this, however. The 1961 elections gave the most votes to the Uganda Peoples Congress (UPC), led by Milton Obote, with its greatest strength among Protestants and smaller ethnic groups in the north that did not have strong memories of pre-colonial state formation. After the elections, Obote's party allied with Baganda traditionalists of the Kabaka Yekka Party (KY) to win the 1962 elections that was followed by independence later in the year. However, the future of independent Uganda was uncertain given the weakness of democratic institutions and the tentative arrangement between northerners and Baganda in the ruling coalition, who were both equally committed to nationalism and separatism. Gukiina writes that at independence, "most Baganda believed that the Buganda Kingdom would not be ruled by the central government."[40] Left out of power was the Democratic Party (DP), which relied heavily on non-Baganda Catholic support in the south.[41]

Obote became Uganda's first prime minister, offering Kabaka Mutesa the country's presidency, appointing five KY ministers, and giving his support to Buganda's demand for full federal status. Obote was willing to make short-term compromises in order to avoid further constitutional crises, believing "modernization" would eventually weaken ethnic loyalties and strengthen national ties. Crisis soon erupted, however, over the issue of the Lost Counties. Obote decided in 1964 to resolve the issue through a popular referendum, an action the Kabaka and the KY opposed. As a result, the UPC-KY alliance was officially dissolved in August 1964, and in November all KY MPs walked out upon the passage of the Lost Counties Referendum Bill. Obote replaced them with DP members to establish a new ruling majority, and the referendum resulted in the return of two counties to the jurisdiction of the King of Bunyoro. In the tense atmosphere following these events, charges of corruption surfaced against Obote, two of his ministers, and Army Chief of Staff Colonel Idi Amin. Parliament almost unanimously passed a motion to establish a commission of inquiry to look into the allegations. When Obote refused to appoint the commission, KY parliamentary representatives demanded his resignation along with two of his ministers.

The crisis continued through 1965 and early-1966, as criticism of Obote spread throughout the UPC and DP as well. Obote eventually decided to take drastic action,[42] arresting five of his ministers and suspending the parliament and the 1962 Constitution. In response, the Lukiiko introduced a motion that ordered all central government personnel off Bugandan soil within ten days. Within a few days, violence erupted in Kampala and on May 24 Obote ordered the military to lay siege to the Kabaka's palace. The Kabaka narrowly escaped to London with his life. More importantly, Obote had embarked on a strategy of single-party rule and military repression, justified, he believed, in order to preserve the state from imminent collapse.[43] Obote made sustained efforts to cultivate new sources of political legitimacy, largely by mounting an attack on the ruling and economic elites of Uganda's kingdoms. He met with leading ecclesiastical leaders, encouraged debate over a new constitution, gave speeches and held rallies, all in an effort to establish popular support for his agenda.

In 1969, Obote announced his *Common Man's Charter*, a further gambit towards legitimacy imitative of Nyerere's *Arusha Declaration.*[44] However, his dependence on the military and his lack of popular support was becoming ever more obvious, particularly in the face of multiple assassination attempts. In order to maintain control over the army, Obote promoted Langi and Acholi soldiers from northern areas most loyal to him. These moves provoked Colonel Idi Amin, who was from the north but neither Langi nor Acholi, to respond. In 1971, while Obote attended the Commonwealth Summit in Singapore, Amin orchestrated a successful *coup*. For the rest of the 1970s, Uganda descended into a long, national nightmare. Amin proved even more unable than Obote to establish popular or legal legitimacy, and his soldiers demonstrated a lack of respect for the property and lives of Ugandan citizens. At first Amin tried to woo religious leaders, and in 1972 he expelled Asians from the country, a move that won him enormous though only temporary popularity. But by the end of that year Amin ran out of options other than terror to stay in power. Amin could only rely upon the support of his own ethnic group, the numerically tiny Kakwa. In 1978 Amin launched a military attack on Tanzanian soil in order to recover some popular support. This last gamble failed disastrously when Nyerere mobilized an invasion that brought Tanzanian soldiers to Kampala and forced Amin into exile.[45]

Tanganyika and Zanzibar (Tanzania)

Tanganyika was unique in its status as a United Nations Trust Territory, obliging the British to answer to the U.N. for its policies. The U.N. Visiting Mission of 1954 recommended Tanganyika obtain independence within 25 years. That independence was achieved much sooner than that, and with less overt political conflict than any other East African territory, was a result of the presence in Tanganyika of a relatively unified African nationalist movement able to win decisively and overwhelmingly at the ballot box. It also resulted from the absence of effectively mobilized immigrant communities and the lack of serious rivalries between African ethnic groups.

Governor Sir Edward Twining arrived in Tanganyika in 1949 charged with the task of accelerating the pace of constitutional reform. By 1952 Twining was committed to the doctrine of multi-racialism espoused in Kenya. Twining was convinced that an immediate transition to African majority rule would discourage foreign investment and lead to an exodus of settlers. In 1955, Twining appointed thirty unofficial members to an enlarged Legco, ten from each racial community. By that year, however, African nationalism was beginning to assume a mass character. The Tanganyika African National Union (TANU) emerged in 1954 from the Tanganyika African Association (TAA), founded as early as 1929.[46] TANU's success in mobilizing territory-wide support was due in part to the widespread use of Kiswahili in the territory, transcending ethnic boundaries. TANU organizers also tapped local grievances over land, taxes, and government agricultural policies, and resentment towards unpopular chiefs and racial privileges. TANU leaders often appeared as more credible leaders in African eyes than local chiefs deeply involved in unpopular government policies.[47] The fundamental message of party president Julius Nyerere and other TANU leaders was that the British had not done enough to develop and modernize Tanganyika, and that it was shameful for any people in the 20th century to be ruled by another. TANU abstained from advocating any issue nationally that might upset the achievement of political unity. Within a few years, TANU nurtured a nationalist consensus not seen in the other East African territories.[48]

In response to TANU's growing strength, Twining used legal and punitive means to try to contain the party. Twining also attempted to encourage the formation of a party that would earnestly defend the government's policy of multi-racialism. The United Tanganyika Party (UTP) gained only limited support, however. Immigrant communities were themselves divided, and many in fact supported TANU out of a sense of enlightened self-interest, realizing that Tanganyika was primarily an African state. In the territory's first elections, scheduled in two stages during 1958 and 1959, each voter was required to cast ballots for three candidates to the Legco, one from each racial community. After Nyerere convinced TANU leaders to cooperate with this multi-racial experiment, TANU-nominated candidates from all three races won decisive victories, capturing 13 of 15 elected seats. These results eliminated the UTP as a viable party and it convinced Twining's replacement, Sir Richard Turnbull, to scrap multi-racialism altogether.[49] Turnbull decided to prepare Tanganyikans for independence after a final round of elections in 1960, in which TANU-supported candidates, whether African, European or Asian, won 70 of 71 contested seats. Nyerere became chief minister in 1960, and on December 9, 1961, Tanganyika became the first East African territory to achieve independence.

TANU's overwhelming electoral strength did not necessarily encourage the endurance of opposition parties after independence. A breakaway party known as the African National Congress (ANC) sought to challenge TANU by making more insistent demands for rapid Africanization of the civil service and the economy, but the party was unable to capture a mass following and it dissolved by 1963.[50] By the mid-1960s, Nyerere made his preference for single-party government clear. He may have been influenced by the embarrassing experience of the 1964 army mutiny, in which he was required to call on British soldiers to restore government authority in Dar es Salaam.[51] Nyerere was also convinced that opposition parties would only lead to needless factionalism and comprised a fundamental threat to the unity necessary for Tanzania to achieve accelerated development. Ethnic conflict and underdevelopment were greater threats to Tanzania in its early history, Nyerere felt, than single-party rule. TANU would, according to the nationalist leader, serve as the primary guardian of the people's interests, and as such, required no rival. Nyerere called for a mass party responsible to and representative of the peasants and workers, working to ensure government acted on behalf of the public interest and not corrupted by private demands. He was convinced competition between political parties would not be consistent with either African pre-colonial traditions or the urgent project of socialist economic development.[52] In 1965 the Tanzanian constitution was amended to enshrine the single-party state into law.[53]

The absence of opposition freed Nyerere to address the political isolation of rural life and work to integrate all citizens into a new national community. These efforts reached their peak in the mid-1970s, when Nyerere's *ujamaa* villagization schemes forcibly relocated over five million Tanzanian peasants to designated village sites.[54] Nyerere called on peasants to move to more centralized locations, and to send their children to schools where they could learn to read and write and absorb TANU party doctrines. Nyerere wanted to "capture" the labor of peasants for nation building projects, and eradicate poverty, ignorance, disease and exploitation.[55] He also believed that he was creating the conditions for Greek-style direct democracy. According to Nyerere in 1962, "living together in villages will also help to perfect our plans for democracy."[56]

TANU evolved into one of the "most extensive party organizations in Africa."[57] TANU's reach in society included a vast system of 10-house cells and local branches, which assumed roles in economic development and in adjudicating local disputes.[58] By 1975, TANU had also dissolved, co-opted, or imposed its dominance over most forms of civil society, including the media, trade unions, and what was once a vibrant peasant cooperative movement.[59] Nyerere initially earned more praise than criticism. His reputation for incorruptibility, as well as having fewer political detainees in his jails than other rulers in East Africa, earned him at least guarded respect among international observers. As in Kenya, elections to the National Assembly were held every five years, with a high rate of turnover. Nominated by their party leaders for voter approval, MPs continued to discuss government policies, but in general they served only to ratify and not to initiate policies. Although TANU was a large tent that included individuals of varying ideological stripes under the shadow of Tanzanian socialism, critical debate was unusual in these "rubber stamp" proceedings.[60]

Tanzanians during the 1970s either accepted or chose not to overtly resist these arrangements. Nyerere's efforts to undermine the emergence of an entrenched bureaucratic bourgeoisie, to nationalize foreign business enterprises, and to provide better education and health services were enormously popular.[61] The most serious criticisms came from TANU party intellectuals and academics at the University of Dar es Salaam, who wanted to transform TANU into a vanguard party that would pursue more aggressive means to implement socialism.[62] They also wanted to adopt more "scientific" means to enhance the nation's productive forces, and they objected to the encroachment of "state capitalism."[63] But Nyerere did not abandon his faith in TANU as a mass party, or his belief in a gradual transition to socialism based upon rural development. Through its extensive Soviet-style party apparatus, TANU was capable of implementing *ujamaa* villagization, one of post-colonial Africa's most ambitious and coercive socialist political projects.

By the end of the 1970s, Tanzania was financially exhausted, economically stagnant, experiencing rapid infrastructure decay, and more dependent on international aid than at the beginning of the decade. Nyerere was increasingly frustrated with the conduct of party and government officials, and with peasants whom he felt lacked discipline and socialist conviction. The gradual onset of economic crisis, the growing authoritarianism and bureaucratization of the state, and its intolerance of organized political opposition, undermined Nyerere's grassroots support. TANU constructed a national consensus in the 1950s by articulating new ideas, and Nyerere preserved that consensus by crafting a compelling vision of a future socialist Tanzania. He also promised that TANU's reforms would benefit ordinary people and attack narrow self-interests. This would be done by promoting economic equality in the new nation and the party would establish a more democratic society than what existed in the capitalist West. But with the failure of many of Nyerere's initiatives, peasants withdrew their involvement in public affairs and sought space free from state intervention. According to McHenry, by the 1980s "cynicism about the party's ability to fulfill popular wishes was widespread."[64] Policies emanating from the center of Tanzanian political life bore little direct relation to peasants' expressed concerns.

Zanzibar, which formed a union with the Tanganyikan mainland in 1964 to create the United Republic of Tanzania, deserves separate discussion due to its somewhat different, yet parallel history with mainland Tanzania. During the colonial era, major ethnic communities on the islands had their own associations, the most powerful of which was the Arab Association. According to the 1948 census, Arabs constituted 19 percent of the population,[65] East Africa's largest non-African community. In the mid-1950s, the British abandoned multi-racialism in favor of common roll elections, partially as a result of pressure from, paradoxically, the Arab Association. Two major party coalitions emerged, the Zanzibar Nationalist Party (ZNP) and the Afro-Shirazi Party (ASP).[66] As the forum for African nationalism, the ASP initially enjoyed significant electoral advantages. The ZNP, however, mobilized a multi-racial coalition of voters under the banner of Islamic non-racialism, allegiance to the Sultan, Zanzibari nationalism, and anti-colonialism. The party was well financed and organized, and it attracted the strong support of Arab and Asian communities, along with a significant number of Africans. As the contest evened, a series of boycotts, evictions, and abusive rhetoric from both sides dramatically worsened race relations.[67] The atmosphere was one of increasing partisan and racial tension, as each side engaged in "exclusionary ethnic nationalism."[68]

The ASP suffered a major blow in 1959 when several of its leading politicians left to form their own Zanzibar and Pemba People's Party (ZPPP), which went on to form an alliance with the ZNP that won elections in 1961 and 1963. The only setback suffered by the ZNP-ZPPP was the exodus of a number of students, workers, and intellectuals from the party who formed the socialist Umma Party in July 1963. Their departure represented growing divisions within the ZNP between conservatives and many younger members who considered the party's rhetoric of racial unity under a common Islamic identity empty when party leaders did not advocate economic reforms in favor of the island's poor African majority. Although limited in size, Umma formed a working alliance with the ASP, and won the sympathy of many in the opposition for its outspoken criticisms of the ZNP-ZPPP. Within a month following independence in December 1963, the new government banned the Umma Party and forced its leaders into exile.[69]

Many ASP supporters were not pleased with the outcome of the 1963 elections, where their party won 54 percent of the popular vote, but failed to win a majority of parliamentary seats. Members of the ASP Youth League (ASPYL) organized a successful uprising in January 1964, only a month after independence. The Sultan fled on his yacht, the ZNP-ZPPP cabinet ministers surrendered, and a reign of terror broke out against their party supporters. The violence, which Sheriff describes as "genocidal in proportions,"[70] singled out Arabs for plunder, rape, exile and execution. The Zanzibar Revolution politically enfranchised Africans who opposed a democratic process they believed had been manipulated by British and Arabs. With the absorption of Umma by the ASP, Zanzibar officially became a single-party state. A new ruling oligarchy emerged, with Abeid Karume originally serving as a *primer inter pares* within the Revolutionary Council. Because he was not personally involved in the uprising, Karume's position was initially weak. Several of his ministers, inspired by their experiences abroad, had specific socialist agendas in mind, and sought to pressure Karume to adopt a more "progressive line." Through the influence of socialist army officers, ministers and civil servants primarily of Umma background it appeared to some that Zanzibar would become the "Cuba" of East Africa. The arrival of military hardware and hundreds of advisors and technical experts from East Germany, the U.S.S.R., and China heightened Cold War tension in the region.[71] The announcement of policies such as land redistribution and the nationalization of businesses and urban properties convinced Western and East African observers the islands were becoming a potential showcase for socialist development in Africa.

Nyerere became personally convinced of the need for action against the perceived threat of a socialist satellite state, a Cold War arms race, the regional spread of racial violence, and a possible invasion of Zanzibar by an Arab counter-revolutionary force.[72] He pressured Karume in April 1964 to accept a union of their two countries, with Zanzibar assuming a junior but autonomous position. While sacrificing independent control over foreign relations, Zanzibar was not required to adapt its domestic policies to those of the mainland. In the years following, Karume gradually consolidated his dominant position in the Revolutionary Council. By the late-1960s, he ruled virtually by personal decree. The Youth League became the primary enforcing agency of the state, which executed four of the nine earliest cabinet members.[73] Karume proclaimed that there would be no elections in Zanzibar for at least sixty years.[74] Definitions of criminal conduct expanded to include a series of offenses such as wearing western fashions or not attending party meetings. Popular memories of the period almost universally describe an atmosphere of fear and petty harassment.[75]

Government policies that imposed food rationing, forced labor, and that caused chronic shortages of basic household commodities were far less popular than land redistribution or the construction of new schools. Thousands fled the islands rather than submit to a regime that imposed on its people a demanding standard of citizenship. Former Umma Party members, who helped shape many revolutionary policies, and who continued to retain their own networks, assassinated Karume in a failed *coup* attempt in 1972. Aboud Jumbe, his successor, subsequently introduced reforms such as the evisceration of the Youth League, and the end of food rations and forced labor. Jumbe established closer relations with the mainland, and he developed a new constitution and a House of Representatives.[76] In his efforts to bring the islands' ruling practices into some conformity with those of the mainland, Jumbe was at least partially motivated by his ambitions to succeed Nyerere as president of Tanzania. Nyerere's ultimate unwillingness to sanction such ambitions led to a personal split and Jumbe's political downfall and retirement in 1984.[77]

Concluding Comments

This chapter's comparative approach yields insights concerning the nature of democratic experiments in East Africa. Despite the region's cultural diversity, the British imposed some policies that were similar. The authoritarian nature of colonialism did not permit African participation in territory-wide representative institutions until the end of World War II. Colonial conservatism, conventional racial assumptions, and the competing demands of politically mobilized immigrant communities combined to deny Africans their political rights. After the war, British governors were pressured by London to institute limited constitutional reforms. Such reforms, however, were complicated by British policies that had favored local "ruling partners" such as the Baganda in Uganda, Arabs in Zanzibar, and white settlers in Kenya. Through indirect rule the British encouraged ethnic fragmentation among Africans in Kenya, Uganda, and Tanganyika. Colonial agents subsequently sought to erase the legacies of favoritism and indirect rule when they attempted to establish multi-racial systems of representation that provoked deep resentment among nationalists in Kenya, Tanganyika, and

Zanzibar. Unable to win nationalist support for this approach to colonial rule, the British abandoned the experiment and finally began to endorse the principle of equal voting rights.

After only a few years of nationalist political mobilization and multi-party politics, by the end of 1963 the British formally withdrew from all four territories in the region. Such a short period, however, did not resolve the contradictions of decades of colonial rule. Nationalists who participated in Lancaster House constitutional conferences possessed perspectives that were unsurprisingly shaped by their long experience with colonial favoritism and indirect rule. Though they may have been liberal in personal conviction, they realized that colonial officials granted these democratic concessions only after long resistance. Political rights, therefore, were not inalienable, they were won by determined struggle. Western definitions of individual rights invited reexamination, and they could also be sacrificed, some believed, for either personal or corporate interests.

Independent civilian regimes in East Africa continued to experiment with different political arrangements in the 1960s; all abandoned multi-partyism in favor of single-party rule. In the era of nation-building, the executive authorities of each state concentrated more power in their own hands, at the expense of legislative assemblies. They increasingly relied either on the military (Uganda), the civil service (Kenya), or the party (Tanzania) to defend their legitimacy and to implement national policies. All four East African territories, meanwhile, officially endorsed some version of African socialism, which justified radical measures to achieve accelerated development, but also legitimized the suspension of civil liberties in the urgent pursuit of nationalist aims. While the espousal of socialism in Uganda and Kenya was either brief or somewhat superficial, in Tanganyika and Zanzibar socialist experiments were to have a profound impact on the everyday lives of millions. In these two territories grassroots participation in a ruling party committee, for example, was considered the embodiment of democracy.

East African regimes also had widely varying success in sustaining political legitimacy. Both Obote and Amin in Uganda were unable, as northerners, to maintain ruling coalitions in the face of ongoing resistance on the part of more numerous ethnic and religious communities in the center and south. While Uganda descended into a cycle of violence that would continue well past the end of the 1970s, the issue of political legitimacy was at least temporarily resolved in Zanzibar through an uprising in 1964, the violence of which systematically eliminated leading opposition elements and intimidated survivors.

In Kenya and mainland Tanzania, coercion and the threat of violence were less necessary in ensuring popular compliance. In the transition to independence, Kenyans and Tanganyikans rallied around the symbolic presence, words and deeds of single, unifying nationalist figures. Nyerere and Kenyatta commanded enormous prestige and trust, and their personal stature dwarfed debates over abstract principles of political rights and morality. Civil society organizations in Kenya and Tanzania could not compete with the power of these two popular leaders, who regarded single-party rule more suitable than multi-partyism. Both were effective in imposing new social contracts, which shared common ground when defining the duties and rights of citizens. In both countries the overall emphasis was as much on corporate duties as on rights. Citizens heard endless and repetitive calls to "build the nation" (*kujenga taifa*). In this context democracy was loosely defined as the ability to participate in the construction of an independent and more egalitarian society; such participation promised direct benefits to both the individual and the community.

Over the past two decades, this version of democratic participation has been largely discredited as a result of economic stagnation, and the spread of neo-patrimonial inequalities. In national debates in Kenya and Tanzania, both socialism and clientalism have been publicly attacked and repudiated. By the 1990s, democratic ideals as defined and propagated by the West had resurfaced throughout the region. The remainder of the book will explore this process in greater detail.

Notes

1 Samwiri Karugire, *A Political History of Uganda* (London: Heinemann Educational Books, 1980), pp. 12 and 14-16.

2 O.A.L.A. Olumwullah, "Government," in William R. Ochieng', ed., *Themes in Kenyan History* (Oxford: James Currey, 1991), p. 95.

3 Olumwullah, "Government," p. 96.

4 The Chiga of Kigezi district in Uganda provide an extreme example of this category: they recognized no communal political power of any kind. The highest sphere of authority was within the family. When disputes emerged which required some form of outside arbitration, an *ad hoc* council of local elders performed such tasks. They did so by invitation only, and had no means by which to enforce their decisions. Rather, fear of loss of respect, disgrace, and social ridicule were enough to induce the Chiga to submit to their rulings. Peter Gukiina, *Uganda: A Case Study in African Political Development* (London: University of Notre Dame Press, 1972), pp. 25-6.

5 Alyward Shorter, *Chiefship in Western Tanzania: A Political History of the Kimbu* (Oxford: Clarendon Press, 1972), pp. 97ff.

6 Isariah Kimambo, *Penetration and Protest in Tanzania: The Impact of the World Economy on the Pare, 1860-1960* (London: James Currey, 1991), pp. 28ff.

7 John Iliffe, *A Modern History of Tanganyika* (Cambridge: Cambridge University Press, 1979), p. 21.

8 John Iliffe, *A Modern History of Tanganyika*, p. 22.

9 Steven Feierman, *Peasant Intellectuals: Anthropology and History in Tanzania* (Madison: University of Wisconsin Press, 1990), p. 46.

10 Karugire, *Political History of Uganda*, pp. 22-3.

11 Mutesa I was able to maintain a standing army and navy of 6,000 men in the mid-19th century for purposes of war and to maintain domestic order. Gukiina, *Uganda: A Case Study*, p. 43.

12 See Abdul Sheriff, *Slaves, Spices and Ivory in Zanzibar* (London: James Currey, 1987).

13 Iliffe, *Modern History of Tanganyika*, p. 66.

14 Karugire, *Political History of Uganda*, pp. 117-8.

15 Iliffe, *Modern History of Tanganyika*, pp. 342ff.

[16] G.S.K. Ibingira, *The Forging of an African Nation: The Political and Constitutional Evolution of Uganda From Colonial Rule to Independence, 1894-1962* (New York: Viking Press, 1973), pp. 26-8.

[17] Norman Bennett, *Kenya: A Political History: The Colonial Period* (London: Oxford University Press, 1963), p. 6.

[18] Bennett, *Kenya: A Political History*, p. 22.

[19] Ibingira, *The Forging of an African Nation*, pp. 21-3.

[20] Ibingira, *The Forging of an African Nation*, p. 26.

[21] Karugire, *Political History of Uganda*, p. 142.

[22] Michael Lofchie, *Zanzibar: Background to Revolution* (Princeton: Princeton University Press, 1965). Legco debates in the 1930s over what to do about the chronic indebtedness of Arab clove planters to Asian financiers raised the issue of whether Arabs could be preserved as the island's landowning elite. By prohibiting further land transfers to Asian financiers, the British demonstrated their willingness to use all necessary means to relieve the insolvency of the Arab planter aristocracy and to sustain the racial *status quo* in Zanzibar.

[23] David Gordon, *Decolonization and the State in Kenya* (London: Westview Press, 1986), p. 90.

[24] Gordon, *Decolonization and the State in Kenya*, p. 92.

[25] B.A. Ogot, "The Decisive Years, 1956-63," in B.A. Ogot and W.R. Ochieng', eds., *Decolonization and Independence in Kenya, 1940-93* (London: James Currey, 1995).

[26] The deaths of eleven Mau Mau detainees under British custody in a "rehabilitation" camp were the object of an official cover-up. Gordon, *Decolonization and the State*, pp. 129-32.

[27] Ogot, "The Decisive Years," pp. 71-2.

[28] John Okumu with Frank Holmquist, "Party and Party-State Relations," in Joel Barkan, ed., *Politics and Public Policy in Kenya and Tanzania* (London: Praeger, 1984), pp. 51-2.

[29] John Okumu with Frank Holmquist, "Party and Party-State Relations," p. 54.

[30] William Ochieng', "Structural and Political Changes," in B.A. Ogot and W.R. Ochieng', eds., *Decolonization and Independence in Kenya, 1940-93* (London: James Currey, 1995), p. 107.

[31] B.A. Ogot, "The Politics of Populism," in B.A. Ogot and W.R. Ochieng', eds., *Decolonization and Independence in Kenya, 1940-93* (London: James Currey, 1995), pp. 187-9.

[32] Ochieng', "Structural and Political Changes," pp. 94ff.

[33] Ogot, "The Politics of Populism," pp. 190-1; Goran Hyden, "Party, State, and Civil Society: Control Versus Openness," in Joel Barkan, ed., *Beyond Capitalism vs. Socialism in Kenya and Tanzania* (London: Lynne Reiner Publishers, 1994), p. 81.

[34] Joel Barkan, "Legislators, Elections and Political Linkage," in Joel Barkan with John Okumu, eds., *Politics and Public Policy in Kenya and Tanzania* (London: Praeger, 1984), p. 72.

[35] Barkan, "Legislators, Elections and Political Linkage," p. 73.

[36] Barkan, "Legislators, Elections and Political Linkage," p. 88.

[37] Christopher Wrigley, "Four Steps Towards Disaster," in Holger Bernt, Hansen and Michael Twaddle, eds., *Uganda Now: Between Decay and Development* (London: James Currey, 1988), pp. 30-1.

[38] Gukiina, *Uganda: A Case Study*, p. 4; Wrigley, "Four Steps to Disaster," p. 32.

[39] Gukiina, *Uganda: A Case Study*, p. 104.

[40] Gukiina, *Uganda: A Case Study*, p. 110.

[41] See D.A. Low, "The Dislocated Polity," in Holger Bernt Hansen and Michael Twaddle, eds., *Uganda Now: Between Decay and Development* (London: James Currey, 1988), p. 41.

[42] Low, "The Dislocated Polity," p. 42.

[43] Gukiina, *Uganda: A Case Study*, p. 133.

[44] Low, "The Dislocated Polity," pp. 43-4.

[45] Low, "The Dislocated Polity," pp. 45-8.

[46] Although the TAA was able to establish a limited network of branches in important towns in the territory, it did not attempt to become a mass political movement with codified demands for constitutional reform.

[47] Feierman, *Peasant Intellectuals*.

[48] Iliffe, *Modern History of Tanganyika*, pp. 507ff.

[49] Iliffe, *Modern History of Tanganyika.*, pp. 560ff.

[50] James Brennan, "The Short History of Political Opposition and Multi-party Democracy in Tanganyika, 1958-64," in Gregory Maddox, James Giblin, Y.Q. Lawi, eds., *In Search of a Nation: Histories of Authority and Dissidence from Tanzania: Essays in Honor of I.M. Kimambo* (London: James Currey, in press).

[51] Brennan, "The Short History of Political Opposition and Multi-party Democracy in Tanganyika."

[52] Dean McHenry, *Limited Choices: The Political Struggle for Socialism in Tanzania* (London: Lynne Reiner Publishers, 1994), pp. 48-9; Joel Barkan, "Divergence and Convergence in Kenya and Tanzania: Pressures for Reform," in Joel Barkan, ed., *Beyond Capitalism vs. Socialism in Kenya and Tanzania* (London: Lynne Reiner Publishers, 1994), p. 16.

[53] Goran Hyden, "Party, State, and Civil Society: Control Versus Openness," p. 93.

[54] Goran Hyden, *Beyond Ujamaa: Underdevelopment and an Uncaptured Peasantry* (Berkeley: University of California Press, 1980), p. 130.

[55] Hyden, *Beyond Ujamaa.*

[56] Feierman, *Peasant Intellectuals*, p. 228.

[57] Okumu and Holmquist, "Party and Party-State Relations," p. 50.

[58] In 1975 the Tanzanian National Assembly officially articulated this through passage of the Interim Constitution of Tanzania (Amendment) Act. Bismarck Mwansasu, "The Changing Role of the Tanganyika African National Union," in Bismarck Mwansasu and Cranford Pratt, eds., *Towards Socialism in Tanzania* (Toronto: University of Toronto Press, 1979), p. 169.

[59] McHenry, *Limited Choices*; Feierman, *Peasant Intellectuals*; Barkan, "Divergence and Convergence," p. 20.

[60] Joel Barkan, "Legislators, Elections, and Political Linkage."

[61] McHenry, *Limited Choices*, p. 51.

[62] McHenry, *Limited Choices*, pp. 51ff.

[63] A.M. Babu, a cabinet minister in Nyerere's government until 1972, was one of his most prominent critics. See A.M. Babu in Salma Babu, and Amrit Wilson, eds., *The Future that Works: Selected Writings of A.M. Babu* (Trenton, New Jersey: Africa World Press, 2002); A.M. Babu in Haroub Othman, ed., *I Saw the Future and it Works* (Dar es Salaam: E & D Limited, 2001); A.M. Babu, *African Socialism or Socialist Africa?* (Dar es Salaam: Tanzania Publishing House, 1981).

[64] McHenry, *Limited Choices*, p. 57.

[65] Lofchie, *Background to Revolution*, p. 72.

[66] In this context, "African" meant indigenous islanders, descendants of slaves, and relatively recent migrant laborers from the African mainland. Those who claimed

indigenous, or Shirazi identity, split their support between the two major coalitions. "Mainlander" Africans gave their strong support to the ASP.

[67] According to the British Colonial Report for 1959-1960, "The political struggle occupied the minds of the people of Zanzibar to the exclusion of everything else. Both men and women took full part in these activities." Haroub Othman and Aggrey Mlimuka, "The Political and Constitutional Development of Zanzibar and the Case Studies of the 1985 Zanzibar General Elections," in Haroub Othman, et al., eds., *Tanzania: Democracy in Transition* (Dar es Salaam University Press: Dar es Salaam, 1990), p. 155. Lofchie observes, "Performance of the most routine daily tasks ... was viewed as an integral facet of the national political struggle ... By 1958 no dimension of social behavior remained politically neutral. Even private quarrels and disputes which had long preceded the formation of modern political parties were absorbed into the pattern of partisan conflict." Lofchie, *Background to Revolution*, pp. 183-4.

[68] Jonathon Glassman, "Sorting Out the Tribes: The Creation of Racial Identities in Colonial Zanzibar's Newspaper Wars," *Journal of African History* vol. 41 (2000), p. 427.

[69] Thomas Burgess, "An Imagined Generation: Umma Youth in Nationalist Zanzibar," in Gregory Maddox, James Giblin, Y.Q. Lawi, eds., *In Search of a Nation: Histories of Authority and Dissidence from Tanzania: Essays in Honor of I.M. Kimambo* (London: James Currey, in press).

[70] Abdul Sheriff, "Race and Class in the Politics of Zanzibar," *Afrika Spectrum* vol. 36, no. 3 (2001), pp. 314-5. According to Sheriff, "There is no doubting the deep-seated wound that it has left in the body politic of Zanzibar."

[71] Babu was quoted as saying in April 1964, "East Africa is a powder keg, and Zanzibar is the fuse." Burgess, "An Imagined Generation."

[72] Amrit Wilson argues American imperialism forced the union agreement as a way of neutralizing communist influence in Zanzibar. See *US Foreign Policy and Revolution: The Creation of Tanzania* (London: Pluto Press, 1989). Archival records in the Lyndon Baines Johnson Library at the University of Texas, Austin, and the National Archives in College Park, Maryland, do not, however, support this view. According to these records, American interests coincided with those of Nyerere; no coercion appears to have taken place.

[73] Othman Shariff, Kassim Hanga, Abdulazziz Twala, and Salehe Saadalla. See Ali Sultan Issa in Thomas Burgess, ed., *Walk on Two Legs: A Memoir of the Zanzibari Revolution*, forthcoming.

[74] Othman and Mlimuka, "The Political and Constitutional Development of Zanzibar," p. 164.

[75] Thomas Burgess, "Cinema, Bell Bottoms and Miniskirts: Struggles Over Youth and Citizenship in Revolutionary Zanzibar," *International Journal of African Historical Studies* vol. 35, no. 2 (2002).

[76] Othman and Mlimuka, "Political and Constitutional Development," p. 169.

[77] See Jan Kees, Van Donge, and Athumani Liviga, "The Democratization of Zanzibar and the 1985 General Elections," *The Journal of Commonwealth and Comparative Politics* vol. 28, no. 2 (1990), pp. 203-4.

Chapter 3

Political Parties and Party Systems

Dean E. McHenry, Jr.

When the "third wave" of democratization hit East Africa in the late 1980s, political activists and academic observers contended that the principal obstacle to the creation of democracy was the domination of the government in Kenya and Tanzania by a single political party and in Uganda by a single political movement. Although there was agreement among the advocates of a multi-party system that the single-party/movement systems had to be eliminated, they were divided over whether a multi-party system was a sufficient condition for democratization to occur. The experiences of these East African countries over the past decade have shown that a multi-party system is not a sufficient condition for democratization. Events have also raised doubts about whether multi-partyism is even a necessary condition. The purpose of this chapter is to examine the East Africa experience to determine the role that political parties have played in the democratization process.

To accomplish this purpose, the chapter is organized into three sections: to reduce terminological confusion, we will seek to clarify the concepts "political party" and "party system"; to provide an empirical basis for a discussion of the relationship between parties/party systems and democracy, we will describe the experiences of the three East African countries since 1990; and, finally, we will summarize observations about the parties-democracy relationship and address the factors that account for those findings.

Defining Political Party and Party System

In East Africa, as elsewhere, the meanings assigned to "political parties" and "party systems," and the related categorization of existing groups and sets of groups have been contentious. For example, there are disputes over whether CCM prior to 1992 was a party or a party-state, since some viewed the ruling party as merely an extension of the state; whether the 1980-85 period in Uganda was one in which a multi-party system existed, since many observers have argued that the UPC dominated the scene and did not permit fair electoral competition;[1] whether the NRM in Uganda prior to its registration as the National Resistance Movement Organization (NRM-O) in 2003 was a party, since many Ugandans considered it was one and the Constitutional Court eventually "declared" that it was; and whether NARC in Kenya is a political party, since many contend that NARC was incorrectly registered as a party since its members are primarily organizations rather than individuals.

The conceptual confusion is reduced, but not eliminated, by defining a political party as "any political group that presents at elections, and is capable of placing through elections, candidates for public office." A party system is "a pluralistic system of 'parts' that forcibly 'express' the opinions of the governed," as suggested many years ago by Sartori.[2] Although these definitions are commonly employed in the literature, they produce additional difficulties. In Kenya, Tanzania, and Uganda, the government agents who register parties and who make the decisions whether a "political group" is a party that can participate in elections, apply different criteria in making their determinations. Thus, the meaning of party varies somewhat from country to country. Also, the assumption that the "opinions of the governed" are expressed through the group of parties present (what is commonly referred to as the party system) is tenuous at best. The degree to which the party system embodies the "opinions of the governed" varies, too. To discuss what are commonly called political parties and party systems in East Africa necessitates a somewhat flexible application of Sartori's definitions.

The Relationship Between Parties and Democracy in East Africa

Assessments of the relationship between parties and democracy in Kenya, Tanzania, and Uganda using empirical data on party evolution and the widely employed Polity IV and Freedom House democracy data sets produce ambiguous images.

Although both data sets employ a liberal definition of democracy, their characterizations of democracy in East Africa differ. In the Polity IV data, the level of democracy does not decline for any year from 1990-1999, while in the Freedom House scale the only country that appears to be more than fractionally higher at the end of the decade as compared with the start of the decade is Tanzania. In addition, the level of democracy in Kenya, Uganda, and Tanzania was approximately the same during the 1970s, when Uganda was ruled by Idi Amin. That the level of democracy in Kenya and Tanzania was no higher than that in Uganda under Amin defies common sense. Nevertheless, if we accept what seem to be imperfections in the dependent variable "democracy," the question about how the character of the parties/party systems is related to the degree of democracy arises.

Multi-party systems have been in existence in Kenya from 1991 to the present and in Tanzania from 1992 to the present, while Uganda has had a no-party system from 1990 to 2003. When we compare the types of party systems (defined crudely by the proliferation of political parties) with the levels of democracy over the decade of the 1990s, we find that according to the Polity IV measure, both a no-party system and multi-party systems seem to be associated with higher levels of democracy; and according to the Freedom House measure, a no-party state and multi-party states are associated with *both* increasing levels of democracy and decreasing levels of democracy.

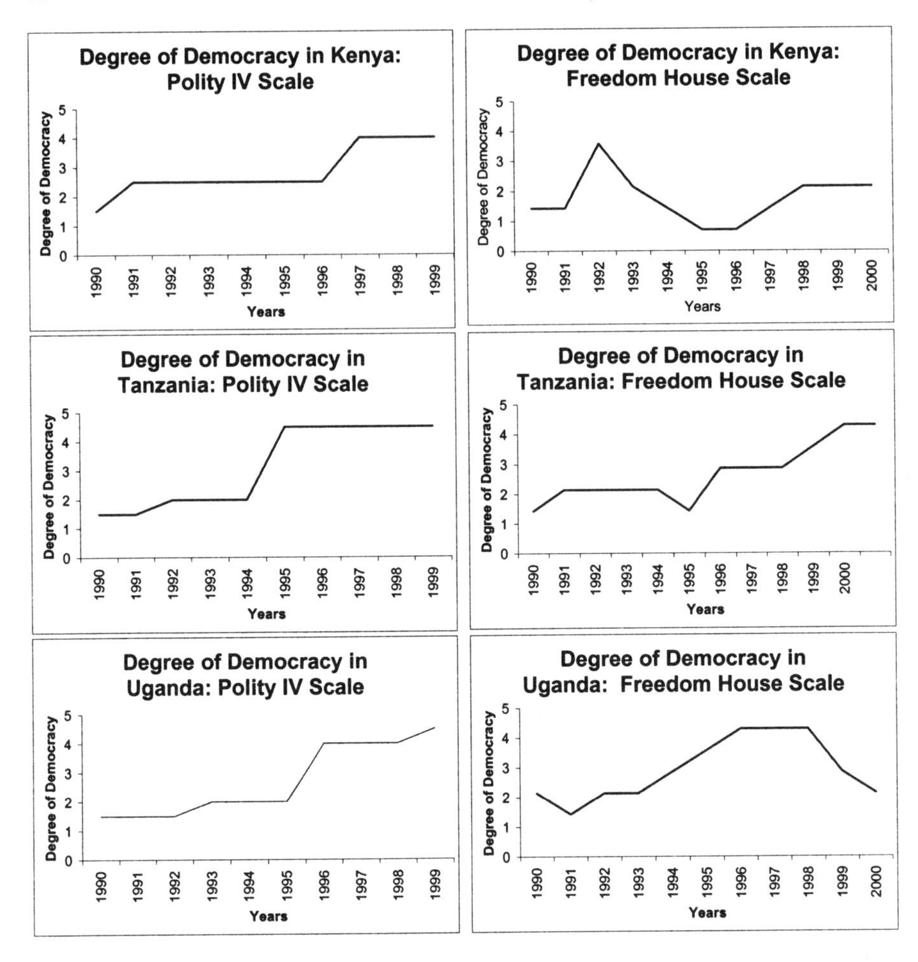

Chart 3.1 Polity IV and Freedom House Measures of Democracy in Kenya, Tanzania and Uganda

Source: The Polity IV data set was compiled by Monty Marshall and Keith Jaggers. An updated version can be found at http://www.cidcm.umd.edu/inscr/polity/index.htm; the Freedom House data set was published by Freedom House under the title "Freedom in the World Country Ratings, 1972-73 to 2000-02." To transform the Freedom House data to a scale of 0 to 10, the political rights and civil liberties scores were summed and subtracted from 14; the result was divided by 1.4. To transform the Polity IV data to a scale of 0 to 10, the autocracy score was subtracted from the democracy score and the result was divided by 2. The dates for the Freedom House data for the first of the two years cited in the set.

The evidence regarding the relationship between the party/party system and the degree of democracy is contradictory. These contradictions suggest the need for a more detailed study of the political parties and their relationship to democracy in Kenya, Tanzania, and Uganda. In examining these experiences, we will focus on the factors leading to the introduction of multi-party/no-party systems, the development of an opposition/opposition parties, the state response to these developments, and how they affected the democratic process in elections, thus enabling us to draw conclusions about the relationship between political parties and democratization in these countries.

Kenya

During the Moi presidency, Kenya became a *de jure* single-party state in 1982. By 1990, though, the challenge to the monopoly of power held by Moi and KANU became intense, fueled by economic decline and charges of corruption.

Shift to a Multi-Party System

In June 1990, the Catholic Bishops' Conference under the leadership of Cardinal Maurice Otunga issued a pastoral letter questioning the single-party system.[3] Although in December KANU voted to maintain its monopoly of power, international pressures to move toward a multi-party system intensified in the months that followed. Meeting on November 25-26 1991, Kenya's major international creditors, the Consultative Group or Paris Club, postponed for six months a decision on Kenya's request for financial assistance estimated at one billion U.S. dollars. The group called for progress in implementing social and political reforms, "in other words, in liberalizing its political regime."[4] Responding to both external and internal pressure, a special delegates conference of KANU approved Moi's decision and endorsed Kenya's reversion to a multi-party state. Later that month, Section 2A of the constitution was repealed and multi-party politics was legalized again.[5]

Throup and Hornsby describe the decision as "a panic reaction by the regime" to the donors' demands and as a step "not based upon a fundamental desire for or understanding of multi-party politics on the part of either the government or the people."[6] In subsequent years, Moi frequently condemned the multi-party system imposed by the international donors and warned that it would lead to ethnic violence. From the beginning, it was apparent that he would resist any challenge to his or KANU's dominance.

Development of an Opposition

A broad alliance of church leaders, civil rights lawyers, professionals, young activists and political elders established FORD a few months before the constitution was amended to allow parties other than KANU to operate. According to one observer, "... the FORD leadership found it challenging to transform a democracy movement into a political party, and they drew on the only model they were really familiar with: KANU. So FORD ended up reproducing KANU's organizational structure."[7] As Throup and Hornsby note in their study of the 1992 election, "all Kenyan political parties are patronage parties and have no independent existence or policy foundation in the absence of the all-powerful leader. Political preferences were based on calculations of personal or local advantage ... "[8] These observations are as relevant in 2004 as they were at the time of the 1992 elections.

FORD's experience in the early years of the return to a multi-party system in Kenya presaged future problems that confronted most parties: frequent leadership battles and numerous ethnic divisions. In October 1992, FORD split into a predominantly Kikuyu FORD-Asili, led by Kenneth Matiba, and a predominantly Luo FORD-Kenya, led by Oginga Odinga. A third major opposition party was the predominantly Kikuyu Democratic Party (DP), led by Mwai Kibaki.

Prior to the second multi-party election, FORD-Kenya split again with the late Oginga Odinga's son, Raila Odinga, breaking away to join the moribund National Development Party (NDP), while the rump party became a multi-ethnic group under the leadership of a Luhya, Kijana Wamalwa. Kenneth Matiba boycotted the 1997 elections, which he determined would be unfair after his newly formed Saba Saba Asili was denied registration. A further split from FORD-Asili led to the formation of FORD-People. The Social Democratic Party (SDP) became a significant participant in both the presidential and parliamentary elections of 1997.

Recognizing that the opposition's inability to successfully challenge KANU's dominance stemmed from its divisions, significant efforts were made to unify the opposition in the year prior to the December 27, 2002 election. In January, five parties, the most significant of which were the DP, FORD-Kenya, and the National Party of Kenya (NPK), joined two civil lobby groups to form the National Alliance for Change (NAC). By June seven more parties had joined; NPK changed its name to the National Alliance (Party) of Kenya; and NAC also assumed that name. In September NAK nominated Mwai Kibaki as its presidential candidate for the up-coming national election. Meanwhile, Moi's selection of Uhuru Kenyatta as KANU's presidential candidate in July led a group of dissidents within the party to form the Rainbow Alliance. Under Raila Odinga's leadership, they left KANU in early October and assumed the identity of the Liberal Democratic Party (LDP). Shortly thereafter the LDP and NAK united to form the National Rainbow Coalition (NARC) to oppose KANU in the December election. The "Memorandum of Understanding" (MOU) defining their union was ambiguous about what was being created. It referred to a "coalition" of LDP and NAK and to the formation of a "single political party" called the National Rainbow Coalition, or NARC.[9] NARC members agreed to support the presidential candidacy of Mwai Kibaki and to run candidates for parliament under the NARC label.

NARC's success in the December 2002 election meant that KANU became the official opposition in 2003. The party found it difficult to adjust to Moi's departure and to its new role as the opposition. By the end of the year, it joined FORD-People in the Coalition for National Unity (CNU). Immediately after its formation, CNU unexpectedly promoted compromise in the Bomas III phase of the National

Constitutional Conference that convened in January of 2004. Although KANU and FORD-People comprised the formal opposition, the most serious opposition seemed to come from within NARC, especially evident in the struggles between NAK and LDP supporters. For the most part, President Kibaki remained aloof from the debilitating struggles within NARC. His occasional calls for the parties in NARC to disband were resisted, especially by the LDP. In a sense, the old opposition to KANU had become both the governors and the opposition.

The Ruling Party and the State's Response

The conclusion of most observers is that KANU used a variety of tools to successfully thwart the challenge of the opposition parties until the 2002 election.[10]

First, Moi lured elements of the opposition into KANU. After the 1992 elections, many opposition parliamentarians crossed the aisle and joined the ruling party. The ease with which this occurred suggests the breadth of the political orientations accommodated by KANU, the weakness of party loyalty, and the desire of parliamentarians for personal benefit. In January 1998, Moi entered into a cooperative arrangement with Raila Odinga's NDP and in June 2001 he appointed Odinga the Minister of Energy, creating a *de facto* coalition government with the NDP. This was followed by a vote of delegates from KANU and NDP to merge the parties. A committee was set up to "harmonize the parties' constitutions and manifestos to create a new party."[11] In March 2002, the NDP formally merged with KANU to form the New KANU. Yet, as we have noted, the anger within KANU regarding the selection of Uhuru Kenyatta as KANU's presidential candidate led to the creation of NARC just before the December 2002 elections.

Second, legal and constitutional tools were employed. Parliamentary districts were gerrymandered in both of the first two elections to the substantial disadvantage of the opposition parties. Just prior to the 1992 election, the rules governing the presidential poll were changed. The victor was required to have a plurality of the total votes and 25 percent of the vote in at least five of the eight provinces. In addition, the president was allowed to form a government from his own party even if he did not have a majority in parliament.[12]

Third, Moi compromised with opponents, especially within his own party. Prior to the 1997 election, a split developed within the party, with one faction identified as KANU-A (dominated by moderates and pragmatists) and the other as KANU-B (composed of hardliners). Moi empowered one faction and then the other depending upon its usefulness in dealing with the challenges to his domination. As the elections approached, Moi shifted support from hardliners to more moderate KANU elements who had joined with some of the opposition leaders to form the Inter-Parties Parliamentary Group (IPPG). This was done in response to the political violence in the Coast Province and mass action by the National Convention Executive Committee (NCEC), which called for comprehensive legal and constitutional changes before the elections. A package of modest electoral reforms and the promise of a constitution review commission after the election was decided upon and finally passed by the National Assembly shortly before the 1997 elections. Ironically, Moi's concession on the review of the constitution led to the National Constitutional Conference, which by early 2004 had become a battlefield where the NAK and the LDP factions within NARC fought over whether the powers of the president would be reduced and those of a prime minister increased (favored by LDP and opposed by NAK), thereby strengthening KANU's relative position.

Table 3.1 Parliamentary Elections in Kenya

Political Party	Percent of Vote in 1992	Number of Seats	Percent of Seats	Percent of Vote in 1997	Number of Seats	Percent of Seats	Percent of Vote in 2002	Number of Seats	Percent of Seats
KANU	24.5	100	49.5	38.5	108	51.4	27.6	64	30.5
FORD-Asili	20.6	31	15.3	1.4	1	0.5	1.4	2	1.0
DP	18.7	23	11.5	21.7	39	18.6			
FORD-Kenya	17.1	31	15.3	10.3	17	8.1			
KNC	1.5	1	0.5						
PICK	0.8	1	0.5						
KSC	0.3	1	0.5	0.3	1	0.5			
NDP				11.2	21	10.0			
SDP				8.3	15	7.1			
SAFI-NA				4.1	4	1.9	3.6	2	1.0
FORD-People				1.9	1	0.5	8.2	14	6.7
Shiriki-sho				0.4	1	0.5	0.3	1	0.5
NARC							50.0	125	59.5
Sisi Kwa Sisi							0.7	2	1.0
Others				1.9	3	1.5	8.2		

Source: For all but 1997 parliamentary percentage of votes and 2002 returns: Dirk Hartmann, "Kenya," in Dieter Nohlen, Michael Krennerich, and Bernhard Thibaut, eds., *Elections in Africa: a Data Handbook* (Oxford: Oxford University Press, 1999), pp. 486 and 488. For 1997 parliamentary percentage of votes: Calculated from Nick G. Wanjohi, "State of Political Parties in Kenya and Transition to Democracy," a paper presented at a workshop on "Transition to Democracy in East Africa" held at the Lake Manyara Serena Hotel, Tanzania, on April 9-10, 2001, p. 20. For 2002 parliamentary percentage of votes and number of parliamentary seats: Calculated, or obtained, from The Institute for Education in Democracy, "Enhancing the Electoral Process in Kenya, A Report on the Transition General Elections 2002, December, 27, 2002" (Nairobi: Institute for Education in Democracy, 2003), pp. 103-104.

Party Success: The 1992, 1997 and 2002 Elections

The multi-party elections since 1990 showed that a majority of people preferred a non-KANU president and non-KANU members of parliament. In the 1992 and 1997 elections, this "victory" of the opposition was not a real victory. In those elections, KANU remained the most popular party in the country, if we assume that the election returns approximate public preferences. It was not until the 2002 elections that KANU lost. The results of the parliamentary election are shown in Table 3.1.

Table 3.2 Presidential Elections in Kenya

Party of Presidential Candidate	Percent of Votes 1992 Election	Percent of Votes 1997 Election	Percent of Votes 2002 Election
Daniel arap Moi in 1992 and 1997; Uhuru Kenyatta in 2002 (KANU)	36.6	40.4	31.3
Kenneth Matiba in 1992; Martin Shikuku in 1997 (FORD-Asili)	25.8	0.6	
Mwai Kibaki (DP)	19.6	30.9	
Oginga Odinga in 1992; Michael Wamalwa in 1997 (FORD-Kenya)	17.1	8.2	
Raila Odinga (NDP)		10.8	
Charity Ngilu (SDP) in 1997; James Orengo in 2002		7.9	0.4
Mwai Kibaki (NARC)			62.2
Simeon Nyachae (FORD-P)			5.9
David Ng'ethe (CCU)			0.2
Others (4 in 1992 & 9 in 1997)	1.0	1.4	

Source: Dirk Hartmann, "Kenya," in Dieter Nohlen, Michael Krennerich, and Bernhard Thibaut, eds., *Elections in Africa: A Data Handbook* (Oxford: Oxford University Press, 1999), pp. 488-489; International Foundation for Election Systems, Results Summary, http://www.ifes.org/eguide/resultssum/kenya_pres02.htm, November 18, 2003.

Three observations may be made regarding the ability of political parties to promote democracy in Kenya. First, the proportion of seats won by KANU was far higher than its proportion of the total vote, indicating the great advantage the party was given by the way districts were drawn. Calculations of the strength of the opposition parties in parliament had parliamentary districts been drawn with an equal number of voters suggest that KANU would have won only 72 (rather than 100) seats in 1992 and 87 (rather than 108) seats in 1997.[13] Clearly, the playing field was tilted against the opposition parties. Second, the disintegration of FORD-Asili, NDP's split from FORD-Kenya, the merger of NDP into KANU, and the subsequent split in KANU during 2002, show the limited degree of institutionalization of parties. Third, the fact that 43 percent of the opposition vote in the 1997 parliamentary election came from parties that received no votes in the 1992 election, while at least 70 percent of the opposition vote in the 2002 parliamentary election came from two new parties, NARC and Sisi Kwa Sisi, is an additional indicator of the impermanence of opposition party organizations. Even though almost as many parliamentary seats were won by opposition parties as were won by KANU in the 1992 and 1997 elections, KANU was the clear winner in the presidential elections in those years. However, in 2002, NARC soundly defeated KANU in both the presidential and parliamentary elections, as shown in Table 3.2.

Did the electoral competition among political parties reflect the growth of democracy in Kenya? The broad consensus seemed to be that the playing field – especially in 1992 and 1997 – was not "level" and that the 1992 election, which Bratton rates as not free and fair, was less accurate than the 1997 election, which Barkan and Ng'ethe describe as "a poorly administered but closely monitored election acceptable to most voters and candidates."[14] The 2002 election was widely viewed as an improvement over previous elections.[15] Yet, to attribute this success to political parties would be disingenuous.

Concluding Observations

The judgment of most observers in the aftermath of the 1992 elections was that the multi-party system was retrogressive as far as democracy is concerned. Ajulu argues that "the result legitimated the Moi regime in a manner that had not been possible during the three previous elections held under a single-party system."[16] Barkan and Ng'ethe contend that "the return to multi-party politics resulted in a protracted five-year stalemate pitting President Daniel arap Moi and his ruling party, the Kenya African National Union (KANU), against an increasingly divided opposition."[17] There were desertions from opposition parties to KANU; ethnic conflict was intensified; and, splits in the opposition parties continued.

The high rates of defections led Makokha to observe that "parties are dying and democracy is not well" because the former "mean(s) little more than a politician's ticket to power." He points out that the main problems with Kenyan political parties are leadership intransigence, popular antipathy towards parties, lack of resources, poor management, disorganization or lack of organizational structures, and lack of ideology. Makokha concludes that "the proliferation of political parties does not point at greater democracy but at the silliness of politicians and their insatiable egos. The parties in place so far are a waste of good paper."[18]

In a perceptive summary applicable to Kenya throughout this period, Nasong'o, argues that "the quest for State House by existing parties in Kenya is not carried out by these parties as political parties per se, but as conglomerates of ethnic interests intent on capturing the state for its own sake."[19] He notes that "in the absence of party ideology in Kenya, politicians have come to perfect the art of the politics of opportunism where they are in one party today, tomorrow they announce their defection to another depending on their own changing political fortunes."[20] Noting the shifting of parties and subsequent reelection of MPs, Nasong'o states "that without an ideology, party allegiance is determined by rational self-interest."[21]

Tanzania

Internal opposition to the single-party state in Tanzania never reached the levels found in Kenya, though the transitions to multi-party systems were relatively simultaneous.

Shift to a Multi-Party System

In February of 1990, Nyerere gave a speech in which he said that a multi-party system should be considered. His principal argument was that the single-party system in Tanzania was no longer serving as a vehicle for democracy.[22] Furthermore, economic problems had undermined CCM's efforts to create a socialist society and Tanzanian leaders were familiar with the changes taking place in Eastern Europe and elsewhere in Africa at the time. Gros suggests that "for Nyerere, multipartyism became the disinfecting solution which would permit CCM to reconnect with the people."[23] In February of 1991, President Ali Hassan Mwinyi appointed the Nyalali Commission to examine the issue.[24] The Commission found that, overwhelmingly, Tanzanians wanted to keep the single-party system. Nevertheless, it recommended a transition to a multi-party system given the problems CCM was facing. In February of 1992, the National Conference of CCM accepted the Commission's recommendation and the National Assembly shortly thereafter enacted the 8th Constitutional Amendment, which allowed for the establishment of a multi-party system.

The National Assembly passed the Political Parties Act, No. 5 of 1992 to facilitate the establishment of a multi-party system. The act prohibits: political parties from advocating the interests of a particular religion, ethnic or racial group, or part of the country; the breaking up of the Union; the use of force; carrying out its activities in only one part of the country; and failing to allow periodic and democratic elections of its leaders.[25] These limitations were meant to prevent the formation of parties that threaten core Tanzanian values. Multi-partyism formally arrived when the Act came into effect on July 1, 1992.

Development of an Opposition

The Registrar of Parties registered parties after a period of provisional registration. During this time, party leaders had to assure the Registrar that the conditions for formal registration were met. Of the six relatively important opposition parties, three were registered in January of 1993: the Civic United Front (CUF), the *Chama cha Demokrasia na Maendeleo* (CHADEMA), and the National Convention for Construction and Reform-Mageuzi (NCCR-Maguezi). The Tanzania Labour Party (TLP) and United Democratic Party (UDP) were registered in the subsequent months. By 2004, there were 16 parties formally registered.

CUF is the strongest opposition party in Zanzibar, although it has a following in both Tanga and the Coastal Region on the mainland. In both the 1995 and 2000 elections, CUF Union presidential candidate, Ibrahim Lipumba, was from the mainland, although the Zanzibar presidential candidate, Seif Shariff Hamad, was the party's most important leader. Conflicts between the mainland and Zanzibar branches of the party have arisen and at one time led to the expulsion of the party chair.[26] The party's center of strength lies on the island of Pemba, as was the case with the ZNP/ZPPP in the pre-revolution period. Observers of the 1995 and 2000 elections suggest that had those elections been free and fair, CUF would have won the Zanzibar presidency and control of the House of Representatives. The party, frustrated by the conduct of the Zanzibar elections, boycotted the House after the 1995 elections and both the House and National Assembly after the 2000 elections. The latter led to the expulsion of members of the party from both bodies and confrontations with police that have shaken Tanzania more than any event since the army revolt in early 1964. However, in October of 2001 the Zanzibar Peace Accord, or Muafaka II, was reached between the CCM government and CUF, restoring a degree of civility to CCM-CUF relations.

CHADEMA was led initially by Edwin Mtei, a former Governor of the Central Bank and Minister of Finance under Nyerere. Mtei was forced to resign following the 1995 elections, because of internal dissention over the use of party subsidies. In the 2000 elections the party entered into an electoral alliance with CUF, and in 2003 CUF sought a continuing alliance with its chairman, Bob Makani.

NCCR-Mageuzi was the strongest of the challengers to CCM in the 1995 multi-party election, but like FORD-Asili in Kenya, it virtually collapsed in the second multi-party election. Among the reasons for its rise were both its early start and the fact that in March 1995, Augustine Mrema, a populist former Deputy Prime Minister and Minister of Home Affairs, resigned from CCM and became its presidential candidate. Among the reasons for its fall are internal struggles, one of which led to Mrema's defection. The party has faced at least three major crises. The first was in early 1995, when a conflict emerged between the Chair, Mabere Marando, and the party Secretary General, Mr. Prince Bagenda. According to Chaligha, "the differences between the two party bosses were caused by ethnic differences."[27] The second followed the 1995 election and involved a conflict between Mrema and other leaders of the party. Mrema accused Marando and others of misusing party subsidies, while Marando and others claimed Mrema did not have the level of education needed by a party leader and presidential candidate. The result was that Mrema left the party for TLP.[28] The third involved a dispute over the misuse of the party subsidy between Marando and the party Secretary General, Dr. Lamwai, a conflict that led to Dr. Lamwai's resignation. He subsequently joined CCM and was nominated by the party to be a member of the National Assembly following the 2000 election.[29]

The TLP became a significant party when Mrema joined it after defecting from NCCR-Mageuzi. Yet, his entry angered founding members of the party so much that they took their dispute to court, which advised them to settle their differences elsewhere.[30] Although TLP's electoral fortunes were enhanced by Mrema's entry, he received only about a third of the votes he obtained when he ran as a NCCR-Mageuzi candidate.

The UDP's membership is primarily comprised of the Sukuma and Nyamwezi. Indeed, its membership is more ethnically defined than that of any other party.[31]

John Cheyo polled about 4 percent of the presidential vote in both elections. Subsequent to the 2000 election, he stood for the Busega by-election in Mwanza Region with the support of all the opposition parties for the first time, yet he lost to the CCM candidate.[32] As was the case in Kenya, the need for electoral cooperation among parties was clearly evident.

Following the success of NARC in the December 2002 Kenyan elections, attempts have been made to build opposition coalitions in Tanzania. One such coalition was "Umoja." Initially, Bob Makani, the chair of CHADEMA, assumed its leadership. In June of 2003, the secretary general of CUF said he was planning a new alliance with CHADEMA, an announcement that surprised Makani, who was quoted as saying "I am the Chairman of our 'NARC'. I can't be a rebel through joining CUF."[33] Yet, he resigned his post as chairman of Umoja shortly after that. NCCR-Mageuzi's chair, James Mbatia, became the acting chair briefly when Makani stepped down. Then in September 2003, John Cheyo, the UDP leader, took over as chair. Eight parties participated, including some very new as well as some that had been around a long time. Although the Registrar of Political Parties said there was no legal provision for recognizing coalitions, CCM's Secretary General, Phillip Mangula, congratulated the parties for forming the coalition.[34] CUF, CHADEMA, TLP and DP did not join the coalition.

Mmuya and Chaligha identify a set of characteristics common to political parties in Tanzania. They are, "by and large socially engineered from the top"[35] since they do not have their origins in mass movements; their leadership is from the *petty bourgeois* class which means that "it is unlikely to have a mutual organic relationship with the masses of the people that comprise the party they claim to lead …";[36] their members "have essentially been drawn from areas that could physically be reached, that is the urban and semi-urban areas";[37] and "the elite character of the leadership and the correlation between the home of the leader and members reduce the new parties to ethnic parochial institutions whose reference will be more to the leader than to the party."[38] Many of these characteristics are shared with Kenyan political parties.

CCM's and the State's Response

The shift from a single-party to a multi-party state in Tanzania brought significant organizational changes to CCM. The party disbanded its official branches in public offices and withdrew from its involvement with the army. It withdrew, also, its supervisory links with labor and the cooperative unions. However, it maintains ties with its women's, youth, and parents' organizations. According to Mmuya and Chaligha, the party's disconnection from the government and the government's support led to closer relations with the business elite and "a return to primordial channels as the basis of political recruitment and gaining of support."[39]

The party in Zanzibar was given greater independence of operation on the islands. At the Chimwaga Congress of CCM in December 1992, an office and secretariat of the CCM vice president for Zanzibar was established. Mmuya and Chaligha contend that this step has given Zanzibar the *de facto* power to act autonomously on issues related to the opposition in Zanzibar.[40]

Paralleling this action, the Tanzanian government created a Zanzibar Election Commission, separate from the Tanzanian Election Commission, to supervise elections in Zanzibar. The government has taken actions that tend to enhance the position of CCM, as well. Following the 1995 election, where the president had to get one vote more than 50 percent of the vote to be elected, a change was made so that the president had to get only one vote more than his/her nearest competitor to be elected. Following the violent protests and demonstrations in Zanzibar and in Dar es Salaam, and the boycott by CUF of the Zanzibar House of Representatives and the National Assembly over the 2000 elections, the National Assembly amended the Elections Act on April 4, 2001, so that a by-election to a vacant seat would not take place until the seat had been vacant for two years rather than the former 20 days. This meant that CUF districts had no representation for two years following the expulsion of CUF members for failure to attend sessions. Still, that did not lead to the disaffection of voters. In by-elections held in May of 2003 on Pemba island to replace the CUF's 15 Union parliamentary members and the 17 Zanzibar House of Representative members, CUF won all but six House seats, where the party's candidates were disqualified because they had missed three consecutive House meetings during the boycott.[41]

Party Success – The 1995 and 2000 Elections

Although local and by-elections were held under the multi-party system in 1993 and 1994, the first national elections under the new system were held in 1995 and 2000.

One of the unique features of the 1995 elections was the attempt to offset the many advantages of CCM by the use of unconditional subsidies for parties. In the discussion of the formation of new parties, it was noted how disputes over the use of the subsidies led to several internal disputes within such parties. By Act No. 11 of 1996, the subsidies were limited to only those parties holding seats in the National Assembly and fielding presidential candidates, a restriction that has meant that only CCM, CUF, CHADEMA and TLP receive such support. A second feature that may be related to the presence of subsidies in the 1995 election and their absence in the 2000 election is the fact that opposition candidates were on the ballots in all of the mainland constituencies for the 1995 election, while there were no opposition candidates on the ballots in 18 of the mainland constituencies for the 2000 elections.[42]

The election results suggest that CCM was much stronger than KANU in the post-1990 period as shown in Table 3.3.

We can draw some tentative conclusions from these data: CCM received a much higher proportion of the seats in the National Assembly than it received of the total vote in both the 1995 and 2000 elections; no party appears able to challenge CCM in Tanzania as a whole; CUF's position in Zanzibar makes it a serious competitor for control of the presidency and the Zanzibar legislature; and the significant fall in the strength of NCCR-Mageuzi and rise in that of TLP between 1995 and 2000 illustrates the personal rather than ideological basis of

Table 3.3 Parliamentary Elections in Tanzania

Political Party	Percent of Vote in 1995	Number of Seats	Percent of Seats	Percent of Vote in 2000	Number of Seats	Percent of Seats
CCM	59.2	186	80.2	69.2	202	87.4
CUF	5.0	24	10.3	11.6	17	7.4
CHADEMA	6.2	3	1.3	3.7	4	1.7
NCCR-Mageuzi	21.8	16	6.9	3.1	1	0.4
UDP	3.3	3	1.3	3.9	3	1.3
TLP	0.4	0	0.0	7.9	4	1.7
NLD	0.4	0	0.0	0.0	0	0.0
NRA	0.9	0	0.0	0.0	0	0.0
PONA	0.3	0	0.0	0.1	0	0.0
TADEA	1.2	0	0.0	0.2	0	0.0
TPP	0.2	0	0.0	0.1	0	0.0
UMD	0.6	0	0.0	0.1	0	0.0
UPDP	0.3	0	0.0	0.1	0	0.0

Source: Amon Chaligha, "State of Political Parties in Tanzania," paper prepared for Research and Education for Democracy in Tanzania (REDET), the fourth workshop on democratic transition in East Africa April 10-11, 2001, Lake Manyara, Arusha Region, Tanzania, pp. 8, 11.

voting for the shift. This is widely attributed to the fact that Mrema left the former and joined the latter party, even though he was unable to bring many of his former supporters to his new party.

The assessments of the validity of these elections as a measure of the strength of parties are not uniform. Most observers, including the U.S. State Department, the Norwegian observer team, the Tanzania Election Monitoring Committee (TEMCO), and Nyang'oro, accepted both the 1995 and 2000 elections as "reasonably fair, except in Zanzibar."[43] Yet in reference to 1995 election, Sandbrook says it was a "highly flawed election;"[44] Gros contents that there were "serious irregularities;"[45] and according to Mukandala, they were "both bungled and sabotaged."[46] Regarding the 2000 elections, TEMCO declared that "the elections on the mainland were free but not fair. The unfairness comes from the big state bias in favour of the ruling party, the heavy-handedness of the police in campaign rallies of opposition parties, and the incomplete separation of state resources from those of the ruling party."[47] The contradictory evaluations in both the 1995 and 2000 elections are due to the difficulty of evaluating the whole from some of the parts and agreeing on what democracy means.

Much thc samc mcasurc of rclativc party strcngth is rcflcctcd in the presidential election results as shown in Table 3.4.

Table 3.4 Presidential Elections in Tanzania

Party of Presidential Candidate	Percent of Votes 1995 Election	Percent of Votes 2000 Election
Benjamin Mkapa (CCM)	61.8	71.7
Ibrahim Lipumba (CUF in 1995 and CUF/CHADEMA in 2000)	6.4	16.3
Augustine Mrema (NCCR-Mageuzi in 1995 & TLP in 2000)	27.8	7.8
John Cheyo (UDP)	4.0	4.2

Source: For 1995, Wolfgang Fengler, "Tanzania," in Dieter Nohlen, Michael Krennerich, and Bernhard Thibaut, eds., *Elections in Africa: a Data Handbook* (Oxford: Oxford University Press, 1999), p. 885. For 2000, "Elections 2000 – President Mkapa's Great Triumph," *Tanzanian Affairs* vol. 68 (January-April, 2001), p. 9.

The aftermath of the 2000 elections in Zanzibar was traumatic. Violence followed a government crackdown in Pemba; refugees fled to Kenya; there were demonstrations in Dar es Salaam that resulted in the use of force by the police and the arrest of the CUF presidential candidate; a major protest march was held in Dar es Salaam with a crowd estimated to number 50,000 people; there were pledges of unity among opposition parties; some CUF members were expelled from parliament; and, eventually, a peace accord was signed on October 10, 2001. This agreement between CCM and CUF sought to create a more level playing field for multi-party politics in Zanzibar. Events since suggest that the agreement is succeeding. Commenting on the May 18, 2003, by-elections on Pemba, the Commonwealth Expert Team observed that "these by-elections should be considered a credible expression of the will and intention of the people of Pemba."[48]

Concluding Observations

After reviewing where Tanzania was, following the 2000 elections, Chaligha concludes that "although the country is *de jure* a multiparty state, it is indeed a *de facto* single party state."[49] Several years earlier Mmuya and Chaligha reviewed the character of the opposition parties and CCM. In this review they suggest that much like advocates of popular democracy, "the future for democracy in Tanzania does not therefore reside with multipartyism alone."[50] It is an observation equally applicable to the Kenyan case as well.

Uganda

The multi-party systems that developed in Uganda after independence in 1962 did not lead to a democratic political system, so when Yoweri Museveni's guerilla forces brought the NRM to power in January of 1986, their re-introduction was rejected.[51]

Adoption of a No-Party Followed by a Shift Toward a Multi-party System

Unlike the cases of Kenya and Tanzania, the democratic opening in the 1990s did not involve a shift from a single-party to a multi-party system. Rather, it involved a shift from the pseudo, multi-party system under Obote and the brief period of military rule under Okello to what the government called a no-party system. In that system, parties were allowed to exist so long as they did not perform the normal functions of political parties. Museveni and others in the NRM explained the utility of this system in Uganda: the country's historical experience with political parties (1962-1966, 1980-1985) was an undemocratic one in which the presence of political parties lead one *away from* democracy; the principal divisions in the country are not economic, but ethnic and religious, which serve as the bases of political party organization; and multi-party systems born and developed in the West, should not be assumed to work universally. The no-party system evolved from a transitional tool to what appeared to be a relatively permanent feature of the vision of democracy in Uganda.[52] The NRM's interim government suspended political party activity for an initial four years; the National Resistance Council extended it for another five years; the 1995 constitution extended it for still another five years until a referendum was held in June 2000; passage of the referendum in 2000 appeared to extend it into the indefinite future. Yet, that was not to be.

The constitutionality of the Political Parties and Organizations Act of 2002 was challenged by the DP. The Act restricted the activities of political parties to Kampala, prohibiting them from opening branch offices, holding delegates' conferences or public rallies, or sponsoring candidates. On March 21, 2003, the Uganda Constitutional Court ruled in a unanimous decision that sections 18 and 19 of the Act essentially created a single-party state and imposed unjustifiable restrictions on the activities of political parties in violation of the constitution. Yet, the court went further. It ruled that the Movement Act, No. 18 (1997) was inconsistent with Article 70 of the constitution and therefore unconstitutional. At a National Executive Committee meeting later that month, Museveni reportedly said that a multi-party system should be allowed. According to one observer his decision "was based on a careful analysis of weaknesses within the Movement as well as external factors. He added that there were some elements within the Movement who had 'a tendency to form cliques.'"[53] His remarks were very similar to Nyerere's 1990 call for multi-partyism in 1990. In rapid succession, party registration began in June; the Movement Act (Amendment) Bill was passed in September; the NRM-O was registered as a political party at the end of October;

and consultations with political parties over the transition to a multi-party system began in January of 2004.

Development of an Opposition

The opposition to the no-party state has included intellectuals, those opposed to Museveni or the NRM's rule, former NRM activists who have become disillusioned, members of the old parties, and international NGOs like Human Rights Watch. Each group sought to convince the government that the no-party state system was not working and/or that the government should allow political parties to operate without the restrictions imposed by the no-party state.[54]

Intellectuals have argued along several lines. Mugaju contends that the historical argument against a multi-party system is unsound since "the pseudo-multipartyism of the 1950s and 1960s and the thuggery masquerading as multipartyism in the early 1980s have been mistaken for real multipartyism."[55] Ssenkumba contends that the president maintains support for his no-party state simply through patronage: "the president himself is like the chairman of some kind of allocation committee, distributing vehicles to religious and traditional leaders, doling out milling machines and heifers to women's groups, ordering the construction of bitumenised roads to communities, and offering the extension of electricity to areas he visits."[56] Kasfir notes that "the NRM leadership's evident lack of interest in its internal democracy further underlines the hollowness of its post-1986 rationales for no-party democracy,"[57] and Muwanga contends that "in the recent years the movement system has degenerated into a sort of oligarchy that will surely not outlive its current members."[58]

Political leaders sought to subtly introduce parties into electoral competition by letting people know their "party" affiliation. The affiliation may be with a specific party, or with a faction supporting multi-party elections. As one observer states, "during elections, candidates albeit standing on 'individual merit' are identified either as multipartists or *movementists*."[59] Thus, when Ssemogerere ran for president in the 1996 election, it was widely known that he was the DP leader.

A variety of other forums to oppose the no-party state idea were used, including "attempting to seek court orders to lift the suspension on political parties, organizing seminars and press conferences airing alternative policies to those of government and refusal to sign the constitution on the promulgation day."[60] In addition to the opposition's success in its challenge of the Political Parties and Organizations Act in March 2003, it successfully challenged the Constitutional (Amendment) Act 13 of 2000. The Supreme Court's unanimous ruling on January 29, 2004 opened the door to many other legal challenges to the actions of the government and parliament.

Human Rights Watch (HRW) published a harsh indictment of the no-party system entitled *Hostile to Democracy*. It claims the movement's rhetoric is simply a sham:

> By denying that the NRM is a political party, the NRM avoids being forced to comply with the regulations imposed on opposition political parties, and by fusing its

structures with the Ugandan state the NRM gains direct access to state funds and the powers of state mobilization.[61]

This is but one of a long list of criticisms raised by HRW. In addition, there has been international pressure exerted foreign representatives, international aid organizations, and NGOs for a multi-party system.

NRM and the State's Response

The NRM/Movement used both carrots and sticks to respond to the multi-party advocates. The sticks have been both legal and constitutional. Legal Notice No. 1 of 1986 formally suspended party activity. It appointed a Constitutional Commission that recommended the no-party system. The Constituent Assembly was elected in 1994 to finalize and ratify the constitution. The 1995 constitution allows parties to exist but prohibited them from "opening and operating branch offices," "holding delegates' conferences," "holding public rallies," "sponsoring or offering a platform to or in any way campaigning for or against a candidate for public office," and "carrying on any activity that may interfere with the movement political system for the time being in force."[62] Those parties in existence before the constitution are allowed to continue, but new ones must be registered in accord with legislation that was not adopted until May of 2002. To be registered, a variety of restrictions apply, many of which parallel restrictions Tanzania has imposed. Parties must have a national character; their membership must not be based on sex, ethnicity, religion, or other sectional division; their internal organization must conform with democratic principles; they must account for the sources and use of their funds and assets; and no person may be compelled to join a party by virtue of his/her membership in an organization or interest group. The constitution also called for the referendum held in 2000 on whether the country would continue to have a no-party system.

The NRC passed the Movement Act 1997 that created structures for the movement which Human Rights Watch claimed "replicates the structures of a political organization that is a party in all but name … creating a state-sponsored political organization disguised as a 'political system.'"[63] Following the Constitutional Court's ruling that the movement was a party, Museveni took several steps to assure that his opponents would not replace him: he dismissed ministers who did not support removal of the constitutional amendment limiting the president to two terms; he registered the NRM-O quickly; he delayed removing a variety of legal restrictions on other parties; and he appointed a government transition team that blocked opposition efforts to "level the field" for fair multi-party competition.

The carrots have involved the appointment of some leading party members to government, the opening of the election process to Resistance Councils, and the opportunity for the opposition to air views in a relatively free press and in bodies such as the Constituent Assembly.

Movement Success – The Elections

There have been elections in Uganda in 1989 (for Resistance Committees from village to NRC), 1994 (for Constituent Assembly), 1996 (for president and councils), 1998 (for the movement), 2001 (for president), and a referendum in 2000 (to decide fate of no-party state). Political parties have not been allowed to formally engage in any of these elections, but the conclusion of observers is that most of these elections have contributed to progress toward democracy. For example, Kasfir observes in his analysis of the February 1989 elections that "generally speaking, though with some notable exceptions, Ugandans considered [these] elections to be fair and democratic – indeed the first general elections in the country's history since independence to receive widespread approval ... on balance, it is reasonable to conclude that the elections did contribute to democratization."[64]

The first direct presidential election was held in 1996; the second in 2001. In 1996 and 2001, the "official" NRM candidate was Museveni; the candidate backed by political parties, Ssemogerere; an "unofficial" NRM candidate, Bisigye; and a few independents. The results are shown in Table 3.5.

Table 3.5 Presidential Elections in Uganda

Candidates	Unspecified "Party" Affiliation	Percent of Vote in 1996 Election	Percent of Vote in 2001 Election
Yoweri Museveni	NRM	74.2	69.3
Paul Ssemogerere	IPC (DP, UPC & NLC)	23.7	
Muhammed Mayanja	Independent	2.1	1.0
Kiiza Besigye	NRM (unofficial)		27.8
Aggrey Awori	Independent		1.4
Others (2 in 2001)	Independents		0.5

Source: For 1996, Siegmar Schmidt, "Uganda," in Dieter Nohlen, Michael Krennerich, and Bernhard Thibaut, eds., *Elections in Africa: a Data Handbook* (Oxford: Oxford University Press, 1999), p. 934. For 2001, "Elections in Uganda," http://www.electionworld.org/election/uganda.htm.

In the 1996 election, Museveni's principal opponent was the leader of the DP who ran against Obote in the 1980 election. The other political parties supported him, so the election was a surrogate of the referendum that was to follow in 2000. In the 2001 election Museveni's principal opponent was someone from the NRM who was challenging its leader. In both cases the opposition candidate lost decisively.

The general assessment of outside observers was that both the 1996 and 2001 elections were "reasonably free and fair."[65] After the 1996 election, Kasfir observed that "most would probably agree that Kenya can hardly be said to be more democratic than Uganda, though the former has 27 parties and the latter has none."[66] After the 2001 elections, the Norwegian observers suggested that "the legal framework and the Ugandan context for political competition favour the sitting president, and make it difficult for challengers to compete on a level playing field."[67] Much the same comment has been made of Kenyan and Tanzanian elections.

On June 29, 2000, a referendum was held to decide whether the no-party system would continue or whether parties would be allowed to participate. A report in the *East African* asserts that whether a movement or a political party system should be adopted had "become the bitterest and potentially most explosive issue in the country for nearly 30 years."[68] The principal issues that voters had to decide were: Should they participate? If so, should they support the movement or multi-party system? Human Rights Watch and some other civil rights advocates argue that the right to freedom of association is a human right, not something to be decided by a majority vote."[69] Therefore, according to this logic, one should not participate in the vote. Most opponents of the movement system, in fact, decided to boycott the referendum. The issues in the debate for and against a movement system had been discussed throughout Uganda for more than a decade. According to the electoral commission, 51 percent of the 9.6 million potential voters voted and 91 percent of them voted for the movement system.[70] According to Mwanga, "the legitimization of the Movement system through the referendum effectively put an end to organized political competition."[71] Organization of African Unity (OAU) monitors declared that the vote "was marked by a high degree of transparency."[72]

The fact that someone from within the NRM challenged Museveni in the presidential elections the following year, suggests, that political competition within the no-party system was possible. Yet, Besigye felt forced to flee the country in August 2001. He first went to Washington to launch a campaign to persuade donors to stop supporting Museveni's no-party system of government and then moved to South Africa.

Concluding Comments

There are parallels between Nyerere's single-party system and Museveni's no-party system. Both may have promoted democracy at one time and hindered it at another time. The ambiguity of Uganda's experience is summed up by Kasfir, who asserted in 1998 that "the NRM leadership may support no-party democracy primarily to help itself maintain its rule in the face of the various local conflicts that it has inherited and to which it must respond."[73] According to Kasfir, "it would be wrong to conclude from this, however, that Uganda is merely a dictatorship with an attractive but misleading façade. In fact, the country is much more democratic than it was before the NRM took power."[74] Two years later, he argued that the movement has been used "to enhance its legitimation and deepen its position of power' rather than to extend the frontiers of democracy ... At the end of the day, their aim has been reduced to self-perpetuation and entrenchment."[75] Whether a multi-party system will do otherwise is yet to be determined.

The Ambiguous Relationship Between Political Parties and Democracy

That there is no consistent relationship between the political parties/party system and the level of democratization in Kenya, Uganda and Tanzania is apparent from a review of the Polity IV and Freedom House data on democracy and an examination of the experiences of each of these countries. Both a rise and a decline in the level of democracy may be associated with a no-party state and a multi-party state. The character and experiences of each country differ. Kenya is the only country that has changed its ruling party/movement since 1990 – and, that was only at the end of 2002. Uganda did not begin to move toward a multi-party system until 2003 – more than a decade after both Kenya and Tanzania. Tanzania has continued with the same dominant party as it did at independence, though that dominance has been seriously challenged in Zanzibar. Democracy in these countries, assessed through experiences in elections, can be interpreted in a variety of ways. Yet, there is no clear link between changes in parties or party systems in the three countries and levels of democracy, almost regardless of how it is measured. In theory, the presence of a variety of political parties should foster the growth of democracy, but the relationship in each East African country is ambiguous. Why?

At least five factors appear contribute to making the political party/party system-democracy relationship ambiguous. First, the concepts of political party and party system, the independent variables, have such flexible meanings that many different types of organization are categorized together. That is, when political parties are related to democracy, a variety of institutions are being related. It is only reasonable that some would relate differently than others. The immense variety encompassed by the terms "political party" and "party systems" is illustrated by the debates in East Africa about whether NARC is a party or a coalition of parties. At one time, Samuel Kivuitu, the Kenyan Electoral Commission Chairman, suggested it was neither. He said it was an "agglomerationconglomeration [sic] of parties, not a coalition."[76] Yet, it was registered as a party. As we have noted, there have been disputes in each country over whether a particular group is a party. The tendency to encompass all within the term "political party" has meant that many different institutions are being related to democracy.

Second, the factors affecting the behavior of political parties differ. For example, during the early 1990s, Uganda was not pressured by external agents to move to a multi-party system, but the opposite was true for Kenya. Tanzania has been quite successful in suppressing ethnic mobilization by political parties, while this has occurred in Kenya.

Third, many parties in East Africa tend to be vehicles used by political leaders for their own advancement or for the benefit of members of a particular region, ethnic group, or religion. Our review of the experiences of parties indicates numerous examples of party mergers and break-ups, of "defections" of party members, and of the creation of new parties for the personal gain of individual leaders. Leaders of many parties tend to appeal to particular ethnic, religious or regional groups on the basis of identity rather than program. One Kenyan commentator has suggested that political parties have become "tribal, or regional advocacies."[77] The use of parties for personal or ethnic purposes may account for the tenuous connection between them and democracy in East African countries.

Fourth, internal party democracy is limited in most East African parties, suggesting that the value placed upon the concept may not be high. Othman contends that the process for the selection of presidential candidates in Zanzibar or for Tanzania has not been democratic.[78] A Ugandan observer notes the lack of internal "party" democracy in the NRM.[79] Similarly in Kenya, as of mid-2003, KANU "had not had elections from the grassroots to the top in the last 14 years."[80] Thus, democracy may not be an important objective of political party leaders for the country as a whole.

Fifth, the concept of democracy applied to East African countries poses a problem, too. There is substantial disagreement on its meaning, exemplified by the differences in the "scores" given by the Polity IV and Freedom House measures for the same countries. Furthermore, the phrase "transition to democracy," widely used since 1990, has much in common with the phrase "transition to modernity," widely used in the 1960s. Both posit an end whose meaning is often taken from Western experience. Selecting a conceptualization of democracy that focuses on procedures evolving out of Western culture may not be viewed as a valuable societal objective.[81] Ake argues bitterly:

> What is being foisted on Africa is a version of liberal democracy reduced to the crude simplicity of *multi-party elections* ... This type of democracy is not in the least emancipatory especially in African conditions because it offers the people rights they cannot exercise, voting that never amounts to choosing, freedom which is patently spurious, and political equality which disguises highly unequal power relations.[82]

Perhaps, it is East Africa's good fortune that political parties/party systems have not consistently produced such a form of democracy.

Notes

1 For example, Justus Mugaju and J. Oloka-Onyango have referred to the period as one of "thuggery masquerading as multi-partyism." See Justus Mugaju and J. Oloka-Onyango, "Introduction: Revisiting the Multi-party Versus Movement System Debate," in Mugaju and Oloka-Onyango, eds., *No-Party Democracy in Uganda, Myths and Realities* (Kampala: Fountain Publishers, 2000), p. 4. Justus Mugaju has referred to it as a period of pseudo-multi-party politics. See Mugaju, "An Historical Background to Uganda's No-Party Democracy," in *No-Party Democracy in Uganda*, p. 22.

2 Giovanni Sartori, *Parties and Party Systems, A Framework for Analysis* (Cambridge: Cambridge University Press, 1976), p. 29. He contends that to treat a single party as constituting a party system is inappropriate even though parts of it may interact with other parts (see p. 44).

3 Emeka Nwokedi, *Politics of Democratization, Changing Authoritarian Regimes in Sub-Saharan Africa* (Munster, LIT Verlag, 1995), p. 130.

4 Nwokedi, *Politics of Democratization*, p. 132.

5 Nwokedi, *Politics of Democratization*, p. 132.

[6] David Throup and Charles Hornsby, *Multi-party Politics in Kenya* (Oxford: James Currey, 1998), p. 4.

[7] Sahar Shafqat, "Opposition Parties in Former One-Party Regimes," a paper prepared for presentation at the Annual Meeting of the American Political Science Association (San Francisco: August 30-September 2, 2001), p. 17.

[8] Throup and Hornsby, *Multi-party Politics in Kenya*, p. 5.

[9] National Rainbow Coalition (NARC), "Memorandum of Understanding, the National Alliance Party of Kenya (NAK) and Liberal Democratic Party-LDP (Rainbow), October 22, 2002, http://www.kenyaelections2002.org/info/002.asp [Accessed November 7, 2003].

[10] For example, Rok Ajulu, "Kenya: The Survival of the Old Order," in John Daniel, Roger Southall, and Morris Szeftel, eds., *Voting for Democracy, Watershed Elections in Contemporary Anglophone Africa* (Aldershot, U.K.: Ashgate, 1999), p. 128.

[11] Emman Omari, "Kanu and NDP Delegates Vote for a Merger," *Daily Nation* (August 25, 2001), http://www.nationaudio.com/News/DailyNation/25082001/News/News65.html.

[12] Ajulu, "Kenya: The Survival of the Old Order," p. 131.

[13] Nick G. Wanjohi, "State of Political Parties in Kenya and Transition to Democracy," a paper presented at a workshop on "Transition to Democracy in East Africa" held at the Lake Manyara Serena Hotel, Tanzania (April 9-10, 2001), p. 19.

[14] On the 1992 election see Michael Bratton, "Deciphering Africa's Divergent Transitions," *Political Science Quarterly* vol. 112 (Spring 1997), p. 78. On the 1997 election see Joel Barkan and Njuguna Ng'ethe, "Kenya Tries Again," *Journal of Democracy* vol. 9, no. 2 (1998), p. 45.

[15] Institute for Education in Democracy, *Enhancing the Electoral Process in Kenya* (Nairobi: Institute for Education in Democracy, 2003), p. 1.

[16] Ajulu, "Kenya: The Survival of the Old Order," p. 134.

[17] Barkan and Ng'ethe, "Kenya Tries Again," p. 32.

[18] *Daily Nation* (March 24, 2000).

[19] Shadrack Wanjala Nasong'o, "The Illusion of Governance in Kenya," in Robert Dibie, ed., *The Politics and Policies of Sub-Saharan Africa* (Lanham, MD: University Press of America, 2001), p. 125.

[20] Nasong'o, "The Illusion of Governance in Kenya," p. 126.

[21] Nasong'o, "The Illusion of Governance in Kenya," p. 126.

[22] Bratton and van de Walle make a number of assertions about the transition that are misleading. For example, they wrongly attribute the principal reason for Nyerere's change of position to a visit he made to Lipsig. See Michael Bratton and Nicolas van de Walle, *Democratic Experiments in Africa, Regime Transitions in Comparative Perspective* (Cambridge: Cambridge University Press, 1997), p. 181.

[23] Jean-Germain Gros, "Leadership and Democratization: The Case of Tanzania," in Gros, ed., *Democratization in Late Twentieth-Century Africa, Coping with Uncertainty* (Westport, CT: Greenwood Press, 1998), p. 103.

[24] Bratton and van de Walle's implication that since the commission's "entire membership" came from CCM, it was somehow illegitimate, makes no sense given the fact that the commission recommended an end to CCM's monopoly of power. See Bratton and van de Walle, *Democratic Experiments in Africa*, p. 113. They fabricate motives, such as the claim that the commission was only appointed because the President believed "in all likelihood that its work could be controlled," for which there is no evidence. See Bratton and van de Walle, *Democratic Experiments in Africa*, p. 165.

[25] United Republic of Tanzania, *The Political Parties Act, No. 5 of 1992*, in Max Mmuya and Amon Chaligha, *Political Parties and Democracy in Tanzania* (Dar es Salaam: Dar es Salaam University Press, 1994), pp. 215-223.

[26] Amon Chaligha, "The State of Political Parties in Tanzania," a paper prepared for Research and Education for Democracy in Tanzania (REDET), the Fourth Workshop on Democratic Transition in East Africa, Lake Manyara, Arusha Region, Tanzania (April 10-11, 2001), p. 19.

[27] Chaligha, "The State of Political Parties in Tanzania," p. 18.

[28] Chaligha, "The State of Political Parties in Tanzania," p. 18.

[29] Chaligha, "The State of Political Parties in Tanzania," p. 19.

[30] Chaligha, "The State of Political Parties in Tanzania," p. 13.

[31] Chaligha, "The State of Political Parties in Tanzania," p. 12.

[32] "President Mkapa Tightens His Grip," *Tanzanian Affairs* vol. 69 (May-August 2001), pp. 15-16.

[33] "Makani Denies Plans to Swap Opposition Alliances," *The Guardian* (June 10, 2003). http://www.ippmedia.com/guardian/2003/06/10/guardian2.asp [Accessed on July 9, 2003].

[34] Ludger Kasumuni, "Mangula Recognizes Legal Foundation of UMOJA," *The Guardian* (September 20, 2003), http://www.ippmedia.com/guardian/2003/09/20/guardian8.asp [Accessed on September 9, 2003].

[35] Mmuya and Chaligha, *Political Parties and Democracy in Tanzania*, p. 47-48.

[36] Mmuya and Chaligha, *Political Parties and Democracy in Tanzania*, p. 55.

[37] Mmuya and Chaligha, *Political Parties and Democracy in Tanzania*, p. 55.

[38] Mmuya and Chaligha, *Political Parties and Democracy in Tanzania*, p. 56.

[39] Mmuya and Chaligha, *Political Parties and Democracy in Tanzania*, p. 131.

[40] Mmuya and Chaligha, *Political Parties and Democracy in Tanzania*, p. 127.

[41] *The Guardian* (Dar es Salaam: May 23, 2003), http://www.ippmedia.com/guardian/2003/05/23/guardian4.asp [Accessed on January 9, 2004].

[42] Chaligha, "The State of Political Parties in Tanzania," p. 5.

[43] U.S. Department of State, "Tanzania Human Rights Practices, 1995," Section 3, paragraphs 2 and 3, March 1996. See http://www.state.gov/www/global/human_rights/hrp_reports_mainhp.html. Geir Sundet, *Democracy in Transition, The 1995 Elections in Tanzania* (Oslo: Norwegian Institute of Human Rights, Human Rights Report, No. 8, June 1996), p. 44. S.S. Mushi, "Conclusion and Recommendations," in Samuel S. Mushi and Rwekaza S. Mukandala, eds., *Multi-party Democracy in Transition, Tanzania's 1995 General Elections* (Dar es Salaam: Tanzania Election Monitoring Committee (TEMCO), Department of Political Science and Public Administration, University of Dar es Salaam, 1997), pp. 291-292. Julius E. Nyang'oro, "Civil Society, Democratization, and State Building in Kenya and Tanzania," in Kidane Mengisteab and Cyril Daddieh, *State Building and Democratization in Africa, Faith, Hope, and Realities* (Westport, CN: Praeger, 1999), p. 188. U.S. Department of State, Office of the Spokesman, Richard Boucher, "Tanzania: Credibility of Zanzibar Elections," November 3, 2000, http://secretary.state.gov/www/briefings/statement/2000/ps001103b.html. Tanzania Election Monitoring Committee, Chapter 10, The 2000 General Elections in Tanzania, How Free and How Fair," http://www.temco.or.tz/docs/freeandfair.html. Chris Tomlinson, "Tanzania in Turmoil After Vote," an Associated Press report at http://seattlepi.nwsource.com/national/tanz31.shtml.

[44] Holly Hanson, "Independent Monitor's Account of Tanzanian Elections," December 11, 1995, http://www.hartford-hwp.com/archives/36/014.html.

[45] Gros, "Leadership and Democratization: The Case of Tanzania," pp. 106-107.

[46] Hanson, "Independent Monitor's Account of Tanzanian Elections."

[47] Tanzania Election Monitoring Committee, "The 2000 General Elections in Tanzania, How Free and How Fair."

[48] Commonwealth Secretariat, "Report of the Commonwealth Expert Team, Pemba By-elections, Zanzibar, United Republic of Tanzania, 18 May 2003," p. ii.

[49] Amon Chaligha, "The State of Political Parties in Tanzania," p. 21.
[50] Mmuya and Chaligha, *Political Parties and Democracy in Tanzania*, p. 199.
[51] Like the multi-party elections prior to Idi Amin's seizure of power in 1971, the UPC's victory in the 1980 elections was widely believed to be unfair, even though the DP accepted the results. The DP seemed able to accommodate itself to almost any regime: it had declared its support for Tito Okello when he overthrew Obote, and for Museveni when he overthrew Okello.
[52] Mugaju and Oloka-Onyango, *No-Party Democracy in Uganda, Myths and Realities*, p. 1.
[53] A. Mutumba Luli, "Museveni Moves to Woo Dissidents Back to Movement," *The East African*, March 31, 2003, http://www.nationaudio.com/News/EastAfrican/31032003/Regional/Regional3103200361.html.
[54] Mugaju and Oloka-Onyango, *No-Party Democracy in Uganda, Myths and Realities*, p. 5.
[55] Mugaju and Oloka-Onyango, *No-Party Democracy in Uganda, Myths and Realities*, p. 4.
[56] John Ssenkumba, "The Crisis of Opposition Politics in Uganda," *Politeia* vol. 15, no. 3 (1996), http://www.unisa.ac.za/dept/press/politeia/153/ssenk.html.
[57] Nelson Kasfir, "'No-party Democracy' in Uganda," *Journal of Democracy* vol. 9, no. 2 (1998), p 61.
[58] Nansozi Muwanga, "The State of the Movement System in Uganda: Monopolizing Political Power or Deepening the Democratic Impulse?" A paper prepared for Research and Education for Democracy in Tanzania, The Fourth Workshop on Democratic Transition in East Africa, Lake Manyara, Arusha Region, Tanzania (9-10 April, 2001), p. 19.
[59] Muwanga, "The State of the Movement System in Uganda," p. 17.
[60] Foster Byarugaba, "The Role of Major Stakeholders in the Transition to Democracy in Uganda: A Descriptive Analysis," European Centre for Development Policy Management (EDCPM) Working Paper No. 35 (June 1997), p. 12, http://www.oneworld.org/ecdpm/pubs/wp35_gb.htm.
[61] Human Rights Watch, *Hostile to Democracy, The Movement System and Political Repression in Uganda* (New York: Human Rights Watch, 1999), p. 3.
[62] Human Rights Watch, *Hostile to Democracy, The Movement System and Political Repression in Uganda*, p. 70.
[63] Human Rights Watch, *Hostile to Democracy, The Movement System and Political Repression in Uganda*, p. 59.
[64] Nelson Kasfir, "The Ugandan Elections of 1989: Power, Populism and Democracy," in Holger Bernt Hansen and Michael Twaddle, eds., *Changing Uganda* (London: James Currey, 1991), pp. 248-250.
[65] Thomas O'hara, "Democratic Representation: A Ugandan Model," in Bamidele A. Ojo, ed., *Contemporary African Politics, A Comparative Study of Political Transition to Democratic Legitimacy* (Lanham, NJ: University Press of America, 1999), p. 105. Carl E. Petersen, "Uganda: Presidential Elections 2001," Working Paper 2001, no. 8 (Oslo: Norwegian Institute of Human Rights [Nordem], May 2001), p. 22. http://www.humanrights.uio.no/forskning/publ/wp/uganda2001.html.
[66] Kasfir, "'No-party Democracy' in Uganda," p. 50.
[67] Petersen, "Uganda: Presidential Elections 2001," p. 22.
[68] Charles Onyango-Obbo, "Uganda Today Is Poorer But No Wiser," *The East African* (July 3-9, 2000), http://www.newsafrica.com/obbo/article397.html.
[69] Human Rights Watch, *Hostile to Democracy, The Movement System and Political Repression in Uganda*, p. 3.
[70] Muwanga, "The State of the Movement System in Uganda," p. 11.
[71] Muwanga, "The State of the Movement System in Uganda," p. 23.
[72] Panafrican News Agency, "OAU Monitors Pleased with Uganda's Referendum" (June 30, 2000), http://fr.allafrica.com/stories/200006300085.html.

[73] Nelson Kasfir, "'No-party Democracy' in Uganda," p. 51.
[74] Nelson Kasfir, "'No-party Democracy' in Uganda," p. 51.
[75] Mugaju and Oloka-Onyango, *No-Party Democracy in Uganda, Myths and Realities*, p. 5.
[76] Gitau Warigi, "Narc's Uneasy Status Brought to the Fore," *Sunday Nation on the Web* (November 16, 2003), http://www.nationaudio.com/News/DailyNation/16112003/Comment/Comment9.html.
[77] William Ochieng, "The Demise of Political Parties in Kenya," *Sunday Nation on the Web* (June 1, 2003), http://www.nationaudio.com/News/DailyNation/01062003/Comment/News_Analysis0106200317.html.
[78] Haroub Othman, "Karume the Son: Resurrection of a Dynasty?" *The Guardian* (January 16, 2004), http://www.ipp.co.tz/ipp/guadian/2004/01/16/3964.html.
[79] Muniini Mulera, "Marx Never Needed a Political Party, We Do," *The Monitor* (November 16, 2003).
[80] Ochieng, "The Demise of Political Parties in Kenya."
[81] The form of democracy that has resulted is widely referred to as "donor democracy."
[82] Claude Ake, *Is Africa Democratizing?* (Lagos: Malthouse Press for Center for Advanced Social Science, 1996), pp. 1-2.

Chapter 4

Political Leadership

Joshua B. Rubongoya

This chapter examines the complex role of national leaders in the democratic transition process, with a particular emphasis on how and under what conditions ruling elites either promote or subvert citizen participation in political decision-making. Do differences in political leadership in Kenya, Tanzania, and Uganda enable us to better understand the scope and content of democratic transitions? This question provides the rationale for a comparative and regional exploration of leadership and democracy in East Africa. While structural, institutional, and global factors are important in shaping the political liberalization process, local elites are particularly relevant because they have organizational advantages and superior access to political and economic resources. They have also demonstrated a willingness to use their positions of power to shape and define regime types, devise strategies for regime legitimacy, and exploit their access to state resources.

Who are the African Ruling Elites?

Schraeder offers a definition of the ruling elite in Africa that is particularly relevant to this study. He defines it as:

> the small, privileged leadership sector of African societies that controls the reign of government and sets the rules of the political system. This ruling elite historically assumed power through either civilian-based independence movements or military-based *coups d'etat.*[1]

Included in this constellation of elites are opposition party leaders, lower and middle ranking military officers, and influential members of the financial and business communities. Schraeder also contends that ruling elites should be distinguished from other elite groups in Africa that comprise the change-seeking opposition, including associational women's, ethnic, religious, labor, and student groups.

This chapter examines political leaders currently in power and those who support their rule, specifically during the democratic transition process. As discussed in the volume's introduction, a transition entails the shift from one set of political procedures to another, from an old pattern of rule to a new one.[2] In the cases under investigation, these shifts involve changes from autocratic and despotic systems of rule to democratic ones that derive legitimacy from the principle of popular sovereignty.[3]

In order to elucidate the role of political leadership in East Africa's democratization process, three main factors are examined. First, what roles do the elite play in determining regime types? Regime types are critical in shaping the extent of political/economic space for citizen participation. To the degree that ruling elites, particularly in Africa, play such a pivotal role in determining regime type, they are thus critical in shaping one of the pillars of democracy, namely the nature and character of state-society relations. The second factor focuses on the role of ruling elites in legitimizing their positions through the institutionalization of state-society relations. Unless political leaders are willing to engage in a process of regime legitimization, democratic transitions in Africa are often tenuous endeavors. The prospects for democracy still depend, for the most part, on the ability and willingness of African ruling elites to create political and economic space. Finally, what is the economic context in which ruling elites seek to monopolize political power to the detriment of democracy? By analyzing these three factors, we will be able to better understand the structure and content of successful transformational leadership in Africa and beyond.

Elite Roles in Historical Context

The first generation of ruling elites in East Africa swept away the vestiges of the Westminster systems of government left behind by the British, and they replaced them with political structures that strengthened the power of the state. These ruling elites, with the presidents in the lead, quickly turned to ideologies of development guided by self-styled concepts of African socialism. In Kenya, self-help through *harambee* became the centerpiece of the socialist experiment; in Tanzania, the principles of African socialism were laid out in the 1967 *Arusha Declaration*; and in Uganda, Obote's *The Common Man's Charter* provided ideological guidance when it was published in 1969. Consistent with the socialist norms of the time, in just over a decade after independence all three countries had abandoned multi-party politics in favor of single-party systems of government.

Elites in each country also elevated the importance of the state to such prominence that it became alienated from the people. As a result, political leaders (particularly in Kenya and Uganda) converted the police, army and paramilitary forces into repressive arms of the state in order to keep law and order. As Schraeder argues, these highly centralized and personalized, single-party systems restricted the range of political debate to such a degree that the single-party ultimately became the means for maintaining control rather than serving as a dynamic tool for promoting change and development.[4] Moreover, as long as African elites did not "slouch to the left," they were assured of tacit support from the West, which was more concerned about winning the Cold War than promoting democratic values abroad.

After the Cold War, elites have had to govern with varying and conditional support from the West. Many of these leaders (both old and new) have been pressured to reform their political systems by allowing regular elections, providing limited space for civil society, and initiating constitutional change. Despite these reforms, political elites have remained key actors in the transition process, often reticent about navigating political change beyond the transition stage.[5]

Elite Roles in Determining Regime Type

According to Bratton and Hyden, "regimes refer to the formal and informal organization of the center of political power, and its relations with the broader political community."[6] These regimes determine who has access to political power, and they structure the relation between those in and out of power.[7] Some regimes facilitate a political transition process that leads to a more democratic order, while others reinforce more autocratic tendencies. Regime types also determine the rules governing power alternation and state-society relations.[8] When the regime type is characterized by formal rules of the political game that are based on popularly accepted principles of participation and sovereignty, the foundation is laid for a functioning democracy. Clearly, political elites are crucial actors in determining the type of regime that emerges in a particular country.

Hyden's libertarian, state-based, and communitarian regime types are especially relevant to this study.[9] The communal model describes political systems commonly found in Africa and in former communist countries. This regime type is often characterized by strong ethnic and community loyalties and,

> is based on the simultaneous participation of a great variety of primary social organizations (more God given than man-made), which clamor for equal access to centrally controlled resources. Community-specific values are encouraged at the expense of others, and governance structures are socially embedded in multi-functional relations.[10]

Communitarian regimes tend to encounter serious political problems because they lack autonomy from other structures in society. A civic realm is hard to develop and institutionalize when formal associational life is weak, and when governance crises emerge due to the incompatibility of unprocessed community demands and limited political resources.[11]

In state-based (or statist) regimes, the state (specifically political elites) plays the primary role in resource and value allocation. Over time, this monopolization and concentration of power by the state is the main cause of a governance crisis. Political elites become unresponsive, thus undermining the potential for either social or political capital.

Finally, market-based or libertarian regimes differ from the previous two in that levels of citizen control are high, and local level governance structures are responsive to citizens' demands. Under libertarian regimes, the market acts as the main mechanism for resource/value allocation and citizens have more freedom of individual action.[12] The libertarian regime type is often beset by two weaknesses that are potential causes of political crisis: the ineffectiveness of ruling elites in aggregating citizen preferences because of the predominant role of special interests and rent-seeking behavior; and the tendency to apply rational-choice approaches such as cost/benefit analyses to policy-making, often at the expense of citizen interest in the political process. Although Hyden warns that no regime is superior to the other, for the purpose of this study, it is clear that the libertarian regime is most conducive for the transition to, and consolidation of, democracy.

Using Martin's models of democratic transitions, Kenya and Tanzania represent "regime change via multi-party elections" and Uganda appears to fall under the "guided democratization" form of political transition.[13] In all three countries, a hybrid statist/communitarian regime persists, even though elites have embraced some elements of the libertarian regime type (more so in Tanzania and Uganda than in Kenya) in facilitating leadership change. In Kenya and Tanzania, political parties seem to promote citizen control in the political transition process while aggregating their demands more effectively relative to single-party or no-party systems. What follows is an analysis of how these models help to explain the role of elites in the shaping of regime types that either promote or subvert the transition to a more democratic order.

Kenya

For a long time, Kenya's political experience exhibited the classic characteristics of a "co-opted" transition:[14] incumbent elites used their exclusive access to the media, electoral machinery and financial resources to co-opt those associational groups in civil society that would otherwise provide formidable and meaningful contestation of power. Political space was limited, with strict government controls over the mass media, non-governmental organizations and other forms of political and non-political organization. Despite the legalization of multi-party politics in 1991, political transition (or regime change) in Kenya did not occur via genuine multi-party elections until December of 2002. The success of the 2002 elections can be attributed, at least in part, to the decision by Moi to honor the constitutional limit to his term in office and because elites showed a willingness (when pressed by civic and international interests) to accept multi-partyism and abandon a strict statist regime type.

The Kenyan state currently exhibits characteristics of both communitarian and statist regime types. It is communitarian because the civic public realm has been difficult to institutionalize given the high level of ethnic fragmentation in the country. Informal governance structures (ethno-religious clientalist networks) that are characteristic of communitarian regime types are likely to continue in Kenya, since Kibaki's administration has stressed the need to make government more efficient, but has not focused on re-imagining the role of the state in Kenya's national life.[15] While the NARC governing elite may rightfully claim a strong mandate since they received over 62 percent of the votes in the 2002 election, the key factor in maintaining this political capital is whether the coalition will remain intact. Serious questions remain about the viability of the NARC coalition, given its "disparate and ideologically unfocussed" composition.[16]

The Kenyan state, despite the 2002 elections, still exhibits strong statist characteristics, with a powerful executive branch that remains a predominant actor in the political realm.[17] This problem might find resolution in the constitutional reform process, but the Kibaki regime has been very slow in moving this process forward. The character of the regime will be determined by a variety of actors, but elites like Kibaki, coalition partners such as Raila Odinga, and members of parliament, will certainly play a central role. Kenya is not yet a libertarian regime type, but it seems to moving in that direction. For now, statist tendencies are likely to be superimposed on communitarian ones, thus creating a statist/communitarian regime type. This hybrid system is more likely to stifle the movement toward consolidated democracy. This partly explains why, as Ndegwa asserts in his chapter, Kenya's constitutional reforms are still stuck in the *process* phase, and they remain far from comprehensively addressing questions of *substance*.

Uganda

The process of democratic transition in Uganda has been quite different from most others in Africa, thus making it more difficult to categorize or classify. Nevertheless, the evidence suggests that Uganda's NRM leadership has chosen "guided democracy" as the model for transition. The NRM, comprised mostly of soldiers from the war of liberation, has attempted to enhance its legitimacy by emphasizing civilian instead of military sources of political support. In so doing, the NRM has tactfully steered political change from above, using populist political techniques while constructing a statist/communitarian hybrid regime.

Uganda has, however, institutionalized some elements of the libertarian regime. For example, elites made several unique decisions that have increased Ugandans' autonomy *vis a vis* the state. The enactment of a new constitution was a major institutional change initiated by the NRM leadership. This decision was key to other regime changes, such as the decentralization and devolution of power, sweeping civil service reform, the legalization of traditional leaders, and the constitutional recognition of women's rights and freedom of expression. Moreover, elites from the executive and legislative branches of government translated these constitutional promulgations into public policy.[18] Through Local Councils (LCs), the NRM broadened its appeal by extending popular democracy to the grassroots, holding regular elections at the local, parliamentary and presidential levels.

Despite the vulnerability to state co-optation, associational groups in Uganda today play a more important role than ever before. The press is more varied and a spectrum of political views continues to shape the civic discourse. The NRM has recently registered itself as a political party following the lift of the ban on party politics that was in place since it came to power. Finally, the decision to liberalize the economy has transformed the market into the vehicle for allocating social values and economic resources. In most of these developments, ruling elites have been at the forefront of transition, dictating the direction and character of changes that have taken place. Although most point toward the emergence of a libertarian regime type, "guided democracy" by definition marginalizes popular participation. As the NRM tenure has been repeatedly renewed, popular voices have slowly been minimized, thus signaling the return of statist policies and pronouncements.

The 17-year ban on party politics has undermined the consolidation of the democratic transition. Furthermore, it is common practice for the Ugandan state to co-opt associational groups, thus weakening their capacity to play a counter balancing role.[19] Museveni now insists (despite loud voices from the opposition) on amending the constitution to allow a third term. Ethnic-based rent seeking has crept back into the system, leading to high levels of corruption and long term poverty. These are all clear signs of statist/communitarian regime types nestled in the underbelly of libertarian social, political, and economic institutional reforms.

Thus Uganda, like Kenya, shows signs of a hybrid regime type. The transition from statism to libertarianism has been constrained by strong communitarian tendencies. While both Kenya and Uganda share statist tendencies inherited from the colonial and immediate post-colonial states, Uganda has moved closer to institutionalizing the libertarian model despite the no-party system. The retrogression toward strong statism is a function of elite decisions regarding the liberalization of the governance realm and the institutionalization of democratic state structures.

It is worth reiterating Uganda's (and Kenya's) hybrid type of regime has mostly been shaped from above. The political leadership, Museveni in particular, is guiding the country through a democratic transition shaped in *his* image and according to *his* own schedule and preferences. The Museveni factor in Uganda's democratic transition is so important, some have wondered whether the country can survive his departure.[20] This observation underscores the primacy of the elite in Uganda's transition and the still unfulfilled role that civic organizations must play in order to consolidate democracy.

Tanzania

Tanzania presents a case study in "regime change via multi-party elections." This form of transition, characterized by a relatively peaceful transfer of power between elites, has occurred twice in Tanzania. The first was from Nyerere to Mwinyi in 1985. This transition period marked the end of single-party rule, which was preceded by an influential speech by Nyerere in 1990, declaring that the single-party was no longer sacrosanct.[21] The second transition was in 1995, when Mkapa was elected president in multi-party elections. Compared to Uganda and Kenya, Tanzania may be the closest to a libertarian regime type. However, it should be noted that the transition process has been closely managed by political leaders from the ruling CCM party; Nyerere continued to exercise significant influence on the incumbent leaders long after he voluntarily relinquished the presidency in 1985. The nature and pace of democratic transformation in Tanzania today depends largely on choices and strategies articulated by Mkapa and Tanzania's ruling elite. Although Tanzania currently has a multi-party system, CCM elites still maintain tremendous influence on the political process. The executive remains the most powerful branch of government, with presidential authority over governmental appointments, ministry creation, and declaration of states of emergency, without seeking legislative or judicial approval. Because of the power of the Tanzanian presidency, CCM has not been quick to respond to demands for changing the political rules that would redefine the regime type in the country.

Nevertheless, the case of Tanzania contrasts with that of its neighbors by emphasizing the positive role that political leaders can play in promoting democratization. The admission that socialism and the single-party state had failed the people, and the willingness of elites to change course toward democracy and free market economics, may have carried Tanzania beyond transition into the early stages of democratic consolidation. Indeed, research done on Tanzania's transition indicates that local citizens are beginning to perceive themselves as autonomous actors.[22] This also demonstrates that Tanzania is moving away from a statist communitarian regime toward a libertarian one in which political institutionalization is replacing personal rule.

Regardless of the political direction taken by the state, the role of the ruling elites is unmistakable, particularly in shaping the nature of transition, and the emerging regime type. Together, these two processes have tended to define the pace and quality of change. Tanzania provides the most promising model of transition and therefore the most democratic regime type in the region. While Uganda's transition is still on track despite the problems mentioned above, it is too early to assess Kenya's prospects. Political party alternation in Kenya was certainly an important step in the process, but the real test is yet to come. Ruling elites in all three countries face three main challenges. The first is how to fulfill the promises made during public gatherings and election campaigns (often articulated in ethnic or tribal terms). The second challenge is to find ways to respond to these demands without resorting to extensive personalization of power. Finally, there is a need to construct effective governance without depreciating the social and political capital needed for the authoritative and legitimate exercise of power.

Elites and Regime Legitimization

The long-term prospects for Africa's democratic transitions depend on how the continent's legitimacy crisis is resolved. This crisis is a function of the poor quality of vertical legitimacy, or the frequently strained relations between society and regime and/or between society and the state. It is characterized by the lack of consensus on the content of the social contract.[23] The second dimension of Africa's legitimacy deficit is the lack of agreement on who constitutes the polity. Across the continent, the domain of the politically defined community that underlies the state is often contested because of ethno-centric forms of participation and representation. This dimension is symptomatic of weaknesses inherent in the quality of horizontal legitimacy.[24] In chapter nine, Conteh-Morgan argues that the legitimacy crisis in East Africa has its roots in the erosion and destruction of local political allegiances to indigenous political systems. Having inherited an illegitimate colonial state, severe economic conditions and weak civil society organizations, post-colonial leaders have not been able to exercise power authoritatively. As Bratton and van de Walle aptly describe:

> Leaders had damaged their own claim to rule by engaging in nepotism and corruption, which led to popular perceptions that those with access to political office were living high on the hog while ordinary people suffered. The erosion of political legitimacy built to crisis proportions because authoritarian regimes did not provide procedures for citizens to peacefully express such grievances and, especially, to turn unpopular leaders out of office.[25]

The legitimacy crisis was heightened by the contraction of economic resources that, together with the loss of political capital, diminished their capacity to co-opt other elites and improve the quality of vertical legitimacy. By the late 1970s, citizen support (or even acquiescence) could only be achieved through coercion and intimidation. Thus, during the current transition, elites in East Africa have sought to gain legitimacy and support using different strategies. Levels of success have varied accordingly.

Uganda

In Uganda, the process of legitimization began before Museveni's NRM came to power. The war to liberate Uganda from the violent authoritarian excesses of the Obote and Okello regimes could not have been successful without the cooperation of the peasantry. By its very nature, guerilla warfare forced the NRA to construct effective structures of horizontal legitimacy by forging deep and meaningful relationships with a cross section of local populations in their areas of occupation. During this period (1982-86), grassroots organizations known as Resistance Councils (RCs) were formed to mobilize popular resistance against Obote's regime. Frequent elections were held to decide who would be in charge of the day-to-day running of community affairs, with security being the most important. This system, with its emphasis on popular democracy, accountability, and transparency, was the building block for establishing a firm basis for vertical legitimacy. During this period, the NRM transitioned from a bush organization exercising power extra-constitutionally, to a fully institutionalized governing body.

Once in power, Museveni's government used *The Ten Point Programme of the NRM* as its ideological mantra. The *Programme* became the cornerstone for the movement system and no-party democracy.[26] The latter was conceived as a remedy for the lack of vertical/horizontal legitimacy, and as a way to reverse the political and economic disintegration that occurred when Amin and Obote ruled the country. The no-party approach was also designed to end (if not manage) the divisive and sectarian nature of party politics. When Museveni took over in 1986, he had to contend with a legacy of gross human rights abuses, violent political massacres, the wanton disregard for the rule of law, and economic crisis. Against this background, NRM elites enacted a number of policies that were effective in legitimizing the regime (and in some ways the state), thus facilitating the emergence of values that support the authoritative exercise of power.

The promulgation of the 1995 constitution using a popular process was one of the most important political developments in Uganda's reconstruction. Several events conducive to state/regime legitimization emerged from this constitutional process: the decentralization of state power; the administration of constitutionally mandated parliamentary and presidential elections in 1996 and 2001;[27] the permission for traditional leaders to restore their kingdoms; the establishment of mechanisms to check human rights abuses, promote transparency in government, and uphold gender balance and women's rights; and the liberalization of the economy.[28]

NRM elite success in reversing Uganda's history of human rights abuse provided the regime (and to some degree the state) with a modicum of political capital and legitimacy. This brought considerable social and economic benefits to many, though certainly not all, Ugandans.[29] These successes, coupled with the often under-appreciated charisma of Museveni, have helped build support for the regime, change the political culture, and pave the way toward democratic transition.

Political change in Uganda has been led by elites in the NRM who have played a crucial role in guiding democracy from above. Uganda's constitutional overhaul, for example, traces its genesis to a little known declaration in the *National Resistance News*, which was developed by Museveni and a small group of supporters in 1981. Although constitutional change was a popular process with wide ranging democratic gains, it has ultimately served the personal interests and political objectives of ruling elites, thus threatening the legitimacy of the Museveni government.[30] There are three threats to legitimacy that deserve particular attention.

First, the on-going effort by the NRM to amend the constitution (via referendum) in order to allow for a third presidential term threatens to undo the entire constitutional precedent set by the leadership. Not only was the development of pluralist democracy delayed by the no-party system of governance, but it is clear that what the elites are "giving" (a return to party politics)[31] is being counter-balanced by a sustained effort to reverse one of the most fundamental principles in the 1995 constitution – term limits. Second, while the NRM spearheaded the process of government decentralization and devolution, they simultaneously created parallel regime institutions such as Resident District Commissioners (RDCs), which tend to undermine (by politicizing) local level decision-making. Third, as the NRM has entrenched itself in power, rent-seeking behavior has given rise to high levels of corruption.[32] The problems associated with political corruption, coupled with a dearth of resources, has exacerbated levels of poverty and ethnic parochialism, thus forcing community interests to be articulated in "raw" (ethnic) terms. Finally, creeping political decay in Kampala is widened by the targeted co-optation of specific sectors of civil society, such as the church, in order to gain their support for unpopular political decisions.

Uganda's experience is a classic example of the pivotal role that elites play in promoting or stifling a democratic transition. In this case, the history and nature of the NRM, and notably what has been described as Museveni's "imperial" executive, has guided the restoration of political legitimacy and movement toward a more democratic order.[33] That this legitimacy may be slipping away is also a function of elite political choices and strategies in the absence of effective civil society organizations. The failure of Museveni's NRM to live up to its original principles of openness and transparency within its own ranks is already beginning to have an adverse effect on civil society.

Tanzania

Political legitimacy in Tanzania has historically flowed from the country's founding father. Tanzania's first leader was best known for his integrity, patriotism, and charisma. Julius Kambarage Nyerere, affectionately called *Mwalimu* (teacher), was one of Africa's most respected political figures because of his principled personality and unrivalled intellect. Nyerere is also fondly remembered as the pan-Africanist leader who provided a home for a number of African liberation movements, including the African National Congress (ANC) and the Pan African Congress (PAC) of South Africa, FRELIMO of Mozambique, and the Zimbabwe African National Liberation Army (ZANLA). He was also instrumental in ending the brutal regime of Idi Amin in Uganda. Nyerere's vision of African socialism, set out in the Arusha Declaration of 1967, was the template for the construction of a democratic Tanzania:

> The objective of socialism in the United Republic of Tanzania is to build a society in which all members have equal rights and equal opportunities; in which all can live in peace with their neighbours without suffering or imposing injustice, being exploited, or exploiting; and in which all have a gradually increasing basic level of material welfare before any individual lives in luxury.[34]

Although Tanzania fell short of these lofty values, Nyerere was perceived as an honest leader in whom citizens could invest their mandate. Immediately following Tanganyikan independence, Nyerere nurtured vertical and horizontal legitimacy for the regime.[35] Years later, Nyerere's integrity was reaffirmed when he acknowledged the limitations of his *ujamaa* ideology and called for its replacement, stepped down from power (only the second African head of state to do so at the time), and embraced pluralism. Nyerere's successors have sought to live up to the high standards that he embodied – at least rhetorically. Whereas Moi followed Kenyatta's footsteps of arbitrary rule, Tanzania's Mkapa has attempted to publicly maintain a high level of integrity and respect for the rule of law and the institutions of government.

Despite having established a single-party state in Tanzania, Nyerere's positive accomplishments are far more tangible than Kenyatta's and Obote's. According to Gros, the single-party socialist state had a high level of legitimacy among Tanzanians, and it had accomplishments that few African countries could claim.[36] Life expectancy was increased from thirty five years at independence to fifty-five by the early 1980s; over the same period, literacy grew from 30 percent to 69 percent;[37] and income inequality between elites and the masses was not as pronounced in Tanzania as it was elsewhere in Africa. Furthermore, Gros argues that on the eve of the government decision to liberalize the political system, a large majority of Tanzanians (77 percent) professed support for the single-party state. Also, the demands for liberalizing the political system were not a product of the people taking to the streets as was the case in Kenya or Zambia. Despite the failures of socialism and the single-party state, Tanzania's leadership could still lay claim to a measurable level of efficacy and legitimacy.[38]

However, post-independence progress in Tanzania has been elite-driven and elite-shaped. While the input of ordinary citizens was solicited, decision-making was limited to elites in the ruling TANU. Even after Nyerere stepped down, he continued to shape political changes so that the party/regime would retain a measure of legitimacy in the political system. This legitimacy began to wane towards the end of the 1980s. It was replaced by, among other things, high levels of government and party corruption, unruly party cadres, and the inability of the ruling party to fulfill the core goal of socialist egalitarianism, along with what Gros has referred to as "centrifugal forces on Zanzibar." However, it was the ruling elite, prompted and led by Nyerere, who initiated the move toward multi-party politics and away from the single-party socialist state. Furthermore, it was the political leadership (with minimal pressure from civil society) that made the *volte face* on economic policy in 1986, when the government turned to the World Bank and IMF, and embraced liberal economic reform.

These policy changes illustrate the dominant role that leaders play in African politics in general, and in democratic transitions in particular. Tanzania's experience demonstrates that choices that favor or oppose legitimation and democratization are often made by elites, especially in places where civil society is relatively weak. Nyerere realized (with minimal pressure from civil society) that the single-party state had decayed beyond reconstruction, and that CCM needed a radical transformation if its traditional focus on democracy and equality were to remain its guiding principles. He thus persuaded incumbent elites to open the door to multi-party politics. This pressured the ruling CCM to radically re-organize in order to compete in a politically competitive environment. As a result, a transition to multi-party politics was institutionalized, which in turn contributed to the emergence of a semi-libertarian regime type. The further consolidation of democracy will depend on continued elite commitment to accountability and transparency.

Kenya

By December 2002, the KANU leadership had run out of social and political capital. It had also lost the support of a broad spectrum of Kenya's civil society. The international community, particularly the donors, had withdrawn financial and moral support. Efforts by the party to reconstruct vertical legitimacy by renewing its appeal via political realignment failed when Raila Odinga's NDP broke away, with a portion of its members joining the opposition National Alliance of Kenya. The past abuses of KANU, and the growing anti-Moi sentiments, were enough to discredit and delegitimize KANU presidential candidate Uhuru Kenyatta.

In the case of Uganda, incumbent illegitimacy had to be solved through a protracted guerilla war. Ruling elites in Tanzania maintained a modicum of legitimacy through regular elections. In Kenya, the character of political transition was partly shaped by Moi's decision abide by the constitutional term limit requirement. To demonstrate how critical elites are in democratic transitions, Ndegwa points out that Moi's decision not to violate the constitutional term-limit mandate transformed the political landscape in very fundamental ways.[39] He argues further that the past practices of political mischief and chicanery by KANU were no longer necessary, the Electoral Commission of Kenya became more assertive and objective, and the constitutional reform process "served the opposition well in smoothing the way toward a compromise settlement with which each significant party could live."[40] The first step in re-establishing the authoritative exercise of power (or vertical legitimacy) in Kenya was successfully completed with a smooth and orderly transfer of power to the NARC coalition in December of 2002. Restoration of meaningful horizontal legitimacy will be a challenge for this coalition government given the ethnic polarization that was the hallmark of Moi's regime.

Clearly, the establishment of a libertarian regime which ensures accountability and transparency will take much longer in a country that has suffered from a long period of statist/communitarian governance. The challenge involves the construction of a civic realm; an environment in which civic institutions, like government departments, political parties, and the media, enjoy respect and legitimacy. Founding father Jomo Kenyatta made progress toward establishing a strong governance realm that linked state and society together in a manner that legitimized the exercise of political authority.[41] The new ruling elite in Kenya might do well to rekindle Kenyans' strong self-help spirit of *harambee* made popular in early post-colonial Kenya. This is a key requisite for establishing meaningful state-society linkages, building what Englebert has called a "consensus on the content of the social contract."[42] Kibaki's government (just like those based in Kampala and Dar es Salaam) will also have to face up to the difficulties of reconstructing this realm. This can only be done by reclaiming the state and limiting the arbitrary use of public resources for private or communal (ethnic/tribal) purposes. This is a challenge facing Uganda and to a much lesser degree Tanzania.

In all three countries, restoring legitimate authority will require effective elite governance (the ability to deliver public goods in an environment of scarcity), and the articulation of a vision that resonates with the population at large. This will entail two related policy and philosophical changes. First, just as Kenyatta was adept at balancing different factional interests within the KANU party without necessarily completely suppressing opposing views,[43] Kibaki and his government must maintain party coherence despite the varied interests that make up the NARC. The second change is related to the issue of state institutionalization. The trend in Uganda and Tanzania has been to institutionalize and legitimize the regime rather than the state. There are signs that Kibaki's government may follow this regional trend, which will further delay the transition to, and consolidation of, democracy.

The struggle to establish political accountability in East Africa has been (and continues to be) contested at different levels. In Uganda, it took a five-year guerilla war to depose an unpopular dictatorship, while in Kenya it took a combination of domestic and international pressure to convince the incumbent to finally step down. In Tanzania, change has come relatively smoothly. What all three cases have in common is the fact that most of these changes were elite controlled. In Kenya and Tanzania, elite decisions to concede past mistakes, and to allow for pluralism and constitutional rule were pivotal in restoring some measure of political capital. What they do next will be important in shaping the nature and character of democratic transition. In Uganda, Obote's stubborn regime had to be uprooted militarily, thereby ushering in a new social and political and economic order. But the imprint of elite roles and interests is unmistakable both in terms of the legitimacy that has been established and the prospects for its decline. Finally, when placed in historical perspective, the more respectable leaders in East Africa, such as Kenyatta, Nyerere, and perhaps Museveni, have benefited from their charismatic personalities as they endeavored to garner citizen support and consent. However, economic performance is also a key pillar in citizen perceptions of effective governance, which in turn bestow elites with the political support they need for good governance.

The Economic Explanation of Power Monopolization

In East Africa (and across the continent), private wealth accumulation has consistently benefited from access to, and control of, the state. For example, the marketing of cash crops such as coffee, cotton and tobacco was initially monopolized by state agencies or parastatals, which became convenient vehicles for elites to extract resources from peasants through price fixing. This unfettered access to the nation's resources can only happen in a state that has minimal transparency and openness. Since a democratic government must by definition have these two elements, African leaders have successfully blocked the transition to democratic systems that limit their unchecked access to state wealth. Some African leaders, such Nkrumah and Kenyatta, were known on a number of occasions to publicly exhort their countrymen to "eat their share of the elephant" or "grab so long as they were not caught." These inauspicious appeals (partly made to garner support and popularity) led the first generation of African elites to monopolize and manipulate public office for personal enrichment and political patronage. In turn, this instrumentalist view of the state became the genesis for institutionalized waste, inefficiency, corruption, and nepotism. As economic crises unfolded, elites became even more interventionist, embracing economic nationalist policies, stifling the spirit of competition and enterprise, and effectively blocking the emergence of an autonomous middle class. The political ramifications were devastating: in Uganda two brutal dictatorships (1971-1986) led the country into economic and political chaos; in Kenya the system became more politically centralized and repressive as interest articulation took on ethnic overtones; and in

Tanzania, despite relative political stability, widespread poverty and corruption in the ruling party resulted in gradual political reform.

The post-Cold War generation of elites has had to address a declining economic resource base and a liberal economic reform orthodoxy dictated by Western governments, the World Bank, and the IMF. While these factors have ameliorated some of the excesses of elite behavior, leaders still view the state as a tool for personal gain and aggrandizement. This helps to explain why they have often subverted democratic reforms, opting instead to steadfastly hold on to the reigns of power.

Uganda

When Museveni and the NRM took power in 1986, the economy was in shambles. The reconstruction of the economy quickly climbed to the top of the agenda in defining the legitimacy of the NRM both at home and abroad. NRM elites eventually initiated monetary reform, economic structural adjustment, poverty alleviation, the extension of rural credit and savings facilities, and the privatization of parastatals. As a result, many state-owned parastatals were sold off, revenue collection increased, and black marketeering in financial trading was curtailed. By all measures, Uganda's economy improved tremendously since Museveni came to power, as evidenced by relatively high GDP growth rates. That Uganda can once again boast of a functioning economy is testimony to the determination of the NRM to restore social order and economic growth. The economic basis of government legitimacy has, however, recently begun to erode with the emergence of political corruption.

The privatization process has been used to pursue private and political elite goals with minimal regard to national interest.[44] A number of scandals have surfaced, exposing corruption in the sale of state assets such as the Uganda Commercial Bank, the Uganda Grain Milling Corporation, Entebbe Handling Services Limited, and the Kampala Sheraton.[45] State-led corruption through institutions like the Public Enterprises Reform and Divestiture Secretariat (PERDS) provides further evidence of how elites have used the state to illegally accumulate wealth, and why, as a result, they often refrain from giving up such power.[46] The wealth that flows from these illicit gains (coupled with donor aid) has been used to finance campaigns and in many instances buy votes. NRM elites (similar to those in Kenya) have used state power to reward like-minded men and women (often from the same ethnic group) with lucrative government portfolios, thus constructing impenetrable patron-client relationships. Given the lack of indigenous capital, these networks now include foreign, often Asian, entrepreneurs who have the resources to purchase state assets.

Tanzania

Despite its socialist rhetoric, TANU gradually coalesced into a *bourgeois* class with exploitative instincts during the *ujamaa* years.[47] Since there was no separation between the party and the state, it was very easy to use this confluence of structural power to direct national wealth toward bureaucratic elite interests.

During the multi-party era, Tanzania adopted policy prescriptions advocated by the IMF and World Bank that resulted in GDP growth from 1.6 to 4.4 percent between 1990-1995 and 1995-2002 respectively.[48] Despite this success, almost six million Tanzanians lived below $1 a day in 1995 while elites with access to state instruments of power were able to live in comparative luxury. The underpinnings of economic planning in Tanzania are no different from the Ugandan experience; privatization has been a central mechanism for the structural adjustment of the economy.

The case of Tanzania also illustrates the dominant role of political elites in using state power to funnel national wealth not only to themselves but also into the electoral system in ways that perpetuate political monopoly. CCM has used access to state resources to maximize its advantages in the multi-party era. Between 1985-1990, Mwinyi did very little to curb the corruption that engulfed political elites and the business interests closely linked to them. The CCM leadership code was cast aside and, similar to the Uganda experience, the predominance of the Asian business interests in the private sector gave them an advantage in the purchase of state enterprises. State/party officials could only resort to using their offices as conduits for kickbacks.[49] Corruption and patronage continued during Mwinyi's second term (1990-95), leading to cutbacks in funding from the World Bank, the IMF, and from key donors such as Sweden. Following President Mkapa's election in 1995, efforts were made to restore fiscal discipline, curb corruption and establish a new ethos. Although the economy rebounded and Mkapa was re-elected in 2000, his actions were not supported by many in the CCM rank and file, an indication that the spirit of reform is not uniformly accepted among CCM followers.

Kenya

Kenya is no stranger to the liberal economic orthodoxy of the post-Cold War era. Moi's repressive state was adept at using economic instruments to monopolize power and marginalize the opposition. Moi and KANU elites used economics to control ethnic group rivalries and their struggles to ascertain resources from the state. Proceeds from the treasury were used to alienate those in the opposition and to reward Moi's supporters, especially those from the Kalenjin and related ethnic groups. The resulting ethno-centric, patron-client relationships became the foundation of Moi's power base and the crucible of state patronage and corruption. Furthermore, these practices increased the stakes for state control and redefining citizenship in ways that were often not democratic in practice.[50] Power was linked to personal and kin-based wealth accumulation. The government often used its resources to influence electoral outcomes through the financing of campaigns, vote buying, the printing of currency (especially during the 1992 elections), or dividing the opposition by offering select individuals with access to the economic largesse of the state. A notable example of this co-optation process was the short-lived NDP-KANU coalition of 2002. The election of Kibaki has not led to rapid reform against graft and corruption, or the further liberalization of the economy. Constitutional reform and cleavages in the ruling NARC coalition have also limited the possibility for fundamental change.

East Africa's elites have, for the most part, failed to create an enabling environment for democracy to flourish in the region. Elites have held the well-founded fear that economically impoverished citizens would quickly ally themselves with the political opposition in a transparent democratic environment. As a result, governments have responded to dissent with either repression or economic co-optation. This economic mismanagement by ruling elites has eroded their legitimacy and the prospects for democratic consolidation. As state resources have continued to decline, so has the capacity of top ranking elites to recruit new members and thus expand their patron-client networks. Ultimately, the ruling class has decreased in size (but not in wealth), become even more insecure, and clamped down on political freedoms.

Concluding Comments

Political leaders in Africa are major stakeholders in any movement toward democratization. They play a central role in shaping transitions that, in turn, determine the kinds of regime types that emerge.

In Uganda, where guided democracy has been the medium of change, the statist-communitarian regime that now exists reflects the priorities and concessions of elite prescriptions. Political leadership has initiated effective political and economic changes, which, in turn, have somewhat improved state legitimization. But prospects for a libertarian regime have been frustrated by elite reluctance to extend political pluralism and allow open contestation of power. As a result, political capital has been squandered and regime legitimacy has suffered.

In Moi's Kenya, a co-opted transition was characterized by elite discomfort with the opening political space and the emergence of a statist-communitarian regime. Elites defined the rules of the political game in ways that reified ethnic identity, marginalized the opposition, and frustrated constitutional reform. Since this occurred in tandem with a relatively strong civil society, this demonstrates the significance of political elites in shaping political change. Kenya's prospects for democratic consolidation rest on the integrity and coherence of the NARC coalition, which has to address the low level of political legitimacy and weak state capacity inherited from the Moi regime.[51]

Elite acceptance of multi-party elections as the path to political change has resulted in the emergence of a semi-libertarian regime type in Tanzania. The absence of large ethnic groups has limited the ethnicization of politics, made mobilization of the masses for development easier, and the struggle for legitimacy less problematic. Similar to its East African neighbors, political elites still play important roles in defining and redefining the boundaries of the state *vis a vis* society, and in deflecting efforts for institutionalizing effective restraints on executive power. In all three countries, the misuse of national resources by the government continues to be a major challenge. As long as elites continue to control the transition by defining regime types, the modes of this transition merit closer attention.

African elites continue to behave as transactional leaders, resisting efforts to embrace the transformational leadership qualities that are necessary for successful democratic transition and consolidation.[52] This comparative analysis demonstrates that elites in all three states have adapted a less progressive, transactional model of leadership in which exchange relationships between leaders and followers characterize the exercise of power. The use of the state to extend patronage in exchange for support has restricted democratic transition and blocked economic growth.

There is a need for further examination of the complex roles that political leaders play in democratic transitions in Africa. The following questions succinctly summarize the dilemmas associated with transition processes that are dominated by political elites. What strategies should co-opted, repressed, and/or marginalized civil society organizations adopt to change the ideological and political inclinations of African elites? What causes leaders to subvert the transition process, and how should opposition forces respond to this elite strategy? Finally, what role should external actors, particularly the donor community, play in keeping the elites true and honest to liberalization and democratization? The cases examined offer tentative answers to these questions, but more research needs to be conducted.

Notes

1. Peter Schrader, "Elites as Facilitators or Impediments to Political Development? Some Lesson from the 'Third Wave' of Democratization in Africa," *The Journal of Developing Areas* vol. 29 (October 1994), pp. 69-90.
2. Michael Bratton and Nicolas van de Walle, *Democratic Experiments in Africa: Regime Transitions in Comparative Perspective* (Cambridge: Cambridge University Press, 1997), p. 9.
3. Bratton and van de Walle, *Democratic Experiments in Africa*, p. 9.
4. Schrader, "Elites as Facilitators," p. 72.
5. Samuel Huntington, *The Third Wave: Democratization in the Late Twentieth Century* (Norman: University of Oklahoma Press, 1991).
6. Goran Hyden, "Governance and the Study of Politics" in Goran Hyden and Michael Bratton, eds., *Governance and Politics in Africa* (Boulder, CO: Lynne Rienner Publishers, 1992), p. 6.
7. Robert Fishman, "Rethinking State and Regime: Southern Europe in Transition to Democracy," *World Politics*, vol. 42, no. 3 (April 1990), p. 428, quoted in Hyden and Bratton, eds., *Governance and Politics in Africa*, p. 6.
8. Jean-Germain Gros, "Introduction: Understanding Democratization," in Jean-Germain Gros, ed., *Democratization in Late Twentieth-Century: Coping with Uncertainty* (Westport: Greenwood Press, 1998), p. 2.
9. Hyden, "Governance and the Study of Politics," pp. 16-17.
10. Hyden, "Governance and the Study of Politics," p. 17.
11. Hyden, "Governance and the Study of Politics," p. 17.
12. Hyden, "Governance and the Study of Politics," pp. 17-19.

[13] Guy Martin, "Preface: Democratic Transition in Africa," *Issue: A Journal of Opinion*, vol. XXI, no. 1-2 (African Studies Association, 1993), pp. 6-7.

[14] This is Guy Martin's third model of democratic transition.

[15] Stephen N. Ndegwa, "Kenya: Third Time Lucky," *Journal of Democracy* vol. 14, no. 3 (July 2003), p. 156.

[16] Ndegwa, "Kenya: Third Time Lucky," p. 157.

[17] Ndegwa points out that campaign promises of free primary education in the run up to the 2002 elections in Kenya became a critical test of things to come when the NARC government was forced to add $47 million to the budget following an influx of pupils into the schools. Ndegwa, "Kenya: Third Time Lucky."

[18] These include The Constitutional Amendment (*Ebyaffe*) Bill; Local Government (Resistance Council) Bill and the Constitutional and Local Governments Act, 1997.

[19] Susan Dichlitch, *Elusive Promise of NGOs in Africa: Lessons from Uganda* (New York: St. Martin's Press, 1998).

[20] Nelson Kasfir, "'No-Party Democracy' in Uganda," in Larry Diamond and Marc F. Plattner, eds., *Democratization in Africa* (Baltimore: The John Hopkins University Press, 1999), p. 209.

[21] Micheal Bratton and Nicolas Van de Walle, "Toward Governance in Africa: Popular Demands and State Responses," in Hyden and Bratton, eds., *Governance and Politics in Africa*, p. 42.

[22] Jean-Germain Gros, "Leadership and Democratization: The Case of Tanzania," in Gros, ed., *Democratization in Late Twentieth-Century: Coping with Uncertainty*.

[23] Pierre Englebert, *State Legitimacy and Development in Africa* (Boulder, CO: Lynne Rienner Publishers, 2000), p. 8.

[24] Englebert, *State Legitimacy and Development in Africa*, p. 8.

[25] Bratton and van de Walle, *Democratic Experiments in Africa*, pp. 98-99.

[26] Nelson Kasfir, "'Movement' Democracy, Legitimacy and Power in Uganda" in Justus Mugaju and J. Oloka-Onyango, eds., *No-Party Democracy in Uganda: Myths and Realities* (Kampala: Fountain Publishers, 2000), pp. 60-78.

[27] President Museveni won the 1996 elections by 74 percent and the 2001 elections by 74 percent of the vote (see Dean McHenry's chapter for source). The NRM also won majorities in parliament in both of these elections.

[28] GDP growth in Uganda averaged 6.5 and 5.7 percent between 1990-95 and 1995-2002 respectively, according to "ICT at a Glance: Uganda," Country Background Information, World Bank and UNESCO, ICT Infrastructure and Access Data, Development Data Group (World Bank, 2001).

[29] Kasfir, "'Movement' Democracy," p. 75.

[30] For example Article 72 of the constitution establishes the right to from political parties, but Articles 269-7 legitimize a movement system that eschews party politics.

[31] The NRM has recently acceded to demands for party politics and has registered itself as a political party [NRM-Organization (NRM-O)] in preparation for the 2005 elections.

[32] Roger Tangri and Andrew Mwenda, "Corruption and Cronyism in Uganda's Privatization in the 1990s," *African* Affairs (2001), pp. 117-133.

[33] See Ndegwa's chapter in this volume.

[34] Julius Nyerere, "Arusha Declaration," in Julius Nyerere, ed., *Ujamaa Essays on Socialism* (London: Oxford University Press, 1971), p. 15.

[35] Tanzania has not had the misfortune of having large ethnic groups capable of threatening the security of others in the business of resource and power distribution. Of course, government policies did help in ameliorating the potential emergence of tensions even among ethnic groups, in particular the Chagga and the rest of the country.

[36] Gros, "Leadership and Democratization," p. 102.

[37] Tanzania's adult literacy rate in 2002 was 77.1 percent. See "ICT at a Glance, Tanzania," Country Background Information, World Bank and UNESCO, ICT Infrastructure and Access Data, Development Data Group (World Bank, 2001).
[38] Gros, "Leadership and Democratization," p. 103.
[39] Ndegwa, "Kenya: Third Time Lucky?" p. 153.
[40] Ndegwa, "Kenya: Third Time Lucky?" pp. 153-154.
[41] Joel Barkan, "The Rise and Fall of a Governance Realm in Kenya," in Hyden and Michael, eds., *Governance and Politics in Africa*, p. 188.
[42] Englebert, *State Legitimacy and Development in Africa*, p. 8.
[43] Englebert, *State Legitimacy and Development in Africa*, p. 8.
[44] Joel D. Barkan, "Divergence and Convergence in Kenya and Tanzania: Pressures for Reform," in Joel D. Barkan, ed., *Beyond Capitalism Versus Socialism in Kenya and Tanzania* (Boulder, CO: Lynne Rienner Publishers, 1994), p. 30.
[45] For an in depth study of corruption in Uganda see Roger Tangri and Andrew Mwenda, "Corruption and Cronyism in Uganda's Privatization in the 1990s"; and Augustine Ruzindana, "Combating Corruption in Uganda," in P. Langseth, ed., *Uganda: Landmarks in rebuilding a Nation* (Kampala: Fountain Publishers, 1995).
[46] See select chapters in the following volumes for detailed studies of the privatization and divestiture program in Uganda: Langseth, *Uganda: Landmarks in Rebuilding a Nation*; Justus Mugaju, ed., *Uganda's Age of Reforms: A Critical Overview* (Kampala: Fountain Publishers, 1999); Apolo Nsibambi, *Decentralization and Civil Society in Uganda* (Kampala: Fountain Publishers, 1998); and Holger Bernt Hansen and Michael Twaddle, eds., *Developing Uganda* (Kampala: Fountain Publishers, 1998).
[47] Issa Shivji, *Class Struggles in Tanzania* (Dar es Salaam: Tanzania Publishing House, 1976), p. 75.
[48] "ICT at a Glance: Tanzania," Country Background Information, World Bank and UNESCO, ICT Infrastructure and Access Data, Development Data Group (World Bank, 2001).
[49] Joel D. Barkan, *Beyond Capitalism versus Socialism in Kenya and Tanzania* (Lynne Rienner, 1994), p. 30.
[50] For a discussion of the complexities of dual citizenship in ethnically divided Kenya, see Stephen N. Ndegwa, "Citizenship and Ethnicity: An Examination of Two Transition Moments in Kenyan Politics," *American Political Science Review* vol. 91, no. 3 (September 1997), p. 18.
[51] Also important to note here is whether Kenya's civil society, united in the face of Moi's repression, will remain so and thus keep Kibaki's government honest to its campaign promises.
[52] R.H. Hall, *Organizations: Structures, Processes and Outcomes* (Englewood Cliffs, N.J.: Prentice Hall, 1996), p. 141.

Chapter 5

Constitutional Reform

Stephen N. Ndegwa and Ryan E. Letourneau

Until recently, East Africans have given scant attention to constitutions and constitutionalism in the current transitions from authoritarian rule to competitive politics. As elsewhere in Africa's democratic transitions, constitutionalism has not received much attention for a number of reasons. Prime among these is the overall preoccupation with elections as the *sine qua non* of democratic transitions. In this regard, incumbency overthrow, regime change, and the survival and performance of new regimes have been the main preoccupations of democracy analysts and of practicing politicians. However, as former monolithic regimes have persisted in power – barely making satisfying changes in rules and practices – opposition politicians and democracy activists have turned greater attention to constitutions and constitutionalism. Especially after initially optimistic opposition groups (parties and civic groups) have suffered repeated electoral defeat since the 1990s, constitutions have become a central concern.

In East Africa, even with liberalization the former single-party or authoritarian regimes have survived electoral opposition for the last decade – with the recent exception of alternation in Kenya in December 2002. The pursuit of constitutional reform in East Africa has arisen out of expedient politics rather than careful and deliberate reflection on the fundamental questions of ordering political life in a modern democratic state. However, this does not diminish the basic questions that these movements have raised or the validity of the consequences they have spawned. While often simply intended to open new fronts for contestation in the hope of wearing down an intransigent regime, recent pushes for constitutional reform have raised new questions on citizenship and re-opened old questions about ordering political power, especially in the ethnic, racial, or regional politics that underlie these fragile nations.

Recent Debates on Constitutional Reform

Three issues are notable in recent debates on constitutional reform in East Africa.[1] One trend focuses on how political power is apportioned, while the second emphasizes citizenship questions, with a particular focus on how individuals and groups relate to state power. The third is a debate over the process by which new constitutions will be formulated. Tellingly, the first two issues tend to be pushed by different and typically opposing actors, although there is some overlap. Overall, the question of how state power is apportioned, especially with regard to decentralizing power, is one pressed most often by politicians, especially those in the opposition or those in putative minority ethnic or regional groups. This rekindles the significant challenge of national unity, bringing sharp relief to the question of identity and power in pluralistic nations. In recognition of this challenge, the first constitutional designs of the post-colonial state addressed federalism (*majimboism*), and the role of traditional authorities.[2] In the contemporary setting, it is usually old parties or their remnants and older politicians who recite these arguments and sometimes actively incite the passions of this era. Importantly, these are now wrapped in the justifications of enhancing democracy. They are positions articulated by those who fear losing incumbency or being overwhelmed as permanent minorities as they anticipate ethnic coalitions in the context of electoral politics (for example, the *majimbo* debate in Kenya).

The second trend draws its leadership and finds strongest articulation among civil society actors, with almost all political parties, except incumbents or their partners, echoing their arguments and values. These organizations press a constitutional discourse that seeks a new formulation of citizenship rights; they are less concerned about the allocation of power between state levels and more about how such power, wherever it resides, is constrained.[3]

The third trend is perhaps even more elemental in that it revolves around the process through which constitutional reform is secured. The debate tends to be especially protracted where the regime receives a threat from the fluidity that would result from retracted state power under a new constitution. In this case, the incumbent regime seeks to retain control of the process by circumscribing the agenda or calibrating the pace of change in order to effectively insulate itself against sudden and catastrophic transformation.

The forcefulness of the push for constitutional reforms in all three East African countries has increased over the last decade, especially since incumbent regimes can make legal, political, and administrative reforms and still manage to subvert competitive politics. Hope has now been placed on the promise of new constitutions, not only as a way to lay out new ground rules for political contest, but also as opportunities to force a public re-negotiation of power and to establish the basic point that those who govern do so at the behest of an empowered citizenry. Opposition groups hope that new constitutions will also provide an opportunity to dislodge incumbents from power by exposing their fictions of responsible government, by easing in new, advantageous rules of contest (especially in elections), or by simply swelling the ranks of supportive citizens who view the opposition as a better governing and rights-upholding alternative.

As we will see in the brief case studies presented in this chapter, the three trends noted above are evident to various degrees in the recent constitutional debates in the region. While the achievements of each movement for constitutional reform are inconsistent, the re-establishment of constitutional discourse as a central issue of the transitions is emphatic. If judgment is to be made about whether these movements have succeeded (and this is perhaps a premature question), it has to be a *caveat*-laden affirmative. The success is less about the actual constitutional changes or even regime changes achieved and more about the initiation of constitutional debate and the emergence of constitutionalism as a key element in the current transitions. Even though much of it has arisen out of the expedient concerns of politicians, constitutional discourse has its own momentum that is difficult to subvert and is likely to inform discourse on transition politics. As the triumph of the Kenyan opposition in December 2002 underscores, the expedient politics of opposition parties now clashes with the fundamental systemic issues pressed by civil society and, swiftly, by former regime members.

Constitutional Reform Debate in Kenya, 1992-2002[4]

When Kenya gained independence from Britain in 1963 it was under a constitution that established a federal (*majimbo*) framework with an executive prime minister and the British monarch as head of state. It was also grounded in liberal institutions such as a bill of rights, entrenched separation of powers, and a delineated balance between regional and central government powers. However, given its overwhelming victory in independence elections, KANU moved quickly to dismantle the federal constitution and establish a sovereign republic with an executive president, reducing and subsequently eliminating the powers of regional governments, and absorbing the largest opposition party in parliament.[5] KANU viewed federalism as unnecessary, expensive, and constraining of its rightful power emanating from its electoral supremacy. While the constitutional debate in Kenya goes back to the challenges of negotiating an independence constitution under the tutelage of the departing British imperialists,[6] we focus on the period between 1992-2002, which coincides with the transition to multi-party politics. While the reforms of 1991 ushered in a multi-party system by lifting the constitutional prohibition against multiple parties, that change was not a result of nor did it produce a broader constitutional debate as witnessed after the 1992 elections, and especially after 1994.

Since 1994, constitutional review has been a central reform priority in the political arena in Kenya. It is the culmination of agitation that started in earnest in 1994 with the publication of the Model Constitution by the Citizens' Coalition for Constitutional Change (4Cs), which took the mantle of pressing for constitutional change following the problematic transition elections of 1992.[7] In many ways, the Kenyan transition that began in 1991 with the repeal of Section 2A of the constitution was woefully incomplete.[8] While the repeal of Section 2A of the constitution allowed for the legal existence of opposition parties, it left in place a matrix of laws (many of which were holdovers from the colonial period, especially the emergency era), which undermined liberal principles necessary for a functional multi-party system. These laws included restrictions on free assembly, sedition laws, and party registration mechanisms controlled by the executive. The constitution itself had been amended over thirty times since independence.[9] The very first set of constitutional amendments in the early 1960s eliminated the federalist framework negotiated just before independence and triggered the nearly three-decade long decline of the balance between central and regional power. Except for the repeal of Section 2A and the 1997 Inter-Parliamentary Parties Group

(IPPG) reforms, all of the amendments restricted the liberties of individuals and groups, while enhancing the power of the executive at the expense of parliament.[10]

As such, civil society groups and opposition parties recognized by 1995 that a response to this negative evolution was necessary. Thus, broad-based constitutional reform became the key goal of most 'progressive' organizations. The momentum started by the 4Cs and related groups gained ground in 1997 when the National Convention Assembly (NCA) and its executive arm, the National Convention Executive Committee (NCEC), began to mobilize for comprehensive constitutional changes before the 1997 elections. With the support of opposition political parties, the NCEC threatened to derail the 1997 elections with mass demonstrations and enlisted politicians to a boycott under the battle cry "no reforms, no elections." As a result, the government was forced to accede to a set of minimum reforms – the so-called IPPG reforms – which allowed elections to take place, with most (though not all) opposition leaders taking part.[11] This agreement included constitutionally entrenching the multi-party system and omnibus legislation repealing most of the repressive laws and administrative regulations. The most significant reform plank was the passage of legislation enabling a comprehensive review of the constitution after the elections. However, even before the formal review was to start, the process proposed in the Constitution of Kenya Review Act became highly contentious and consumed much of the energy in the political arena after the elections of December 1997 in which the ruling party KANU retained power.[12] By late 1998, this process had been derailed and in the next two years, a protracted battle ensued to decide the process of constitutional reform.

The process of constitutional review spelled out in the 1997 act was as follows. A Constitution of Kenya Review Commission consisting of 29 commissioners was to be appointed by the president from a list of 45 submitted by various stakeholders. This commission would collect and collate the views of Kenyans by traveling across the country holding public hearings. The act delineated three stages for the establishment of the commission but made no mention of how it would actually work. The first stage involved the submission of names of potential commissioners to the attorney general by any organization from a list of eleven 'stakeholders' or sectors of the political and civil society. The stakeholders were identified as: registered political parties, religious organizations, 'institutional' organizations, professional associations, trade unions, business representatives, farmers, women's organizations, youth associations, associations of disabled persons, and NGOs.[13]

The second stage required the Attorney General to compile and submit the names offered in the first stage to ten specific stakeholders drawn from the sectors in the first stage. For example, among registered political parties only those with elected members in parliament could participate in this second stage to select forty-five names to be recommended to the president. In addition to the parliamentary parties, the other organizations expected to be involved in the second stage were the National Council of Churches of Kenya (NCCK), the Evangelical Fellowship of Kenya, the Muslim Consultative Council, the Supreme Council of Kenya Muslims, the Hindu Council of Kenya, the Association of Professional Societies of East Africa, the Kenya Women's Political Caucus, and the NGO Council. It is from the forty-five names chosen in this second stage that the president would pick twenty-nine to sit on the commission, appointing one of them as chair.

After this stage, however, it was not clear how the commission would operate. Issues related to the modalities of commission operation, along with the concern of the president's unfettered final say on the composition of the commission, became the center of contention between civil society, some opposition parties and parliamentarians, on one side, and the incumbent regime on the other. Much energy was spent on the process because it was recognized that it had a great deal of influence on the ultimate content of the revised constitution. The opposition and civil society asserted that the *status quo* as spelt out in the act privileged the incumbent government in that it would control the composition of the commission, and the analysis and drafting of the recommendations to parliament and would thus render parliament and civil society roles only as advisory.

The opposition and civic lobby groups opposed the process stated in the 1997 act based on several additional issues. First was Kenya's history of presidential commissions, which have typically not been participatory, transparent, or independent. For example, many of them have not published their final reports, indicating that when the regime perceives commission findings as threatening it simply ignores them. The experience of the Saitoti Commission of 1990 – which was constituted to collect views from Kenyans on whether to reform the single-party constitution – was an example of how compromised and ineffective such commissions were. While the commission received views from the public and politicians urging a change, its report asserted that Kenyans were generally happy with the single-party state and sought only minor modifications. A few months later, under the president's direction and responding to growing pressure, the party changed the constitution to allow multi-partyism.[14]

More substantively, the reform lobby had particular preferences that were at odds with what the incumbent KANU sought. The NCEC and its allies, such as the 4Cs, saw the best option of constitution making as a convention which would express the popular will and which would retain sovereign authority to re-make the constitution in more fundamental ways than a presidential commission could.[15] The NCEC's position was based on an assumption articulated in its campaigns against the state (for example, in its stance against the 1997 elections), that the KANU regime was illegitimate and held power against the will of the majority of Kenyans. However, given the interests of the political class to retain institutional continuity, and the institutional interests of the newly inaugurated parliament which could not be expected to legislate itself out of existence, the possibility for a convention remained a distant one.

The opposition and reform lobby groups had a clear agenda to promote the recognition of popular sovereignty. The reform lobby preferred a process that allowed for a fundamental review and re-writing of the constitution, not just on the grounds of the substantive deficiencies of the current document, but equally to serve as an assertion of popular sovereignty. For instance, the NCEC took the liberty to expansively interpret Section 10 of the 1997 Act by asserting that the commission "will or may entail making an entirely new constitution."[16] A strong element of the reformers' thinking, therefore, was the idea that before any review is undertaken there ought to be some agreement about the vision of Kenya that Kenyans share, and which then would be the standard against which proposals presented to the commission would be judged. In the process spelled out in the 1997 act, there was no indication about how a commission would determine this national vision. Partly to this end, it was widely suggested that a broad-based civic education campaign be undertaken to educate the population about the constitutional review process. The reform lobby sought to make this a joint civil society and government mandate and to conduct an impartial civic education campaign – at least from their perspective. Without civic education the input from the grassroots, of which both government and opposition were so solicitous (at least in word if not in action), would not be informed or effective.

The incumbent regime preferred minimal reforms and feared that if the process was opened up, the revisions demanded and enacted would be so radical that its hold on power – and especially control of the presidential succession – would be threatened. Moreover, the then incumbent KANU itself represented many diverse interests, some of which had different preferences with respect to constitutional change than those held by the party's dominant faction.

On the matter of substantive constitutional models or concrete plans, the debate in Kenya between 1992-2002 lacked any of these and instead focused on issues of process and of the larger goals that different factions pressed as critical precursors. Few organizations offered concrete plans for the content of constitutional change or proposed any particular constitutional model. Indeed, the 4Cs' 1994 model constitution stood out as the most coherent and most comprehensively discussed option. The 4Cs, however, asserted the model was not offered as a concrete option but as an example to highlight some of the values and principles that it would like to see debated and ultimately reflected in any new constitution.[17]

Although the debate on the content was of less immediate importance to most stakeholders given the preoccupation with process, certain principles seemed to be central. Essentially, the vision articulated by the reform movement was first and foremost an assertion of constitutionalism as a mechanism for checking state power. The constitutional reform process was prompted by the decay in the respect accorded the constitution over a three-decade period. This disregard for constitutional restraints included state manipulation of the constitution through numerous amendments such as the one establishing a single-party state in 1982.

Second, the constitutional reform lobby sought to promote certain substantive values expressive of the liberal tradition. These emphasized individual sovereignty and rights, limited government, and checks and balances against executive power, especially with regard to promoting and preserving the supremacy of parliament and the judiciary.[18] While these values did not excite much disagreement from the incumbent party, they did ignite a debate centered on the fears of the ethnic communities that perceive themselves as minorities and/or as vulnerable against the dominance of the larger ethnic communities – a re-enactment of the constitutional debate at independence.[19] This concern has been reflected in the multi-party political discourse and, tragically, in the recurrent ethnic clashes in 1992, 1997, and 1998. For instance, discussions of electoral systems (constituency demarcation and distribution, presidential vote calculus, etc.) invariably revealed fundamental divisions coinciding with the large/small community cleavage.[20]

Finally, these debates revived notions of center-peripheral power balances, which invariably are articulated in ethnic terms. For example, the *majimbo* option originally introduced in 1991 to counter multi-party activists was evidently a ploy to threaten dismemberment of the nation, an idea considered as an anathema by the opposition, especially given its implication of a much weaker central state. Yet, it encapsulates the central question of how smaller ethnic groups would survive and access state power, resources and protections in the context of electoral politics that are ethnically patterned and exclusive.

The Kenya case illustrates the significant battles over *process* that characterizes constitutional reform attempts in the current transitions. The debate over the process of reform was particularly strident in Kenya but, as will be seen below, much more muted in the Uganda and Tanzania. This is arguably dependent on the incumbent regime's estimation of the peril of an open process. Thus, in the Kenyan case where the transition has been much more protracted, the Moi government was viewed as dominated by minority ethnic groups. The government was also besieged by an opposition that accused it of having unraveled the prosperity achieved during the first two decades of independence, and forcing electoral victory by violence and by guile. The fact that the opposition collectively gathered more votes at all levels in the 1992 and 1997 elections underscored the possibility that a more open process of constitutional review could lead to the KANU's loss of power.

Given the prolonged debate over the process of reviewing the constitution, the other two trends identified earlier appear much more muted in the Kenyan case. For example, the debates over *majimboism* appeared only sporadically and seemingly only as a tool to further consolidate support for the KANU regime among minority groups to bolster its preference for a more controlled and contained constitutional review. Finally, although the issue of constraining state power was a constant pre-occupation among civic groups (in fact their preference for a more open and participatory constitutional review process was an extension of this agenda), it was subsumed under the debate over the process, which defined not only how expansive the review would be but whether it would take place at all. As will be evident in the next two cases, where the process of review was less contentious, these more substantive debates assumed center stage with perhaps more definitive results.

The Constitutional Reform Debate in Uganda, 1994-2004

While a complete constitutional history of Uganda must start at least at the struggles for establishing the independent federal constitution,[21] our focus here is on the specific struggles over the reconstruction of constitutional government since 1986. For all its other shortcomings, the NRM regime has overseen the most expansive constitutional reform in Uganda's history. While it can claim to be progressive in this aspect, it is clearly pushed to constitutional reform by the necessity to ensure legitimacy, pressed by its own insecurity as an initially un-elected regime and later as an elected regime losing support steadily as it governs.

In Uganda, constitutional reform has ignited an animated debate over the nature of the state and the most appropriate political system, and on the substantive division of state power. The debate on the process of reform has been less animated. Like neighboring Kenya, Uganda's constitution suffered early setbacks under the independent government. When Uganda gained its independence from Britain in 1962, it had a federal constitution that framed a republic balancing several ethnic and sectarian interests, including the traditional monarchies. However, in 1966 the first government of President Milton Obote unilaterally changed the constitution and installed a new one in 1967, abolishing the Buganda monarchy and extending the life of parliament without elections.[22] The 1971 overthrow of Obote by Amin was initially seen as a necessary halt to the steep decline into authoritarianism under Obote, but it eventually resulted in fifteen years of unmatched terror.[23]

When the NRA swept into power in January 1986, Ugandans had seen the worst of Amin and several successor regimes. The NRM leaders saw themselves as "revolutionary democrats" even as they moved in through armed force to depose the last of the serial caretaker governments in place since the fall of Amin in 1979. Indeed, this self-perception is an important subscript to the Ugandan constitutional debates, for it enables advocates of the no-party movement system to view themselves as irrevocably linked to the orderly pursuit of a democracy. However, in its disdain for the established parties and politicians preceding it, the NRM reveals its intolerance for the free-for-all that liberal democracy institutionalizes. Instead, the NRM exhibits a penchant for constraining options it considers a danger to the fragile fabric of the nation, a form of tutelage similar to that of typical authoritarian regimes.

When the NRM assumed power in 1986, its *Ten Point Programme* initially served to guide the early years of political reconstruction in Uganda.[24] Among its priorities was the 'democratization' of Ugandan public life (with a great emphasis on participatory democracy rather than the institutionalization of democracy in polyarchic terms). This was best exemplified by the creation of participatory organs ranging from the lowest Resistance Councils (RC) at the village level to the National Resistance Council (NRC). While the RC acted as a local governing council and dealt with day-to-day issues at the local level, the NRC acted as a supreme national organ and as a legislature. In between these were several councils at the parish, sub-county, county, and district levels. While the lower councils had always been elective, even during the war in the second decade of NRM rule, these councils continued to be democratized as the NRC was replaced by an elected parliament.[25] The democratization of these arenas of post-reconstruction power via elections was induced by the political imperatives of responding to demands for greater legitimacy.

As elsewhere in Africa, the 1990s brought radical pressure on the NRM regime to allow competitive politics. The usual demands were on single-party and/or military regimes: for greater opening up of political space, for the extension or revival of extinguished political and civil rights, and for the introduction of competitive elections.[26] The NRM leadership, notably President Museveni, was willing to open up to competitive politics but not to political parties. On the human rights issues, the NRM was widely believed to have vastly improved on the horrific records of its preceding regimes. In fact, the regime had distinguished itself by appointing a human rights commission as soon as it came to power and later entrenching it in the new constitution.[27] However, in succeeding to provide a safe political environment for the NRM, the regime also provided the conditions for the emergence of an opposition. This was particularly so with regard to the question of multi-party politics, which became the defining feature of the constitutional reform debate in a slowly liberalizing Uganda.[28]

In terms of process, the constitutional review debate was less heated than in Kenya. This is consistent with the regime's calculation of its relative popularity *and* potential to overwhelm the opposition. Uganda has tried to re-write its constitution using both the more constrained Constitutional Commission and the more participatory Constituent Assembly. The Constitutional Commission was set up in 1989 – a time of general agitation in the region and almost contemporaneous with the Saitoti Commission in Kenya. The commission, headed by a high court judge and composed of academics and lawyers, worked for three years to collect and collate views. Subsequently, a Constituent Assembly was directly elected in March 1994 to craft a new constitution. Even though the NRM had stated its objection to political parties (and it was unclear if it would accept a constitution entrenching parties), it allowed parties to be represented by two delegates. Thus, unlike Kenya, the process itself remained relatively uncontentious, although the nature of the resulting democracy – especially whether multi-party or no-party as the NRM preferred – became the most critical debate.

Under the 1995 constitution the NRM established the no-party system in which competitive elections are held but parties are not allowed to operate and candidates are not allowed to campaign on the basis of their party affiliation. Instead, all are considered members of the movement which is entrenched in the constitution, whose Article 70 pronounces it "broad-based, inclusive, and non-partisan."[29] Although the right to form political parties is guaranteed under Article 72, their operation is prohibited so long as the movement system is in place. The movement system itself can be changed through an act of the elected parliament passed by 2/3 of the MPs and followed by a referendum. In 2000 a referendum approved the continuation of the movement system as the fundamental system organizing state power in Uganda. Moreover, the 2001 election of Museveni in relatively free and fair but tense elections indicated that Ugandans still broadly accepted the movement system. Ugandans seem to support it less for its adherence to its ideology of inclusiveness and more as approval of the NRM government's achievements – turning a desolate, brutalized population and a defunct economy into a relatively peaceful country with the highest economic growth rates of the sub-region.[30]

NRM insistence on a no-party form of electoral democracy has recently been revised given the January 2004 court decision discussed by Rubongoya in the previous chapter. However, the question of the nature of the political system appropriate for Uganda remains a contentious issue. It is important to point out that it belies a significant question about the nature of the state and of the nation. NRM opposition to political parties has been based on its belief that they are vehicles of ethnic and regional balkanization of Uganda: "There is a strong belief in the country that political parties have been responsible for the ethnic, regional, and religious polarization and conflict which have bedeviled the country since independence."[31] The opposition parties, including the old parties (and politicians) associated with the authoritarian regimes of the past vehemently oppose this position. Whether this notion of political parties as balkanizing entities is fabricated by the incumbent regime to retain power (as is Moi's self-fulfilling prophecy of ethnic conflict in pluralistic politics in Kenya) is an open question.

However, constitutional reform in Uganda is fraught with pitfalls, some of which portend a dismal future. For example, the aim of the Museveni government to combine popular democracy and parliamentary democracy spawns internal contradiction. While the *Ten Point Programme* of the movement suggests the possibility of partyless local councils and multi-party competitions at the national level, the Constitutional Commission rejected this in 1992.[32] Part of this stems from the balance Museveni must strike between allowing sufficient democratic space through participatory organs and the imperative to contain the excesses of partisan competition based on ethnicity, regionalism, and religion.

The apparent connection between constitutional reform and immediate political balances skews the calculations behind constitutional choices such that the expedient supersedes the fundamental. Thus, as Kasfir points out, it is paradoxical that even given its claim to inclusiveness – which it has achieved by bringing to its fold several opponents – the NRM has resisted internal democratization.[33] Morever, in its attempts to ensure that constitutional reforms do not endanger its hold on power, the regime has traveled the well-worn path of subverting central principles of constitutionalism. For example, the NRM has never held elections for its top officers, repeatedly conflates the state with the movement (thus seeking state privileges for the latter), and declared the president the chair of the movement to avoid his exposure to the test of an election.[34] Thus, the constitution has become part of the battleground that confronts a successful savior regime fast approaching the limits of its uniqueness and unsure of its ability to survive in a new political and constitutional order. Under these circumstances, as in Kenya, further constitutional reform may become a casualty of the politics of regime survival. Thus, as attested by the tense presidential election of 2001 (which Museveni won handily), electoral competition has become the proxy battle over the constitution, since winning elections and especially the presidency is the surest way for the opposition to re-work the constitution to advantage parties other than the NRM.

Substantively, as in neighboring Kenya, the balance between the executive and the other parts of the state has emerged as a critical issue in the attempt to re-write constitutional rules to further entrench democracy. Although this is muted by the overall focus on the movement question, it is also intertwined with it since the issue is inseparable from the founding revolutionary, Museveni, whose presidency defines the "imperial" executive.

The 1995 constitution went a long way in re-establishing a balance of power among the different organs of the state. However, the practice of this separation is doubtful, especially in the shadow of the prohibition of the operation of opposition parties. Gingyera-Pinycwa argues that this situation is due less to the absence of enabling legislation and more to the holdover from a system steeped in authoritarianism.[35] Gingyera-Pinycwa shows that presidential dominance has survived despite the changes in the 1995 constitution. For example, he points to the case of parliament passing a bill to raise the nomination fee for candidates intending to run for parliament and to institute direct elections for district women representatives instead of indirect election by electoral colleges. When Museveni vetoed the bill, parliament buckled and reversed itself to support the president's position. More recently, Ugandans have debated constitutional proposals to allow Museveni to have an unprecedented third term. With a submissive movement hierarchy, opposition has been strongest among civil society and the issues remained unresolved in mid 2004.

Another episode cited by Gingyera-Pinycwa regards the dispute over the June 2000 referendum on the movement system. In this instance, the opposition sued the state in the Constitutional Court, charging that the procedure used to adopt the Referendum Act was flawed. In reaction, the parliament, with the collusion of the president, proceeded to pass the act in a day in order to make moot any attempt to stall the process.[36] While both instances reflect action within the legal purviews of each institution, the fact that the substance of the action limited options and was invoked with patently political concerns is suggestive of the privilege given political imperatives over constitutional ones. As Gingyera-Pinycwa concludes, the executive has maintained a "domineering profile within the political system" while parliament remains "too timid and too deferential" to the executive "to make for a vigorous and robust power balancing."[37]

The Uganda case exemplifies two of the notable trends in constitutional debates unfolding in African transitions, one focusing on the nature of the state, and the second exploring the relationship between different institutions of the state. Even though the question of whether and how to proceed with constitutional review has seemingly been settled, Uganda confronts an even more fundamental question about how state power should be organized. The contention that liberal multi-party politics hosts several dangers to the fabric of the nation is seemingly backed by the history of dictatorship, decay, and violence but it also echoes the problematic justifications offered by the first generation of single-party states in the region. As such, the movement question excites as strong an opposition as was the case in Kenya among activists seeking to force a more open process for constitutional review. However, the concern still exists that the no-party system would pave the way for institutionalizing single-partyism and weaken checks and balances. Substantively, the debate over the relationship between the presidency (traditionally the core of an authoritarian edifice) and parliament (viewed as the first bulwark against authoritarianism) is an extension of the debate over the nature of the state. It further underscores the active efforts to restrain state power, especially executive power. Separately but related to this has been the effort to revive a federalist framework, whose credibility remains shadowed by its close association with the Buganda monarchy and especially with royalists who seek a more powerful role for the kingdom. This debate, which addresses the concern for restraining state power, remains muted as the focus remains on the better clarified (and personified) movement system.

The Constitutional Reform Debate in Tanzania, 1995-2004

Tanzania has the distinction of being one of the very few successful constitutional unions attempted in post-independence Africa. It is also peculiar in that the Union occurred when most other countries were threatened by break-ups. Formed from mainland Tanganyika, which gained its independence in 1961, and the Zanzibar isles of Unguja and Pemba, the United Republic of Tanzania came into existence in 1964. The mainland, given its size and leadership in the relationship has always been the dominant partner, although the islands have had a degree of independence. Constitutionally, Tanzania moved to a single-party state very early as a result of the supremacy of TANU's resounding electoral success at independence. In 1963, TANU appointed a commission to examine the modalities of moving to a single-party state and in 1965 the constitution was changed to establish one. It would be another three decades before Tanzania would hold competitive multi-party elections.

Opposition to the single-party state peaked with demands for a more liberal political system in the early 1990s. As a result, the CCM government appointed the Nyalali Commission to review the political system and recommend whether to move to a multi-party system.[38] While the main constitutional changes were implemented in 1994 to establish a multi-party system and open the way for the first multi-party elections in 1995, the debate on constitutional reform took a new urgency after the opposition lost the 1995 elections. The elections, especially in Zanzibar where the main opposition party (CUF) was strongest, revealed how entrenched CCM was and how the nature of state power assured the incumbent party continued dominance. In particular, in spite of the change to multi-party politics, it became clear that several issues remained outstanding and were viewed as best addressed by constitutional reform.

In October of 1995, Salmin Amour of CCM was declared the Zanzibar President over Seif Shariff Hamad by a margin of only 0.4 percent. The results of the election escalated contentious relations between mainland Tanzania and Zanzibar, and their respective major political parties with regard to political reform in Tanzania. Amid outcries of election fraud, demand came for constitutional reform and a review of election practices. Broken promises made in the post-election glow of Tanzania's first "democratically" elected leader in 1995, and those made prior to the October 2000 election, fueled the clamor for review.

While the Zanzibar elections and the broader Union questions were the epicenter of the constitutional review movement, the foundations for the call to review the constitution were laid during Nyerere's regime. A substantially powerful presidency, weak judiciary and legislative branches, and a divestiture of power in the local levels of politics are imprints of over three decades of single-party rule under CCM.[39] The more recent call for reform has been spearheaded by CUF, several scholars, and local legal and rights associations.[40] Three issues animate reform calls: presidential power, a change in election procedures, and the relations between the mainland and Zanzibar.

The Presidency

The structure of the national presidency of Tanzania has not changed substantially since 1985 when Nyerere left office. Under Nyerere and his successors Mwinyi and Mkapa, the Tanzanian presidency has remained overwhelmingly powerful relative to other branches of government. States of emergency can be declared without the approval of the parliament, while key appointments to positions in the cabinet, the prime minister, and chief justice, are also not subject to the approval of parliament. Inherent problems with this method of selection are cronyism and positional incompetence. It is not uncommon for this to happen in Tanzania due to the heavy reliance on patronage to attract and retain votes and political support. Reformists press for the addition of parliamentary vetting for cabinet appointments, for the creation of new cabinet posts, as well as approval for the declaration of states of emergency.[41] They also seek to empower parliament to impeach the president to check executive excesses.

Electoral Reform

Allegations by CUF (and other opposition parties) and international observers regarding extensive irregularities during the 1995 and 2000 elections, serve as the basis for the call for electoral reform.[42] The elections in 2000 were dubbed "a shambles" and included irregularities such as polling stations opening hours late, missing paper ballots, and sudden increases in the number of ballots.[43] Proposed election reform focuses on Zanzibar and Tanzania more generally (since there are national elections inclusive of Zanzibar and the mainland along with separate elections in Zanzibar). Specifically, reformists have emphasized the need for more independent electoral commissions, more transparent voter registration processes, and the legalization of independent candidates. During the two multi-party contests in 1995 and 2000, the national and Zanzibar electoral commissions were comprised of party officials, few of whom, if any, were viewed as independent of CCM.[44] Reform of both commissions is currently the subject of debate in preparation for the 2005 elections, with progress specifically being made in the reformation of the Zanzibar Election Commission.

Currrently, independent candidates do not have the right to run for office. The reformists argue that this is inimical to democratic principles and to the freedom of association provision in the constitution. They argue that no candidate should feel obligated to join a political party they feel is impotent in order to run for the presidency.[45] Another contested issue is the requirement of a majority rather than a plurality to determine the winner of the presidential election.[46] Prior to this change, the Tanzanian government had amended earlier laws to allow for a simple plurality. Additionally, reformists argue that a coalition government be formed if a majority winner emerges after two rounds of elections. It should come as no surprise that election reform has not been a CCM priority, since the ruling party has most to lose from the proposed changes.

The Union

The state of the Union between mainland Tanzania and Zanzibar is the third major reform issue. In the current system, a president is elected for the Union, and a president is elected for Zanzibar. The Zanzibar president, who also serves as vice president of the Union, is responsible for matters that solely pertain to the semi-autonomous islands of Unguja and Pemba that comprise Zanzibar, whereas the Union president has jurisdiction over matters germane to the mainland and the Union. The reformists propose a more federalist style of government in which Zanzibar and the mainland would each resemble states falling under the ultimate control of the Tanzanian government.[47] Both Zanzibar and the mainland would have powers that were specifically delegated to them, while the Union government would retain powers that were particular to it. One of the problems this seeks to resolve is the enduring ambiguity over what specifically constitutes "matters that are particular to Zanzibar."[48]

The debate over the reform of the Union belies a more fundamental disquiet about its general condition. One of Zanzibar's primary complaints is that it does not benefit from the joint sovereignty as much as the mainland does. This stems in part from Zanzibar not receiving a proportionate share of tangible benefits such as aid, grants, and loans.[49] Zanzibari leaders also complain about a lack of autonomy when it comes to economic issues that it sees as solely related to the island itself. Other complaints from the Zanzibaris include a lack of representation in Union government institutions and foreign missions. Moreover, there are claims that new articles in the constitution were drawn with total disregard for Zanzibari interests.[50]

The mainland believes that Zanzibar violates the constitution of the Union with certain provisions in its own constitution. Some of these provisions and actions are more symbolic than substantive, such as Zanzibar receiving foreign leaders and giving them a twenty-one-gun salute, establishing special brigades with military features, and joining small regional groups independent of mainland Tanzania.[51] The Zanzibari government is also accused of not transferring its accounts to the Central Bank of the Union, and failing to meet its annual financial contributions for running Union affairs. Finally, until the recent changes, there were constitutional disputes over the privilege given to the Zanzibar president to automatically become the Union vice president. Thus, the Zanzibar president could become the un-elected Union president in the event of incapacity or death of the incumbent. The Bomani Commission, which recommended the abolishment of the two vice presidencies, addressed this anomaly and this was adopted in an amendment to the constitution.[52]

Overall, the opposition and reform activists in Tanzania have had a difficult time getting the reform agenda moving. CCM, much like Uganda's NRM, has interpreted its overwhelming electoral success, especially on the mainland, as a mandate for the *status quo* and only allowed slow-paced reforms to its advantage. The ruling party argues that the 1977 constitution is the proper instrument for the administration of the country as a whole. CCM activists argue that discarding the constitution would disown the positive foundations on which Tanzania was established.[53] The CCM has also made it known that a new constitution should be drafted only if Tanzania falls into a state of total collapse. Not unlike Kenya's KANU – another former single-party monolith that stalled reform for a decade – CCM is particularly opposed to national conventions and constitutional assemblies, deftly dismissing them as inefficient and given to producing political vacuums.

CUF's response to these assertions is that the *ujamaa* assumptions of the 1977 constitution are no longer applicable and rather outdated in today's capitalist world.[54] CUF also contends that the modalities of single-party governance by the ruling CCM need an overhaul. The disregard the ruling party has shown for widespread pro-reform views has created serious animosity between the ruling CCM and the opposition, especially CUF. On occasion, this has flared up in the form of protests and riots. Between 1998 and 2001, CCM enacted legislation outlawing some forms of protest, and jailed opposition party members on questionable treason charges.[55]

After particularly bloody clashes in Zanzibar in January 2001, an attempt was made to end the animosity between the leaders of CCM and CUF as they signed a peace agreement in October 2001. Under the agreement, the opposition made some gains on the reform agenda. For example, permanent voter registrars have been established, and electoral laws were revised, and by-elections were successfully held in Zanzibar for the seats the CUF had vacated following the October 2000 parliamentary election amidst allegations of election improprieties.[56]

The political climate for reform in Zanzibar and Tanzania as a whole is unlikely to change in the near future. The ruling CCM government has bought itself some time by undertaking the least reforms sought by CUF, thus reversing the increasingly untenable position of not discussing reform at all. In early 2003, CUF and like-minded opposition parties continued to see the delay in constitutional and judicial reforms as a sign of CCM not wanting to relinquish its hold on power. CUF won the May 2003 by-elections in Zanzibar, allowing it to reassert its status as the dominant party of Zanzibar. The animosity between CUF and CCM and between Zanzibar and the mainland continues to flare up in the context of interpretations of the constitutional spaces each occupies. Some of these arguments continue to be symbolic, but meaningful to the citizenry. For example, while in Switzerland for hipbone replacement in December of 2003, Mkapa gave his weekly radio instead of allowing the vice president to fill in. This created a stir among opposition groups, who argued this was the constitutional duty of the vice president since Mkapa was out of the country. The opposition also doubted if any documents concerning a temporary transfer of powers were ever drafted.

Constitutional reform in Tanzania thus projects two of the three trends identified in the beginning. While process concerns seem to be underplayed given the incumbent party resistance to comprehensive reforms, the debate is dominated by concerns about reformulating the nature of the state through restructuring the Union and, to a lesser extent, by containing the power of the state *vis-à-vis* citizens and organized groups. Part of the reason the constitutional debate, especially in the mainland, has been less strident in Tanzania than in Uganda or Kenya (especially) is the fact that the initial constitutional review under an appointed commission (Nyalali Commission) resulted in the elimination of many of the problematic laws and practices that have derailed liberal politics elsewhere.

Indeed, the heat in much of the current constitutional debate emanates principally from the leftovers of such undemocratic practices evident in the domineering posture of CCM, especially in Zanzibar, where it is threatened by a credible opposition. The subversion of the popular will in the isles (as evidenced by the electoral malpractices in 1995 and 2000) incites the perennial question of the relationship between the mainland and the islands, a question important in its own right but given added urgency by the sense of disenfranchisement evident from the two disputed electoral outcomes. It is unclear whether Mkapa's successor in CCM will support any fundamental changes to the constitutional landscape. One of the more popular would-be successors is Salim Salim, chair of the Nyerere Foundation, a former three-term Secretary-General of the OAU, and former Tanzanian Prime Minister. His links to Nyerere and his political and diplomatic skills make him a favorite among CCM party elites – but therefore unlikely to fundamentally alter the regime perception on Union questions or CCM dominance more narrowly.

Concluding Comments

Clearly, constitutional reform has become a central agenda item in the current transitions in East Africa. While democratic transitions seem to have stalled in several other ways, principally in the failure of opposition groups to dislodge incumbents (with Kenya's late exception), there is evidence of constitutional reform. Even though the constitutional reform movement in all three countries has not gained much ground in terms of substantive changes, they have all established at least three important principles. First is related to the process of reform, second is the logic of restraining state power, and third is the significance of reformed constitutions as both new scripts to underwrite nationhood and to secure the path to democratic societies.

On process in all three countries, the opposition and reform activists have insisted on an open and participatory process. While in Uganda this has been achieved to a large degree, in Kenya and Tanzania the incumbent regimes (whose historical practices were decidedly non-participatory) fought the process at every turn. In all three countries, the incumbents effectively resisted the impulse by civil society to create sovereign national conferences or conventions to re-write constitutions. The actual option adopted was the presidential or parliamentary-appointed national commission. While in Uganda this was expanded to open deliberation in a constituent assembly, in Kenya and Tanzania the incumbent governments saw parliament (where ruling parties dominated) as the final arbiter of new constitutions.

In spite of this slow progress toward substantive reforms, it is clear that the priority item on the agenda is restraint of state power. This takes on several guises driven by historical relations within each of the three countries. For example, the issue of federalism reappears throughout East Africa as it did in the first decade of independence. In Uganda it is in relation to the restored Buganda monarchy, in Kenya as the *majimbo* debate, and in Tanzania as a reconsideration of the Union. Within each debate, driven as it is by the immediate political fortunes of individual politicians, is an important issue of restraining central state power and preserving areas of autonomy short of the central state. This relates to the larger question echoed broadly within each transition of local determination of critical issues in the public arena, of balancing ethnic interests, and of localizing power as an antidote to the corruption and despotism from the center.

Finally, in all three countries the constitutional debates make important symbolic and concrete claims to the supremacy of citizens. Unlike constitutions bequeathed these nations at independence (which were negotiated under the tutelage of an interested but disengaging imperial power) and unlike subsequent constitutions (with mutations wrought to fit authoritarian regimes), the present constitution making, if successful, will result in compacts grounded in a local political process. The very notion that the people – as represented by civic groups, political parties in and out of power, and self-selected individuals – can participate in formulating the kind of government they want is a radical idea given the history of these countries. Thus, the fact that there are open debates about the constitutions is an important step forward in the democratization of these countries. In particular, it is a significant step in unraveling the ingrained the notion of East Africans as subjects at the mercy of the state and asserting their status as participatory and rights-endowed citizens of democratic republics.[57]

Notes

1 This assessment is principally based on a close familiarity with the protracted case of constitutional reform in Kenya and parallel trends seen in other countries. It does not pretend to list all the issues that dominate debates in every instance or in every country. See Stephen N. Ndegwa, "The Relevance of the Electoral System," *African Journal of Political Science* vol. 2, no. 1 (1997), pp. 12-40; and Stephen N. Ndegwa, "National Dialogue in Kenya: Religious Organizations and Constitutional Reform, 1990-2000." Report prepared for Management Systems International (Washington, D.C.: March 2001).

2 Jan Jelmert Jorgensen, *Uganda: A Modern History* (New York: St. Martins Press, 1981).

3 For example, the Citizens' Coalition for Constitutional Change in Kenya, the Zanzibar Elections Monitoring Group, the Tanzania Elections Monitoring Group, and the Uganda Law Society. These organizations have pursued activities such as election monitoring, electoral law reform, constitutional and legal reviews meant less to supplant a particular government (although often this is implicit) and more to establish limits on state power.

4 This section focuses on the period before the demise of the KANU regime following the December 2002 elections. The coming to power of the opposition coalition produced much activity in constitutional reform after a brief period of inaction but also spawned several controversies. At the time of writing, it is difficult to assess whether these controversies are significant, whether the constitutional review process itself will survive the acrimony of the coalition, and whether the review process is sufficiently robust to contain emerging fundamental questions of state power, citizenship, and competition. It

is probably too early to fathom any patterns in the ongoing controversies and imprudent to suggest any analytical clarity.

[5] Bethwell Ogot, *Historical Dictionary of Kenya* (Metuchen, NJ: Scarecrow Press, 1981).

[6] Tom Mboya, *Freedom and After* (Boston, MA: Little, Brown 1963).

[7] Joel D. Barkan, "Kenya: Lessons from a Flawed Election," *Journal of Democracy* vol. 4, no. 2 (July 1993), pp. 85-99.

[8] John Harberson, "The Future of Democracy in Kenya," *Africa Today (Special Issue)* vol. 45, no. 2 (April 1998), pp. 161-258; Stephen N. Ndegwa, "The Incomplete Transition: The Constitutional and Electoral Context in Kenya," *Africa Today (Special Issue)* vol. 45, no. 2 (April 1998), pp. 193-212.

[9] Institute of Education in Democracy, *Election Handbook* (Nairobi, Kenya: IED, 1997).

[10] Ndegwa, "The Incomplete Transition."

[11] Ndegwa, "The Incomplete Transition."

[12] Republic of Kenya, *Kenya Gazette Supplement: The Constitution of Kenya Review Act, 1997* (Nairobi: The Government Printer, 1997).

[13] Republic of Kenya, *Kenya Gazette Supplement: The Constitution of Kenya Review Act, 1997.*

[14] Maloba Barasa, "Constitution: Why the People are Supreme," *East African* (Nairobi), May 1, 2000.

[15] Ndegwa, "The Incomplete Transition"; Stephen N. Ndegwa, "Rethinking Citizenship in Africa," *Africa Today* vol. 45, no. 3-4 (1998), pp. 351-367.

[16] Republic of Kenya, *Kenya Gazette Supplement: The Constitution of Kenya Review Act, 1997.*

[17] Ndegwa, "The Incomplete Transition"; Ndegwa, "Rethinking Citizenship in Africa."

[18] Citizens Coalition for Constitutional Change, "Model Constitution for Kenya," Nairobi, Kenya 1994, unpublished report.

[19] Stephen N. Ndegwa, "Citizenship and Ethnicity: An Examination of Two Transition Moments in Kenyan Politics," *American Political Science Review* vol. 91, no. 3 (September 1997), pp. 599-616.

[20] Ndegwa, "The Relevance of the Electoral System"; Joel D. Barkan, "Towards a New Constitutional Framework in Kenya," *Africa Today* vol. 45 (April-June 1998), pp. 161-258.

[21] Jorgensen, *Uganda: A Modern History*; D.W. Nabudere, *Imperialism and Revolution in Uganda* (London: Onyx Press, 1980).

[22] Dirk Berg-Schloser and Rainer Siegler, *Political Stability and Development* (Boulder, CO: Lynne Reinner, 1990); A.B.K. Kasozi, *The Social Origins of Violence in Uganda, 1964-1985* (McGill-Queens University Press, 1994).

[23] Kasozi, *The Social Origins of Violence.*

[24] Yoweri K. Museveni, *What is Africa's Problem?* (Minneapolis, MN: Minnosota University Press, 2000).

[25] Nelson Kasfir, "No-Party Democracy in Uganda," *Journal of Democracy* vol. 9, no. 2 (April 1998), pp. 49-63.

[26] Michael Bratton and Göran Hydén, eds., *Governance and Politics in Africa* (Boulder, CO: Lynne Rienner, 1992).

[27] Kasfir, "No-Party Democracy in Uganda."

[28] *Africa Confidential*, "Uganda: One Party, All Party," *Africa Confidential* vol. 50, no. 15 (July 21, 1995).

[29] Republic of Uganda, *Uganda Constitution* (Kampala: Government Printer, 1995).

[30] Anonymous, "Uganda: Kaguta Yekka!" *Africa Confidential* vol. 41, no. 3 (February 4, 2000), p. 6; Michael Bratton Gina Lambright, "Uganda's Referendum 2000: The Silent Boycott," *African Affairs*, vol. 11 (2001), pp. 429-452.

[31] Emmanuel Kirenga, "A Home-Made Model: Democracy in Uganda," *The Parliamentarian* (January 1997), pp. 19-21.
[32] Kasfir, "No-Party Democracy in Uganda."
[33] Kasfir, "No-Party Democracy in Uganda."
[34] Kasfir, "No-Party Democracy in Uganda."
[35] G.G. Gingyera-Pinycwa, "Birth Pangs of Transition to Democracy in Uganda," paper prepared for Research and Education for Democracy in Tanzania, the Fourth Workshop on Democratic Transition in East Africa, Lake Manyara, Arusha Region, Tanzania (April 9-10, 2001), p. 11.
[36] Gingyera-Pinycwa, "Birth Pangs of Transition to Democracy in Uganda," p. 14.
[37] Gingyera-Pinycwa, "Birth Pangs of Transition to Democracy in Uganda," pp. 14-15.
[38] Jennifer Widner, *Building The Rule of Law* (New York: W. W. Norton, 2001).
[39] Paul J. Kaiser, "Zanzibar: A Multi-Level Analysis of Conflict Prevention," in Chandra Sriram and Karin Wermester, eds., *From Promise to Practice: Strengthening U.N. Capacities for the Prevention of Violent Conflict* (Boulder, CO: Lynne Rienner Publishers, 2003), pp. 101-133.
[40] *The Nation*, opinion, "Isn't it Time Tanzania Rethought it's Union?" http://www.hartford-hwp.com/archives/36/361.html, February 4, 2001.
[41] Ngila Mwase and Mary Raphael, "The 1995 Presidential Elections in Tanzania," *The Roundtable* (2001), pp. 245-269.
[42] CNN, "Mkapa pledges to act on Zanzibar, Fight Corruption," November 20, 2000, http:edition.cnn.com/2000/WORLD/Africa/11/20/Tanzania.president.reut/index.html.
[43] CNN, "Mkapa pledges to act on Zanzibar, Fight Corruption," November 20, 2000, http:edition.cnn.com/2000/WORLD/Africa/11/20/Tanzania.president.reut/index.html.
[44] Paul J. Kaiser, "Structural Adjustment and the Fragile Nation: the Demise of Social Unity in Tanzania," *Journal of Modern African Studies* vol. 34, no. 2 (June 1996), pp. 227-23; Mwase and Raphael, "The 1995 Presidential Elections in Tanzania."
[45] Saffari, Abdallah J., "The Constitution of United Republic of Tanzania: Salient Considerations" (Dar es Salaam, Tanzania: 2001), unpublished paper.
[46] Saffari, "The Constitution of United Republic of Tanzania: Salient Considerations."
[47] Mwase and Raphael, "The 1995 Presidential Elections in Tanzania."
[48] Mohammad Bakari, "The Union Between Tanganyika and Zanzibar Revisited" in Ulf Engel, Gero Erdmong, and Andrew Mehler, eds., *Tanzania Revisited: Political Stability, Aid Dependency and Development Constraints* (Hamburg: Institute of African Affairs, 2000), pp. 133-148.
[49] Bakari, "The Union Between Tanganyika and Zanzibar Revisited," p. 141.
[50] Mwase and Raphael, "The 1995 Presidential Elections in Tanzania."
[51] Bakari, "The Union Between Tanganyika and Zanzibar Revisited," p. 143.
[52] Issa Shivji, "Problems of Constitution-Making As Consensus-Building: The Tanzanian Experience," presented at the Sub-Regional Workshop on Land Tenure Issues in Natural Ressources Management in the Anglophone East Africa witha Focus on the IGAD Region, Addis Abbaba, Ethiopia, March 11-15, 1996, http://www.gtz.de/orboden/oss/sh22_b.htm.
[53] Max Mmuya, "Constitutional Debate, the Status of the Union and Decentralization," in Ulf Engel, Gero Erdmong, and Andrew Mehler, eds., *Tanzania Revisited: Political Stability, Aid Dependency and Development Constraints* (Hamburg: Institute of African Affairs, 2000), p. 119.
[54] Mmuya, "Constitutional Debate, the Status of the Union and Decentralization," p. 116.
[55] TOMRIC News Agency, "Mkapa Unveils Intervention Dilemma In Isle Crisis" (May 26, 2000).
[56] Kaiser, "Zanzibar: A Multi-Level Analysis of Conflict Prevention."

[57] Mahmood Mamdani, *Citizen and Subject: Contemporary Africa and the Legacy of Late Colonialism* (Princeton, NJ: Princeton University Press, 1996); Ndegwa, "Citizenship and Ethnicity."

Chapter 6

Civil Society

Samuel A. Nyanchoga

The concept of civil society has been the subject of scholarly debate since the advent of Western political thought, with more recent permutations of this concept offered by scholars and practitioners studying African politics. The emergence of authoritarian, single-party regimes unresponsive to the popular will facilitated the emergence of organized, non-state, grassroots efforts to meet basic needs and services that the state no longer provided effectively. These initiatives have been analytically captured by the term civil society, which is used in this chapter to describe non-governmental organizations that make social, cultural, religious, economic or political transactions independent of the state, including, but not limited to, clubs, societies, clans and ethnic associations.

Civil Society During Pre-Colonial Times

The concept of civil society in Africa is rooted in pre-colonial societies, gradually acquiring new dimensions as society became more complex in the colonial and independence periods. During the slave trade, centralized political organizations on the continent rarely justified their existence based on their capacity to meet the needs of individuals in society. The ancient kingdoms of Ghana, Mali, Songhai, Benin, Asanti, Dahomey, and Fulani marginalized rural masses and rarely involved them in governance matters. Slave-based societies often perpetuated intra-state violence and compromised individual security. Societies controlled by social groups or classes, such as the Baganda and Bunyoro Kitara in Uganda, concentrated power and prestige at the expense of peasants and artisans. Societies under male gerontocracy, such as the Mijikenda of Kenya and the Nyamwesi, Chagga, and Hehe of Tanzania, were also authoritarian in rulership.[1]

In the light of these circumstances, individuals sought to attain security and welfare needs through kinship institutions, which counter-balanced the pervasive powers of the state. In societies such as the Turkana of Northern Kenya, the age-set institution was the composite of civil society, able to influence gerontocratic leadership. The *Utani* institution among the Kamba and Taita of Kenya, and the Nyamwesi of Tanzania, contributed to the leveling of social hierarchies and autocratic tendencies. This institution also enabled children and grandparents to be classified as equal and therefore created the political space necessary to encourage freedom of expression.[2] Many of the civil society organizations that existed in pre-colonial Africa served to counteract non-participatory leadership tendencies.

The colonial state was also not answerable to the people it ruled, but rather to the colonial leaders residing abroad. In African colonies, local migrant workers in urban settings and on settler farms found voluntary associations indispensable to their daily lives. These associations served as mutual aid societies, lending money to members, arranging funerals, and taking care of marriage arrangements for urban migrants.[3] The activities of these associations were cultural, economic, and political.

In Kenya, the Kikuyu Central, the Kavirondo, and Taita Hills Associations were ethnically based and they were formed during the inter-war period. These associations defended the interests and articulated the grievances of their ethnic constituencies. The associations stood against racial segregation policies, punitive taxes, native registration ordinances, the *Kipande* system, and the overall process of land alienation. They also demanded that the colonial government provide land title deeds and education for Africans.[4] Similarly in Tanzania, ethnic-based associations such as the Bukoba-Bahaya Union and the Kilimanjaro Native Planters Association focused on self-improvement for their members.

Beginning during the inter-war period, regional associations also emerged in East Africa. Some of them were class-based, such as the East African Trade Union Movement which brought together labor unions in the region and organized concerted efforts to petition regional governments to improve labor conditions.[5] Associations such as the Tanganyika African Welfare Association and the Kenya African Union restricted membership to educated Africans. There were also urban-based associations whose interests ranged from social welfare to politics to economics. They included the Usangi Sports and Welfare Club (1946), the Bukoba Native Corporation Union (1949) and the Victoria Federation of Cooperative Union. These associations wrestled control of cotton marketing from Indian agents who paid African farmers lower prices for their produce.[6]

During the late 1950s, some associations transformed themselves into political parties that struggled for independence and eventually assumed political control in the newly independent countries. The Tanganyika African Association, the Kenya African Union, and the Uganda Peoples Congress/Kabaka Yekka evolved into political parties that ruled in Tanzania, Kenya and Uganda immediately after independence from Great Britain.

The Fall and Rise of Civil Society Since Independence

During the early years of independence, the ruling parties (TANU, KANU, and UPC) institutionalized themselves in power, simultaneously demobilizing and alienating civil society organizations from the political process. During the Cold War era, Western countries and their allies often supported non-democratic, pro-West regimes in Africa for the sake of safeguarding the liberal economic and political order against the perceived threat of communism. Many African countries suffered serious democratic hemorrhages during this period. The ruling KANU,

UPC, and TANU/CCM parties maintained power through a combination of force, corruption, clientalism, and neo-patrimonialism. Throughout the 1990s, unresponsive states gave way to the rebirth of associational life throughout the region that contested the legitimacy of incumbent regimes in power emerging with newfound urgency and popular attention.

During a democratic transition process, the locus of power often shifts from the state to the citizenry. This did not happen in East Africa because the ruling elite created a strong state that restricted democratic practice. In 1989-1990, the Moi government embarked on repressive measures against pressure groups such as the FORD.[7] In Uganda, the incumbent government was accused of rigging the 1983 election and entrenching itself in power.[8] Tanzania's government either demobilized non-governmental organizations that articulated people's interests or co-opted youth, women and workers organizations into the CCM government. As the following case studies demonstrate, this led to the emergence of defiant civil society organizations that sought participation in the political space of the public realm, with the ultimate goal of replacing incumbent regimes with more responsive governments.

Kenya

During Kenyatta's rule, the Central Organization of Trade Unions (COTU) was placed under government control together with other sectors of civil society, thus limiting the freedom and impact of associational life.[9] In 1982, the Moi government, through parliament, amended the constitution making Kenya a *de jure* single-party state. After an abortive *coup d'etat* in 1982, the government outlawed politically active civil society organizations, such as the *Mwakenya*, the Kenya Patriotic Front, and the Kenya Revolutionary Movement. Members of these organizations were accused of plotting to overthrow the government and were either detained or forced to flee into exile.

By 1989, the political space of the public realm was completely monopolized by the KANU government. Secret ballots were replaced by a queue voting system in parliamentary and civic primary elections. In doing so, the government undermined the voting rights of many citizens who were afraid to stand behind photographs of candidates known to be critical of government policies. At times, candidates with the shortest queues were declared winners in broad daylight due to their support of the Moi regime.[10] The government also removed the security of tenure for High Court judges, members of the Public Service Commission and the Auditor General. Outspoken publications such as *Beyond*, *Development Agenda*, *Financial Review* and *The Nairobi Monthly*, were banned or forced to close down. Organizations such as *Maendeleo ya Wanawake* were co-opted into KANU.

In 1990, the government passed a law to establish a framework of operation for NGOs. The act established two administrative structures: a board to administer the act; and an NGO council to advise this board on NGO issues. The membership of the board was drawn from government departments and the NGO council was subordinate to the board. All NGOs were required to submit their constitutions to the board, and they were not allowed to amend their constitutions or affiliate with foreign groups without the consent of this body. Virtually all civil society organizations, including children's homes, church groups, trade unions, and environmental organizations, were subject to the requirements of the act. This enabled the government to increase its surveillance powers and restrict the advocacy activities of civil society organizations that were not in the "national interest" of the country. As a result, the board often used this act to threaten, ban, or de-register civil society groups which were critical of government policies. For example, between 1989-1990, the National Council Churches of Kenya (NCCK) and the Green Belt Movement were threatened with de-registration for raising potentially explosive political issues. The Green Belt Movement successfully prevented KANU from erecting a skyscraper in a public park, and NCCK condemned government rigging of general elections in 1989.[11]

In response to these government initiatives, a defiant civil society emerged that advocated economic and democratic freedoms, albeit with different ideological agendas. Civil society organizations in the country had one thing in common; a belief that democratic change would not be brought about only by constitutional means; organized protest was also necessary. FORD organized mass demonstrations against the state prior to multi-party elections in 1992, thus emerging as a pro-active organization competing for political space with the KANU government.

The Law Society of Kenya (LSK) served as a powerful and independent professional association. Members of the association had an independent source of income, thus providing them with the resources necessary to challenge the state without the risk of economic dislocation. In the late 1980s, the LSK became increasingly vocal about human rights abuses and the administration of justice. As a result, human rights lawyers were detained for criticizing government violations of human rights. In 1988 the LSK, together with the NCCK, formed the Justice and Peace Commission of Kenya to agitate for democracy and peace. The government responded by promulgating regulations requiring lawyers to obtain annual trading licenses. This was an attempt to bar politically active lawyers from legal practice, thus curtailing their financial independence. In 1989, the government unsuccessfully tried to affiliate the LSK with KANU in order to limit the efficacy of the organization. In 1990 and 1991, the government attempted to stop LSK from electing pro-democracy lawyers into leadership position in the organization. When these government strategies did not succeed, four members of the LSK, acting on behalf of the government, successfully sued the LSK and restrained it from making political statements.[12]

Despite this, the LSK remained politically active by agitating for political pluralism and calling for the repeal of contentious sections of the constitution, such as the Public Security Act that empowered the president to detain without trial those perceived to be anti-government. The lawyers also advocated for a democratic society through the media. *The Nairobi Law Monthly*, an independent magazine, openly criticized the government for its inconsistent application of the rule of law, violation of human rights, and corruption in the civil service. The government banned the magazine but rescinded its decision after international and domestic pressure. The magazine became a popular forum for expressing the views of pro-democracy activists.

Churches were also active in building a democratic culture in Kenya, reaching out to rural and urban populations. More than many other civil society organizations, churches were able to reach rural areas where most of the population lives. During the 1980s, the government often resorted to violence to silence clergymen who criticized the government's human rights record. According to widely circulated press reports, Bishop Alexander Muge of the Church Province of Kenya (now the Anglican Church of Kenya [ACK]) died in mysterious circumstances, and Reverend Timothy Njoya of the Presbyterian Church of East Africa (PCEA) was transferred from his Nairobi church to Tumu Tumu due to his outspoken views on government repression and election irregularities. However, these actions did not stop church leaders from confronting the government. In 1988, the Catholic Church set up the Peace and Justice Commission (PJC), which addressed issues of corruption, injustice, and poverty in the country. In the same year, the NCCK, LSK, PJC, the Kenya National Union of Teachers (KNUT), and the COTU, condemned the queue voting system that had replaced the use of secret ballots.[13]

In a 1990 sermon, Reverend Njoya challenged the government to introduce political pluralism. In April of the same year, Bishop Henry Okullu of the ACK called on the government to amend the constitution and limit presidential terms to two five-year terms. These views were supported by the LSK.[14] By August 1990, the KANU-government yielded to pressure from civil society and political activists, and it abolished queue-voting system. In addition, the 70 percent rule for KANU parliamentary and civic nominations was abolished. According to this rule, a candidate receiving more than 70 percent of votes caste during the nomination exercise was declared the winner of the civic and parliamentary elections.[15] In August 1990, FORD was formed, and it pushed for the introduction of multi-party politics. The government responded by arresting the founders of the pro-democracy movement, including Oginga Odinga, Masinde Muliro, and Martin Shikuku. A year later, the donor community suspended aid to Kenya due to lack of progress in implementing political and economic reforms. In December 1991, the Kenyan government repealed the controversial section 2A of the Kenya Constitution and allowed multi-party politics.[16]

Civil society organizations began to prepare the groundwork for establishing a participatory democratic system. The remainder of this section builds on the analyses of constitutional reform in Kenya provided by Ndegwa in the previous chapter, specifically focusing on the role of civil society organizations in this process.

The NCCK published manuals and organized seminars on electoral processes countrywide and launched a weekly series of newspaper articles on the theme, "towards multi-party democracy and election process in Kenya." The NCCK educational campaign targeted an array of pro-democratic pressure groups (including women's and youth organizations), promoting dialogue on issues related to the 1992 elections. KANU won these elections in a tense and controversial environment that included reports of state-sponsored violence in the Rift Valley and Coast Province, and voting irregularities.

The NCCK and Catholic Episcopal Conference (CEC) specifically condemned the 1992 ethnic clashes in the Rift Valley and the Coast Province. The opposition claimed that these ethnic clashes were politically engineered to validate claims by the ruling political elites that multi-partyism would sharpen ethnic cleavages and lead to civil violence in the country. The NCCK task force report on ethnic clashes implicated high profile personalities in the Moi administration as the possible instigators of the clashes. The ethnic clashes forced non-Kalenjin ethnic communities to flee the Rift Valley region of Kenya, leaving KANU to enjoy substantial voter support. The NCCK was threatened with de-registration immediately after its report on ethnic clashes was made public. The Parliamentary Select Committee that examined the 1992 ethnic clashes came to similar conclusions but its report was rejected by the KANU-dominated parliament.

Overall, civil society organizations were involved in initiating dialogue among the contending parties, denouncing violence, resolving conflicts, calling for the rehabilitation and settlement of victims of clashes, and encouraging participatory democracy. In 1995, opposition political parties supported the move for constitutional changes as a way to assure that subsequent elections would serve a the guarantor of democracy in the country. The following year, civil society, together with mainstream opposition political parties, formed the Citizen Coalition for Constitutional Changes (4Cs), and they planned a constitutional conference in May of the same year.

The 4Cs established the National Convention Assembly, with representatives from NGOs, trade unions, political parties (KANU refused to attend), churches, and the business sector. In April 1997, the National Convention Assembly formed the National Convention Executive Committee (NCEC) to spearhead constitutional reforms.[17] NCEC advocated mass action, strikes, and boycotts to force the government to accede to constitutional reforms.

Consequently, the government agreed to engage in dialogue with opposition political parties regarding constitutional reforms. The KANU government argued that constitutional changes should be carried out through a commission mandated by the National Assembly. The NCEC, however, believed that the reforms should be negotiated in an arrangement that would allow representatives from a broad spectrum of civil society organizations to participate in the process. This division did not augur well for meaningful dialogue between the protagonists, who declared August 8, 1997, a day of national protest. This forced the KANU government to seek dialogue with moderate opposition groups in parliament which resulted in the formation of the Inter-Party Parliamentary Group (IPPG). The IPPG resolved to repeal all laws relating to detention without trial and to establish a commission to review the Kenyan Constitution. The IPPG also agreed on minimum electoral reforms before the December 1997 general elections, including the selection of nominated members to parliament according to the proportion of elected seats in the National Assembly. Previously, this was the prerogative of the president. Another reform that was agreed upon was a procedure to refer election petitions to the Court of Appeal.[18] Kenya entered the second multi-party elections with a few political changes that ultimately resulted in a reduced KANU majority in parliament.

In 1998, the agitation for constitutional reforms started again. Opposition political parties argued that the act establishing the Constitutional Review Commission was flawed and should be repealed. The IPPG organized meetings where representatives of the opposition were invited to share their views about how the constitution should be reviewed. A three-tiered system was agreed upon by all stakeholders. This included the District Forum (DF), National Forum (NF), and the Constitutional Review Commission (CRC). The District Forum was to collect views from the people and pass it to the Constitutional Review Commission. The National Forum, with representation from each district in the country, was to ensure that all recommendations were included in the draft constitution before presentation in parliament. This agreement ended in stalemate. The KANU government capitalized on the stalemate and, by virtue of its membership majority in parliament, referred the constitutional review process to this legislative branch of government. Attorney General Amos Wako was instructed to develop a workable formula for a comprehensive constitutional review. The Attorney General asked political parties with representation in the National Assembly to review the constitution. It ended in yet another stalemate because KANU wanted majority membership on the committee and the party wanted to sideline civil society organizations in the constitutional review process. This prompted these organizations to regroup under NCEC, asserting that the constitutional review process should include representation from the population at large. This new stand was supported by the Catholic Church, NGOs, and opposition political parties such as the DP and the SDP.

In November 1999, the NCEC launched "A Vision for National Renewal", in which it proposed the establishment of a caretaker government with representatives from the civil society, political parties, and the Kenyan armed forces.[19] The KANU government, as expected, rejected the proposal outright. The following month the religious community met at *Ufungamano* House in Nairobi under the chairmanship of Bishop John Njue of Kenya Episcopal Conference (KEC). At this meeting, religious leaders affirmed their commitment to a "people-driven" constitutional review process. The KANU government acted swiftly, and with the support of the National Democratic Party (NDP), an opposition political party, instituted a 27 member parliamentary select committee headed by Raila Odinga to collect views from the public on how the constitutional review process should proceed.[20]

The *Ufungamano* initiative, guided by a steering committee composed of religious leaders and headed by the head of the Anglican Church, Archbishop David Gitari, condemned the Parliamentary Select Committee for lacking moral authority and a mandate from the public to proceed with constitutional review process. Many representatives of civil society felt that the parliamentary select committee was satisfying the narrow interests of the ruling political elites.

The people-driven constitutional review approach gained support from lawyers, the women's political caucus, opposition political parties and university student associations. High profile Kenyans, such as Archbishop Ndingi Mwana a

Nzeki, the head of the Kenya Catholic Church, rejected an invitation to share their views before the Parliamentary Select Committee on Constitutional Reform. In January 2000, religious communities and civil society organizations organized a prayer meeting in Nairobi's Uhuru Park, and they officially launched a parallel constitutional review initiative to the Parliamentary Select Committee. The parliamentary select committee was condemned for being beholden to a political clique of the ruling elite, therefore lacking a legitimate mandate from the public to spearhead the constitutional review process.[21]

As the constitutional review process stalled, a multitude of organizations accused the KANU government of inefficiency, corruption and a general mismanagement of the economy. The teachers' union, KNUT, accused the government of ruining the country's educational system while the Kenya Coffee Growers Association (KCGA) accused it of interfering in the coffee industry. At one point, coffee farmers from central Kenya violently took control of coffee factories and withheld coffee from the mills, citing poor management and corruption.[22] Representatives of civil society organizations cautioned the international community not to resume financial assistance to Kenya until adequate economic and political reforms were enacted. The IMF and World Bank team visiting Kenya at this time impressed upon the KANU government the need to initiate more economic reforms and to open the political space of the public realm to other stakeholders. The team remained non-committal on aid resumption until adequate reforms were in place.

In 2000, *Muungano wa Mageuzi*, or the Movement for Change, emerged under the leadership of political activists such as James Orengo, Mukhisa Kituyi, Kipruto arap Kirwa, and other political activists. *Muungano wa Mageuzi* saw little hope in the parliament-appointed Constitutional Review Commission since it was seen as serving the narrow political interests of the ruling party. The movement focused on organizing nationwide political allies to build a broad consensus in the country on the question of political reform. It also challenged the government to make the constitutional reform process as consultative and participatory as possible before the 2002 multi-party elections. The government acted swiftly by declaring the movement illegal and it was banned from organizing political rallies.[23]

In the 2002 general elections, many civil society organizations endorsed NARC presidential candidate, Mwai Kibaki. Organizations such as the Kenya Human Rights Commission, the Green Belt Movement, the Citizen Coalition for Constitutional Changes, the National Constitution Executive Council and Federation of Women Lawyers were openly supportive of the opposition party alliance.[24] When NARC came to power, many key leaders of civil society organizations joined the government. As a result, this has limited the effectiveness of civil society organizations to carefully monitor the government like they did during the 1990s. It remains to be seen if this will undermine the fragile democratic process currently underway.

Tanzania

During the years immediately following independence, TANU demobilized and co-opted civil associations to work for the state. In 1963, the National Executive Committee of TANU resolved to make Tanzania a single-party state and, by 1965, Tanzania became a *de jure* single-party state. With the institutionalization of its supremacy through the Arusha Declaration of 1967, TANU compelled or recruited locally organized groups to work with the ruling party. Leaders of civil society organizations were co-opted to support the TANU government and its policies. The organizations that were captured and absorbed into the state included the Cooperative Union of Tanzania, the Tanzania Parents Association, the Tanzania Women Organization, and the Youth League of the Union of Tanzanian Workers. The state also created mass organizations, such as rural cooperatives. The policies of these organizations were realigned to reinforce those of the party and the government. These organizations also drew substantial financial support from the state treasury, ultimately becoming an important way for the government to mobilize the general population politically. Overall, the political space of the public realm was controlled by a single-party state that seriously constrained associational life and genuine democratic competition.

After 25 years of single-party rule, a variety of proactive civil society organizations emerged to contest political dominance by CCM. For example, the *Susungungu* movement emerged in Mwanza and Shinyanga, and the *Wasalama* movement gained momentum in Tabora. These two movements openly defied state authority and the judicial system by operating autonomously in their areas of origin.[25] There was also an upsurge of civil society organizations dealing with environmental issues, along with professional, religious and social problems.[26] The adoption of World Bank/IMF recovery programs during this period were unmistakably against the tenants of *ujamaa* and self-reliance, promoting private sector initiatives at the expense of Tanzania's large public sector. In the era of structural adjustment and economic reform, individuals were expected to pay for social services that were subsidized during the *ujamaa* period. Tanzania suffered from bureaucratic incapacity to act on critical areas and problems facing society, including corruption, shortages of basic goods, economic stagnation, budgetary constraints due to decreasing production for export, and limited donor support.

The government attempted to control civil society through legislation and bureaucratic control. Civil society organizations were brought under one umbrella body, the Tanzania Association of Non-Governmental Organizations. The registration process for NGOs enabled the government to strengthen its surveillance capacity and restrict the advocacy work of civil society.[27]

In February 1990, the Tanganyika Law Society (TLS) organized a workshop on the democratic limits of a single-party system. This was followed by another seminar in early 1991 on the multi-party system. The workshop was attended by representatives of University of Dar-es-Salaam Academic Staff Association, the Sokoine University Academic Staff Association, the Zanzibar Legal Services Center, the Legal Rights Movement, the Movement for Constitutional Reform, members of foreign missions operating in the country, among others. The 1991 seminars led to the launching of the National Convention for Construction and Reform (NCCR) to coordinate the activities of opposition groups and civil society. The NCCR then resolved that the government should be dissolved and it proposed the formation of a transitional government leading to multi-party democracy. The NCCR also asked the government to organize a national convention to discuss constitutional reforms that would pave the way for multi-party politics in the country. The government rejected the proposal and consequently NCCR broke up, leading to the proliferation of various groups, such as *Kamahuru, Chama Cha Wananchi*, National Convention for Construction and Reform-*Mageuzi* (NCCR-M). NCCR-M advocated the establishment of a federal system of government, the supremacy of parliament, the independence of the judiciary, free education and health services, state regulation of economy, de-linking of the military from politics, and a vibrant civil society.

The CCM government rejected these proposals and it argued that opposition groups were not registered and therefore they did not have the legal status to review the constitution with the government. Pressure from the media, opposition groups, and civil society organizations compelled the government in February 1991 to establish the Nyalali Commission to collect views from the public on the merits and drawbacks of single and multi-party systems. In February 1992, the commission recommended: the adoption of a multi-party political system; independence of judiciary and parliament; freedom of association; and the de-linking of the civil service and the armed forces from CCM. The commission also recommended the repeal of Sections 3 and 10 of the Union constitution, which declared Tanzania a socialist, single-party state. Other sections that were to be repealed on the recommendation of the commission included the Prevention of the Detention Act, the Mass Media Act, the Newspaper Act, and the Political Parties Act.[28]

In February 1992 the CCM government convened a national conference and ratified the Nyalali recommendations, thus adopting multi-party politics in Tanzania. Two months later, the Union parliament repealed the sections of the constitution granting CCM party monopoly over political affairs of Tanzania.[29] Female membership in parliament was to be increased to 15 percent of the total number of members, and presidential cabinet nominations were to be approved by Parliament. The Nyalali Commission ushered in a new era of competitive politics in Tanzania.

Civil society organizations embarked on civic education initiatives to enlighten the public on the electoral process. The Tanzania Media Women Association (TAMWA) held seminars and workshops on civic education. Similarly, the Zanzibar Legal Services Centre (ZLSC) and Tanzania Gender Networking Program (TGNP) carried out voter education projects in some districts to enable voters to participate fully in the electoral process.[30] Despite these efforts, the 1995 elections on the mainland were administratively problematic, and the Zanzibar elections were contentious, as the opposition Civic United Front party, along with local and international observers, called into question whether the exercise was "free and fair".

During the period preceding the 2000 multi-party elections, the CCM government dissolved the Tanzania Union Federation of Workers (TUFW) to weaken the union movement, which had been politically vocal. The aim was to tame and demobilize politically active organizations in the country.[31] The 2000 elections were also marred in controversy, with CCM winning the elections amidst accusations of rigging and police brutality. International observers, opposition political parties and media organizations, such as the *Habari* Corporation, accused the CCM government of stealing votes in Zanzibar using police intimidation and a politically biased electoral commission.[32]

Civil society political activism seems to be evolving slowly in Tanzania compared to Kenya. The Arusha Declaration entrenched single-party supremacy and state ownership of property and resources, hence disempowering the civil society organizations and denying them the resources necessary to operate independently of the central government. As a result, many civil society organizations have focused on "non-political issues" not directly related to the transition process, such as environmental preservation, business planning, community development, and education.

Uganda

From 1962-1966, the Obote regime adhered to constitutional arrangements that were established during the transition to independence. After 1966, Obote introduced a republican constitution that gave the military a larger role to play in politics, and he relegated political parties and civil society organizations to the background.[33] The army increasingly became the arbiter in civilian conflicts. For example, the *Rewenzururu* Movement, composed of the Baamba and Bakonzo ethnic communities, demanded increased participation in the local Toro government, and they were suppressed. As a result, there was widespread violent confrontation between the state and supporters of this movement. According to local press reports, many Baamba and Bakonzo supporters were detained, and state security forces killed others. Leaders in Kampala never accepted their demands for participation in the local Toro government. Instead, the government enhanced the militarization of politics as a crisis management strategy. Uganda's political landscape was further polarized along ethnic lines, ultimately leading to the overthrow of Obote in 1971 by military force. Military rule in Uganda plunged the country into chaos, with mass murders, the suspension of the constitution, the expulsion of Asians, and the general destruction of economic, political, and social institutions.[34]

During the 1970s, Yoweri Museveni formed the Front for National Salvation (FNS) that was dedicated to overthrowing the Idi Amin government.[35] In 1980, after the controversial election that led to the victory of the UPC, Museveni's renamed NRM gained the momentum necessary to eventually gain state power.

The NRM presented a ray of hope after the brutal regimes of Amin and Obote. It was seen as a panacea to Uganda's internal problems and it quickly received the backing of the international community. Tanzania and Kenya, prior to multi-party politics, were relatively peaceful, and there was the latent fear that support for the proactive agents of political change could lead to chaos. Hence, the international community was cautious about supporting the movements and organizations that wanted to overturn the *status quo*.

The decay of state institutions under Amin and Obote, and the creation of a monolithic political system, undermined the credibility of the state as the provider of basic services for its citizens. The rise of civil society organizations in the 1980s and 1990s was an effort by people to create their own space of operation and provide immediate solutions to the social, economic, and political crisis in Uganda.

Once the NRM captured state power, a decentralized local council system was established.[36] The administrative structure of the local councils began from the village to the district level, and every Uganda citizen was obligated to participate in the activities of this movement system.[37] In dismissing a multi-party system as a key ingredient of a democratic political system, Museveni developed the no-party system.

The resurgence of the civil society in Uganda was due in large measure to pressure from the international donor community, which assumed that non-governmental actors were closer to the people, therefore enabling them to provide efficient services to people at the grassroots level.[38] Organizations such as the Danish International Development Agency (DANIDA), Swedish International Development Cooperation Agency (SIDA), and the United States Agency for International Development (USAID), among others, recognized the role that civil society could play in mass mobilization, and they channeled substantial resources through them.

There are several broad categories of civil society groupings in Uganda relevant to this study. The National Organization of Civil Education and Election Monitoring is comprised of professional non-governmental organizations and human rights groups,[39] and the National Council of Independent Monitors (NCIM) includes independent religious institutions (including organized churches and mosques) and student groups. Some gender-related organizations include the National Association of Women of Uganda (NAWOU), Action for Development (ACFODE), the Uganda Women's Organization Network (UWEONET), the Federation For Women Lawyers (FIDA), and the Forum for Women in Democracy (FOWODE). These women's organizations have played an important role in the political transformation process in Uganda. For example, ACFODE successfully lobbied for the formation of a ministry dedicated to women's affairs in 1988 and also for the establishment of a Department of Gender Studies at Makerere University. FIDA has been instrumental in the campaign against domestic violence, rape and defilement, and UWONET successfully lobbied for a land bill to make it illegal to follow the practice of barring women's access to land inheritance. FOWODE, through its training programs, has strengthened women's advocacy and lobbying skills.

These organizations provided alternative political organization and plurality, and they constituted a challenge to the monopoly of the ruling elite. In an effort to respond to this proliferation of politically active civil society organizations, the NRM declared a moratorium on competitive politics and it invited those in the opposition to share in the broad based government, provided they accepted the leading role of NRM in the coalition.

The 1989 NGO Registration Statute provided guidelines on the operation of civil society organizations in Uganda. The statute established an NGO regulation board, whose members were drawn from government ministries (Internal Affairs, Relief and Social Rehabilitation, Justice, Lands and Survey, Planning and Economic Development, and the President's Office). The Board regulates NGO activity and has the power to de-register any NGO that does not act on behalf of the public interest. The process of registration involves the Resistance Council and District Administrators for security clearance.[40]

In the mid-1990's, a number of civil society groups questioned the monopoly of the NRM in the political space of the public realm. They contended that the NRM lacked the ability of self-criticism and that those associating with the movement were doing so out of political expediency and individual self-interest, not on principle. In 1996, the politically conscious group called the Inter-Political Forces Committee (IPFC), led by James Rwanyarare and Godfrey Lule, among others, called for multi-party politics and good governance in Uganda. The IPFC advocated the establishment of a participatory democratic and accountable government involving all stakeholders. The IPFC called upon the NRM government to recognize the Lukiiko and the Kabakaship not merely as a part of the cultural heritage of Uganda, but also as genuine institutions of governance in Uganda.[41]

One particularly contentious issue in Uganda was the referendum in 2000. It was expected that passage of the referendum would allow for political space to be opened for competitive politics, thus bringing an end to the monopoly of the NRM in politics. Civil society organizations were at the forefront of struggling for the return of competitive politics to Uganda. A consortium of NGOs established the Monitoring Cluster, which included the Uganda Joint Christian Council (UJCC), the National Organization for Civic Education and Monitoring (NOCEM), the Uganda Association of Women Lawyers (UAWL), the Uganda Women Network Community, and the Agency for Social Inquiry. This consortium of civil society groups wanted the passage of legislation to allow for the restoration of all political organizations, including political parties, to participate in the referendum process. These organizations worked to liberalize the state owned-media to give equal press access to interested parties, to ensure that there was no censorship of information, and also allow for freedom of association and public meetings without intimidation. Similarly, the electoral commission was called upon to be fair and impartial in processing the outcome of the referendum. The Monitoring Cluster also wanted civil society organizations and international observers to monitor the referendum process without fear or threats from the state.[42]

Ultimately, the passage of the referendum in 2000 severely limited political choice and it left the advocates for political pluralism with limited opportunity to influence democratic change. With low voter turnout, the NRM system of government received 80 percent of the total votes cast. Multi-party advocates accused the NRM government of intimidation and violence throughout the referendum process. They felt that the Museveni government used referendum results to entrench a single-party system of government under the guise of the movement system of government.[43] Consequently, the donor community and the UJCC, an umbrella organization for Protestant and Catholic churches prevailed upon the NRM government to allow political parties to exist in Uganda.[44] In November 2000, the government introduced a Political Organizations Bill (POB) to grant limited freedom to political parties.[45] During the 2001 presidential elections, several political aspirants declared their interest in assuming the presidency in a post-Museveni political order. However, Museveni won the election easily, garnering over 70 percent of the votes cast.

The January 2004 Supreme Court ruling calling into question the NRM political dominance offers interesting opportunities for civil society organizations to agitate for political change. However, there is no guarantee that all non-state actors will follow this path. For example, the Catholic Church is calling upon Museveni to seek a third term, urging him that "revolutionary leaders do not desert the struggle."[46] Politically active civil society organizations such as the East African Law Society, the Uganda Law Society, and the Pentecostal churches have offered platforms for discussion of Uganda's current leadership and a more inclusive democratic process.[47]

The Impact of Civil Society in Democracy in East Africa

The case studies examined in this chapter clearly demonstrate that governments in the region have adopted an expansive, proprietary attitude towards the political space of the public realm, and they view civil society organizations as intruders to this political space. This has often forced these organizations to affiliate with political parties (opposition or incumbent), depend on donors for survival, and/or to balkanize into elite or grassroots entities. These scenarios often compromise the effectiveness of civil society in promoting democracy.

Political Party Affiliation

Civil society organizations are often dominated or controlled by the governments in power, or they become affiliated with opposition parties. In the case of Tanzania, several opposition political parties in the 1990s emerged from civil society organizations and some of the existing ones are linked to opposition political parties. The Civil and Legal Rights Movement changed to the People's Party while the University Academic Associations (UDASA and SUASA) were ideologically linked to the NCCR-*Mageuzi*. In Kenya, the Green Belt Movement linked itself to FORD-Asili in the 1992 general election although its founder did not stand for parliamentary election on the party ticket. Several civil society organizations maintain a strong link with the current NARC government of Kenya. Once civil society organizations become linked to opposition parties or the government, it becomes difficult for them to remain independent advocates for a free and fair democratic transition to multi-party democracy. Independence enables civil society to compete with the state and opposition political parties for political space, and hence cultivate a genuine democratic culture.

Donor Relations

Civil society organizations have also been impacted by close relations with donors entities abroad. When the IMF and World Bank depict good governance in terms of anti-corruption and efficient management,[48] many NGOs respond by tailoring programs to meet these objectives in lieu of questioning government policies that have contributed to the collapse of the agricultural sectors and transportation infrastructure each country.

Civil Society Divisions

Civil society is often polarized into elite and grassroots segments. Grassroots actors lack power, authority and the capacity for independent work, while elite-based organizations are often urban-based, and removed from agricultural areas where the majority of East African populations reside. In Kenya, the most politically active civil society groups such as the National Executive Convention are urban based, with minimal grassroots support. Similarly, in Tanzania and Ugandan many civil society groups are urban based, and are not able to reach the rural population. Moreover, these organizations are pre-occupied with service delivery rather acting as a countervailing force between the excesses of state power and the aspirations of other political actors, such as political parties. Because of these limitations, political parties, particularly the ruling parties, are able to mobilize the rural population with party propaganda and at the same time discredit politically active civil society groups as foreign agents intent on overthrowing constitutionally elected governments. This leaves civil society alienated from the rural population and at times is treated with suspicion.

This study demonstrates the centrality of civil society in building a democratic culture in the face of weak opposition political parties in the region. But civil society groups must overcome the limitations examined in this chapter if they are to successfully contain the proprietary attitude of the state towards the political space of the public realm. Nevertheless, civil society has become an important alternative to weak opposition political parties in building and maintaining a democratic culture in East Africa.

Notes

1 K. Mkangi, "A Critical Reappraisal of the Social Cultural Background to the Anti-Democratic Culture in East Africa" in Oloka-Onyango, et al., eds., *Law and the Struggle for Democracy in East Africa* (Nairobi: Clari Press Ltd., 1996); C. Coquery–Vidrotich, *Africa: Endurance and Change South of the Sahara* (California: Berkeley Press, 1953).

[2] A.S. Nyanchoga, "Party Politics in Kenya," in Aseka et al., eds., *The Political Economy of Transition in Kenya* (Nairobi: Eight Publishers, 1999); Mkangi, "A Critical Reappraisal," 1996.

[3] E. Stitcher, *Migrant Labour in Kenya* (Harlow: Longman Group Ltd. 1992).

[4] S. Makhan, *History of Kenya's Trade Union Movement to 1952* (Nairobi: East Africa Publishing House, 1969), p. 13.

[5] Makhan, *History of Kenya's Trade Union Movement to 1952*, pp. 185-200.

[6] Ali Mazrui and M.C. Tidy, *Nationalism and New African States* (London: Heinemann, 1984), pp. 100-104.

[7] *Weekly Review* (February 22, 1990), p. 3.

[8] G.P. Okoth, "The Historical Development of Democracy in Uganda: A Review of the Problems and Prospects," in Oloka Onyango, Joseph Oloka-Onyango, Kivutha Kibwana, and Peter Chris Maina, eds., *Law and the Struggle for Democracy in East Africa* (Nairobi: Clari Press Ltd, 1996), p. 57.

[9] D. Gillies and M. Mutua, *A Long Road to Uhuru: Human Rights and Political Participation in Kenya* (London: West Minister Foundation, 1993), p. 12.

[10] *Weekly Review*, vol. 29 (April 1988); Nyanchoga, "Party Politics in Kenya," 1999.

[11] For more on the Green Belt Movement, see Stephen Ndegwa, *The Two Faces of Civil Society: NGOs and Politics in Africa* (West Hartford, CT: Kumarian Press, 1996).

[12] Gillies and Mutua, *A long road to Uhuru*, 1993, p. 24.

[13] J. S. Nabende, "The Church and Kenyan Politics" in Aseka, et al., eds., *The Political Economy of Transition in Kenya* (Nairobi: Eight Publishers, 1999), p. 137.

[14] *Weekly Review* (January 12, 1990); Nyanchoga, "Party Politics in Kenya," p. 109.

[15] *Weekly Review* (December 7, 1990), p. 15.

[16] Nyanchoga, "Party Politics in Kenya," p. 110.

[17] H. Kiriama, "Fundamental Constitutional Changes in Kenya" in Eric Masinde Aseka, J.S. Nabende, and Martha Wangari, eds., *Political Economy of Transition in Kenya* (Nairobi: Eight Publishers, 1999).

[18] Kiriama, "Fundamental Constitutional Changes in Kenya," p. 130.

[19] *Daily Nation* (November 5, 1999), p. 7.

[20] *Daily Nation* (December 5, 1999).

[21] *Daily Nation* (January 10, 2000).

[22] *Daily Nation* (February 2, 2000).

[23] *Daily Nation* (December 8, 2000).

[24] *Daily Nation* (December 30, 2002).

[25] K.I. Tambila, "Transition to Multi-party Democracy in Tanzania: Some History and Missed Opportunities," in Oloka Onyango, ed., *Law and Struggle for Democracy in East Africa* (Nairobi: Clari Press Ltd., 1996), p. 41.

[26] Max Mmuya, ed., *The Functional Dimension of the Democratization Process: Tanzania and Kenya* (Dar es Salaam: Dar es Salaam University Press, 1994).

[27] Tambila, "Transition to multi-party democracy in Tanzania," p. 42.

[28] Mmuya, *The Functional Dimension of the Democratization Process*, p. 108.

[29] Mmuya, *The Functional Dimension of the Democratization Process*, p. 112.

[30] F. Maghimbi, *Women Participation in National Affairs: The Case of Tanzania* (Dar es Salaam: Tema Publishers Company, 1996), p. 338.

[31] *The East African* (July 3-9, 2000), p. 3.

[32] *The East African* (November 6-12, 2000), p. 2.

[33] D.M. Mudola, "The Problems of Institutional Building: the Uganda Case" in Paul Wiebe and Cole P. Dodge, eds., *Beyond Crisis: Development in Uganda* (Mekerere University MISR African Studies Association, 1987), p. 20; Okoth, "The Historical Development of Democracy in Uganda," p. 20.

[34] Mudola, "The Problems of Institutional Building: the Uganda Case," pp. 55-66; G.P. Okoth, "The Historical Development of Democracy in Uganda," pp. 52-53.

[35] Okoth, "The Historical Development of Democracy in Uganda," p. 67.

[36] A. Dicklich, "Indigenous NGOs and Political Participation" in Hansen B. Holger and Twaddle Michael, eds., *Developing Uganda* (Oxford: James Curry, 1998), p. 152.

[37] N. Baraza, Contemporary Civil Society and Democratization Process in Uganda: A Preliminary Exploration (Kampala: CBR publication, working paper No. 54. 2000).

[38] G.E. Kyarimpa, *Civil Society and Political Participation in Uganda: Prospects for Consolidating Democracy* (Makerere University, 2001), p. 8.

[39] Including the Uganda Law Society (ULS), the Uganda Lawyers Association (ULA), the Uganda Journalist Associations (UJA), the Makerere Law Society (MLS), and the Foundation for Human Rights Initiative (FHRI).

[40] F.W. Jcaho, "Political Parties, NGOs and Civil Society" in Oloka Onyango, Joseph Oloka-Onyango, Kivutha Kibwana, and Peter Chris Maina, eds., *Law and the Struggle for Democracy in East Africa* (Nairobi: Clari Press Ltd, 1996), p. 194.

[41] *The New Vision* (February 2, 1996).

[42] *The East African* (March 13-19, 2000).

[43] *The East African* (July 3-9 2000), p. 1.

[44] *East African* (July 10-16, 2000).

[45] *The East African* (November 6-12, 2000).

[46] *The Monitor* (February 4, 2004).

[47] *The Monitor* (February 4, 2004).

[48] M. Mamdani, "Democratic Theory and Democratic Struggles" (CODESRIA Paper, 1992); M. Mamdani "McNamara's Speech: A Rejoinder" (CODESRIA BULLETIN No. 2, 1991).

Chapter 7

Structural Adjustment and Economic Reform

Stephen F. Burgess

In the 1980s, most African states suffered economic downturns and had little choice but to adopt stringent economic reforms, guided by IMF currency stabilization and IMF/World Bank structural adjustment programs (SAPs).[1] Subsequent austerity measures brought unrest targeted against many regimes, which helped bring political liberalization and paved the way for the third wave of democratization, which arrived on the continent in the early 1990s.[2] Since then, African leaders have grappled with economic reforms, while struggling to negotiate democratic transitions. In this chapter, the comparative impact of economic reform on the democratic transition process is evaluated in East Africa.[3]

At issue is whether economic reform has played, on the whole, a more positive or more negative role in the democratic transition process. In Tanzania, internal and external pressures led the ruling party to implement simultaneous economic and political reform, which eventually brought multi-party democracy and economic growth. Before the reform process, the ruling party had developed substantial popular support and ethnic cohesion, so that it did not fear losing power or overreact against the social stresses that economic reform brought. In Kenya, external economic and political pressures and internal popular pressures led to a decade-long struggle that helped end the Moi regime. His successor Kibaki came to power committed to democracy, transparency, and economic reform; however, the new ruling coalition has been fragmented and slow to reform. Uganda has benefited the most from economic reform, but Museveni has used this success to resist pressures for a multi-party democratic transition.

Contending Positions on Economic Reform and Democratic Transitions

In addressing the impact of economic reform on democratic transitions, there are three contending positions: one that favors simultaneous economic reform and democratization; one that stresses economic reform first; and one that advocates debt forgiveness.

The "Reform-Democratization" Position

Western governments and, to some extent, the World Bank and IMF, have promoted simultaneous economic reform and democratic transition in Africa.[4] Most donors have claimed that economic reform strengthens the democratic transition process and that democratization enhances economic reform. Supposedly, reform produces economic growth, which enhances political stability and the conditions for peaceful democratic competition. Growth also enables political incumbents to rely less on patronage in campaigning for reelection and, instead, emphasize their records in office. Privatization disperses economic power, removing it from the state elite, and opens the way for the building of a middle class of entrepreneurs. Reform can bring the reduction of "urban bias,"[5] reducing the income gap between urban and rural areas and helping empower rural dwellers, the majority of Africa's population.

Donors also claim that "good governance" enhances economic reform and growth.[6] Supposedly, democratic transitions replace corrupt dictatorships with governments that practice good governance, are more accountable to the public, and are more willing to revitalize entrepreneurship, promote growth, and alleviate poverty.

The "Reform First" Position

Advocates contend that African states are too poor to sustain economic reform and democratic transition at the same time and that economic reform and growth must take precedence. This position has its roots in "modernization theory" of the 1950s and 1960s, which stressed the development of state capacity to cope with popular mobilization and demands for public goods and services.[7] While Western donors, including the IMF and World Bank, have publicly supported simultaneous economic reform and democratic transition, in practice they often support the "reform first" position. When faced with the choice, they would rather see sustained economic reform and a less than successful democratic transition than multi-party democracy with failed economic reform.[8]

Skepticism exists about the viability of multi-party democracy in least developed countries (below $1,000 per capita).[9] Poverty and ethnic competition prevent economic reform and democratic transition from advancing together. A shortage of resources and ethnic divisions compel leaders to monopolize political power and disburse patronage in neo-patrimonial systems.[10] Economic reform governments in poor multi-party democracies are vulnerable to anti-reform coalitions, which campaign against austerity and, upon gaining power, revive clientelism. Neo-patrimonial leaders organize resistance to economic reform, so that they can maintain or regenerate their patronage networks, especially to benefit the ethnic groups that support them. Control over the state and restrictions on politics help leaders to exclude competitors who aspire to expand their own patronage networks. Finally, poverty inhibits the development of alternative loci of economic and political power, which intensifies the struggle for control of the state.

The "reform first" position posits that African states first must develop their economies and administrative capacity before they can sustain democracy, and that poor states must maintain consistently high rates of growth to attain an economic level where multi-party democracy and greater equality can eventually be consolidated. Therefore, the top political priorities for an economic reform regime are the building of state capacity and the maintenance of autonomy from neo-patrimonial forces.[11]

The "Debt Forgiveness" Position

This approach gained prominence during the debt forgiveness campaigns of the 1990s.[12] The United Nations Economic Commission for Africa (ECA) and the African Union, among others, contend that African economies are fragile, dependent, and overly indebted. As a result, austerity and liberalization degrade emergent democracies, social services, infrastructure, and domestic industry.[13] They contend that debt forgiveness and the opening of industrialized economies to African imports must take precedence over economic reform and that reforms must be protracted. Advocates of this position also contend that debt forgiveness would provide the resources, services, and space necessary for the development of democratic institutions and healthy economies.

Definitions of Economic Reform

The World Bank has defined economic reform as sustained improvement toward the attainment of a "good" macroeconomic policy stance, which includes: (1) the adoption of a flexible, stable, and realistic exchange rate policy; (2) a monetary policy with low inflation (preferably in the single digits); and (3) fiscal policies with low budget deficits and higher revenue collection.[14] Successful reform should bring sustained economic growth, defined as Gross Domestic Product (GDP) growth rates of at least six percent, necessary to offset three percent population growth rates in most African countries. States that sustain reform then should attract foreign direct investment, which reduces dependence on foreign aid and produces industrial development and higher growth rates. States that initiate but fail to sustain reform regress into high budget deficits, high inflation and over-valued currencies, coupled with a slow-down in economic growth. Would-be reformers in Africa have found that cutting government size and lowering budget deficits to be especially problematic. The inability to balance budgets continues to produce inflation and high interest rates and discourages investment.

In the 1980s, the IMF and World Bank developed one economic blueprint for more than 30 different African economies. However, most were weak and could not withstand the "shock treatment" that structural adjustment programs imposed.[15] With the lowering of import protection, the domestic manufacturing sector in Africa found it difficult to compete with foreign goods. In many countries, as privatization was implemented, insufficient private capital existed to keep many formerly state-owned industries running, and many workers lost their jobs. The rural sector lacked the infrastructure and capital necessary to develop an agricultural market economy, and production declined. Often, user fees were instituted for schools and health clinics, which left many without access to basic education or health care. Food subsidies were slashed, which caused higher food prices and social unrest. SAPs caused unemployment and impoverishment, which generated a wave of protests against the World Bank, IMF, and governments that were implementing austerity measures. In the 1990s, the former two adjusted to criticism of SAPs and conditionality standards, though the World Bank proved more flexible than the IMF.

The first wave of economic reform came in response to the economic downturn and debt crisis of the 1980s and was largely forced on African states. Most of the first wave or "large improvement" countries in the 1994 World Bank study failed to sustain the pace of reforms and were unable to move to the adequate or good levels. The second wave of economic reform occurred in tandem with the third wave of democratization of the early 1990s.[16] The opening up of the democratic process coincided with massive dissatisfaction with and protests against decaying neo-patrimonial regimes and widespread economic failure.[17] Regimes fell or were chastened, and all promised a change of course, resulting in the widespread initiation of new economic reform programs. The most successful second wave economic reform case was Uganda, which, by 1991, had scored "small improvement" and a "fair" policy stance and from that year on made "large improvement," leaping forward towards a "good" stance, which was sustained throughout the 1990s.[18]

In 1996, the IMF and World Bank launched the Highly Indebted Poor Countries (HIPC) program, responding to indebtedness and poverty partly engendered by SAPs. In the first three years of the program, tough standards were applied for debt relief under the HIPC program, including the formulation of acceptable poverty reduction strategies, and only Uganda and four other countries qualified. In October 1999, after considerable pressure from African leaders and a wide range of forces in developed countries, the IMF and the World Bank agreed to the expansion of HIPC.[19] Since then, more than a dozen African countries have qualified. The IMF's sensitivity to the poverty alleviation issue was underlined by the creation of Poverty Reduction and Growth Facilities (PRGFs), which replaced Enhanced Structural Adjustment Facilities (ESAFs), the cornerstone of SAPs. Also, PRGFs promised to be targeted at attracting foreign direct investment.[20]

The IMF and World Bank, in their 1996 HIPC initiative, acknowledged that successful reformers remained encumbered by unsustainable levels of debt and needed relief and assistance. In April 1997, the World Bank designated Uganda as the first country that would receive debt relief. All five first wave HIPC states managed to reach the "completion point" of the "original framework" and received debt relief. The five then moved on to the "enhanced framework," which provided additional debt relief.[21] Uganda progressed further and reached the completion point of the enhanced framework in March 2000.[22] No other country has been able to match Uganda's progress. After meetings in September 1999, the IMF and World Bank lowered HIPC standards, and, in 2000, Tanzania and 12 others became HIPC candidates.

Uganda: Economic Reform, Blocked Democratic Transition

Since President Museveni and the NRM came to power in January 1986, Uganda carried out IMF and World Bank-supported economic reforms and achieved high rates of growth. At the same time, Museveni limited democratic transition and curbed political party competition, contending that a no-party state was essential to Uganda's ethnic cohesion and important for economic growth and stability. Uganda's rapid economic growth, around the recommended six percent mark for more than a decade, bolstered Museveni's arguments that growth, development, and ethnic cohesion should not be jeopardized by multi-party competition and full democracy. As long as Uganda progressed with its economic reform program and practiced "good governance," Western donors generally accepted Museveni's position on multi-partyism and did not exert undue pressure for greater democracy, preferring sustained economic reform to democratic transition.

The Ugandan economy was developed under British rule to export agricultural commodities, with coffee as the main cash crop. South Asians were brought to build the East African Railway and rose to prominence in the private sector. After independence in 1962, the Obote regime sought to harness the cash crop economy to industrialize and to expand social services. As Obote increasingly concentrated power in his hands, he began the nationalization of private enterprises and moved the country towards socialism. When Amin seized power in 1971, he drove the economy into the ground, especially after he ordered all Asians expelled and their businesses expropriated in 1972. After Amin was overthrown in 1979 and Obote restored, civil war aggravated Uganda's economic woes. In the early 1980s, Uganda remained one of the worst rated macroeconomic performers. With its GDP in continuous decline, Obote agreed to reforms, giving the IMF considerable control over the Ugandan economy.

The basis for Uganda's economic reform was established in the early 1980s, when the NRM mobilized large numbers of Ugandans, especially peasant farmers, to fight the second Obote regime and set up rural political and economic structures. As NRM guerrillas operated among peasant farmers and learned that their demand was to freely produce and market, and that they were opposed to socialist agriculture and state intervention, Museveni and the NRM discarded Marxism, Maoism, and socialism, and devised *The 10-Point Programme* as a blueprint to reconstruct Uganda, based on a "mixed economy."[23]

When Museveni and the NRM came to power they were still wary of capitalism, Western donors, the IMF, World Bank, and transnational corporations. Before the Museveni government could begin implementing *The 10-Point Programme*, IMF officials presented a stabilization plan with a ready-made package of policy recommendations. World Bank officials soon followed with reconstruction assistance, especially for rebuilding Uganda's shattered infrastructure. As the NRM regime initiated negotiations with the IMF to stabilize the economy and reconstruct the devastated country, Museveni and his colleagues realized that they lacked the technical expertise to challenge the IMF package and that *The 10 Point Programme* was not a well-developed alternative. As a result, the regime responded to IMF demands and began the adjustment process.[24] Museveni was also influenced by the economic success of the newly industrialized countries in East Asia, which emphasized economic growth and national unity before multi-party democracy.[25]

In May 1987, IMF shock treatment was applied, and the NRM regime began implementing an Economic Recovery Program (ERP) that included the devaluation of the Ugandan shilling. Once sufficient stabilization was achieved, the IMF, World Bank, and Western donors made an ESAF available in September 1988.[26] As coffee prices fell and war continued in northern Uganda, the ESAF/ERP helped to keep a very fragile economy from collapsing.

In the late 1980s, foreign aid maintained Uganda's economic recovery and the NRM regime's commitment to economic reform. The return of Ugandan Asian businessmen and the arrival of foreign direct investment sparked economic growth and bolstered support for reform. In the 1990s, aid became less significant in maintaining support for reform, as foreign direct investment increased and growth accelerated. Once the ESAF/ERP was implemented and began to produce positive results, the Museveni government continued its commitment to reform and began cutting the size of government in the face of considerable societal pressure. According to Brett, "the Ugandan leadership has incorporated opposition representatives into the regime, compromised its own ideological assumptions, maintained economic discipline, threatened powerful vested interests, and supported the small group of key officials who have had to enforce the unpopular decisions required to sustain their SAP."[27]

In the 1990s, the economic reform program became "Ugandan-owned," as the Museveni government built a pro-reform coalition, including farmers and entrepreneurs. The government elevated local technocrats to decision-making positions, and welcomed a working relationship with experts from the IMF, World Bank, and other foreign agencies.

In the 1980s, the NRM initiated Resistance Councils (RCs) as a basis for self-help schemes and "grass roots" economic development.[28] In 1989 and 1992, the NRM organized local and district non-partisan RC elections, which enabled people to vote unpopular incumbents out of power, combat corruption, and exercise political voice. The encouragement of local level participation through the RCs, NGOs, and self-help schemes fostered economic recovery, development, support for economic reform, as well as the rebuilding of civil society and grassroots democracy.[29] According to Schurmann, "the families, villages and markets of Uganda are the primary fuel energizing the country's recent high growth rate. Uganda has had a tradition of rural credit going back many decades. And recently some of the 1,000-

plus NGOs operating in the country are going into rural credit, savings and education."[30] The "bottom up" nature of economic development in Uganda augmented the growth of the pro-reform coalition.

The NRM's government of national unity (GNU), which maintained restrictions on multi-party competition, and adeptly maintained a pro-reform coalition, prevented elites from effectively challenging the ERP.[31] The NRM regime was able to resist distributional demands by elites and interest groups. Also important in economic reform was the discipline developed during five years of guerrilla warfare and exhibited by NRM cadres in fighting corruption and preventing dissension when the reform path was chosen. This discipline, augmented by popular participation and a relatively free press, maintained government accountability and autonomy from elites and it helped build confidence in government promises of good governance.

The NRM regime implemented cuts in the size and expenditures of government, as well as market liberalization and privatization. A notable example of cuts came in the early 1990s, when the NRM regime demobilized more than 30,000 NRA soldiers. This occurred without unrest and at a time when the army was fighting rebels in the north. The government demonstrated its commitment to market liberalization by permitting private firms and cooperative unions to compete against the parastatal Coffee Marketing Board (CMB) in marketing coffee, though the CMB maintained its monopoly over coffee processing. The World Bank assisted in injecting private sector competition against powerful political and bureaucratic interests in the marketing of coffee and did the same for cotton, grain, and other crops.[32]

Privatization proved to be the least successful aspect of the economic reform program. When the NRM came to power, there were about 150 publicly owned companies. In the early 1990s, the NRM's drive to privatize over 40 public enterprises faced a strong challenge in the National Assembly over its questionable legal basis and over the restoration of property to Ugandan Asians.[33] As privatization proceeded, the lack of clear guidelines allowed "corruption and cronyism" to taint the process.[34]

Despite the halting privatization process, by the mid-1990s, Uganda had become the most successful African country in implementing market-oriented reforms and achieving high growth rates. Increased investment led to the expansion of manufacturing, as well as a rise in production capacities. State institutions revived, and policy coordination in the various ministries improved. However, Uganda remained encumbered by extraordinarily high levels of debt that could not be overcome by expanding exports. As late as 1992, Uganda's debt burden was contributing to net capital outflow.

Donors, the IMF, and World Bank met at the May 1992 Paris Club Consultative Group and committed $800 million to Uganda, though much was used to service a mountain of debt.[35] Ugandan leaders, technocrats, and NGOs worked with donors, the IMF, and World Bank to establish the Ugandan Multilateral Debt Fund (UMDF) in 1995, which became the predecessor of the HIPC program launched in 1996.[36] Subsequently, Uganda experienced a net inflow of capital, with $311 million repatriated in 1997.[37]

With the country moving in a positive economic direction, Museveni called for elections for a constituent assembly in 1994 and for parliament and president in 1996. In both elections, economic reform, austerity, and government corruption were issues. However, the growth and development provided by reform helped to bring high voter turnout, mainly assisted parliamentary candidates favorable to the NRM, and helped elect Museveni. Afterwards, the new parliament supported the economic reform and anti-poverty programs. At the same time, the parliament investigated the privatization scandals and other improprieties.

After the 1996 elections, economic reform continued, as Uganda was selected as the first HIPC candidate. In 1997, Uganda enjoyed the largest improvement of any country in the Institutional Investor ratings.[38] By 1998, that government had met all the requirements in order to receive debt relief, including the formulation of a poverty alleviation program, the 1997 Poverty Eradication Plan. In January 2000, the Ugandan government presented a Poverty Reduction Strategy Paper in qualifying for the Enhanced HIPC initiative.

Uganda had already made progress in the 1990s in reducing poverty. Economic reform brought the reduction of urban bias, which led to rising agricultural production and rural incomes and reductions in poverty. Uganda's anti-poverty programs were targeted mainly at the rural areas. They were formulated and administered by local NGOs, and they proved to be more effective than other African anti-poverty programs. By 1998, UNDP estimated that 55 percent of the population was under the poverty line,[39] in contrast to 69 percent in 1990.[40] By 2000, the World Bank estimated that the poverty rate diminished further to 35 percent in zones where war was not taking place.[41]

Uganda's Poverty Eradication Plan increased primary education, health care, and road building, mainly in the rural areas. The education reform program required checks for school expenditures to be sent directly to local parent-teacher associations. One result of government programs was that 80 percent of children went to primary school by the end of the 1990s, as opposed to 40 percent at the beginning of the decade.[42]

HIPC assistance, in conjunction with comparable action by other creditors, enabled Uganda to reach a debt-to-export ratio of 150 percent in mid-1999.[43] Therefore, the government was able to redirect resources to poverty reduction efforts and economic development. Economic reform brought diversification of the economy away from dependence on coffee exports and also brought investment in manufacturing and sustained economic growth.

Privatization accelerated after the 1996 elections, with over 80 companies listed for sale. The lack of standards and transparency led to benefits for high ranking government officials, including Museveni's brother, and Ugandan Asian businessmen. The Ugandan parliament and press investigated and exposed wrongdoing. Subsequently, institutional reforms improved the privatization process, so that the 2000 sale of Uganda Telecom Ltd. occurred in a "fair and transparent process." However, the main suspects in previous privatization improprieties were not brought to trial.[44]

Corruption in the privatization process was matched by growing improprieties in other aspects of government. The situation worsened from 1998 to 2003, when Museveni ordered the Ugandan army to intervene in the Democratic Republic of the Congo (DRC) to combat rebel insurgencies. While defense spending increased and placed an additional burden on the economy, army leaders set up business operations in the DRC and profited from the intervention.[45]

Uganda's June 2000 referendum on multi-partyism was, in many ways, a referendum on the popularity of Museveni and the economic reform program. The verdict was mixed, due to an opposition boycott and low turnout. During the 2001 presidential campaign, Museveni stressed his economic record, while his opponents emphasized the regime's corruption and arrogance.

At the end of 2003, the economy was still growing, but the speed of growth had slowed from six percent to about 4.5 percent per year. At issue was whether the slowdown was temporary, due to bad weather and low coffee and cotton prices, or permanent, reflecting an end to the fifteen-year reconstruction and recovery phase. In addition, urban populations continued to benefit more than rural ones, and much of the growth remained concentrated in the central region, around the capital, Kampala.

Whatever the long-term prognosis, government plans to reduce poverty (including a new anti-poverty plan) and reduce reliance on donors (which pay for 53 percent of Uganda's budget) by increasing local tax revenue and export income were adversely affected by the economic slowdown. The government had already cut welfare budgets in 2002 in order to divert funds to fight rebels in the north, which angered donors. In response to the slowdown, the Ugandan finance minister called for a focus on strengthening institutions – such as commercial courts – and eliminating corruption and promoting growth. Museveni and all his ministers published statements of their assets. President George W. Bush's trip to Uganda in July 2003 demonstrated continued external faith in Museveni and his government as economic reformers as well as leaders in the fight against HIV/AIDS.

It continues to be unclear whether or not the slowdown and continued economic reform efforts will weaken the government and permit the opposition to gain in strength and push for a multi-party democratic transition. Whatever the case, Uganda is better positioned economically to undergo a transition to multi-party democracy than a decade earlier. If a full democratic transition had happened earlier, Uganda would have taken longer to recover economically, given its fragility. On the negative side, the postponement of full democratic transition allowed corruption and arrogance to infect the regime, which is affecting the economy. It has been ironic that Museveni was flexible and cosmopolitan enough to try a new formula for economic reform in the 1980s but rejected pressures for democratic transition and multi-partyism. As long as the economic reform has produced growth, Museveni has used it as an excuse for delaying democratic transition and multi-party competition.

Tanzania: Economic Reform and Democratic Transition

Tanzania is one of the few African states able to manage economic reform and develop multi-party democracy at the same time. Economic reform in Tanzania helped to initiate the democratic transition and made a positive impact on the political reform process, especially in diminishing corruption. While the World Bank designated Uganda as the premier economic reformer by naming it the first Highly Indebted Poor Country (HIPC) in April 1997, Tanzania was named as an HIPC candidate in March 2000, after considerable pressure from leaders and friends of the country. Although the democratic transition has been limited by the continuing dominance of CCM, the Tanzanian case affirms the position of many Western donors that economic reform and multi-party democracy can advance together.

Like Uganda, the Tanzanian economy was built on agricultural exports, including coffee, sisal, and Zanzibari cloves, with tourism and mining as potential growth areas. In 1967, President Nyerere abandoned the export-oriented development strategy promoted by international agencies and announced, in the Arusha Declaration, the turn towards *ujamaa* socialism and self-reliance. Self-reliance was to be achieved through state-owned import substitution industries. The state redistributed wealth from more prosperous peoples and regions to the less advantaged. A leadership code was also established to encourage ruling party officials to remain close to the people and prevent those officials from engaging in corrupt practices or in business. On the political front, Nyerere argued that a single-party state was essential for economic development and that multi-partyism was divisive and detrimental to development.[46]

Ujamaa socialist experimentation contributed to an economic downturn, with declines in investment, export agriculture, and GDP per capita, along with a mounting debt crisis. As early as 1979, the IMF intervened and offered funds for stabilization in exchange for macroeconomic policy change. Nyerere led resistance to the IMF's conditions. However, no donors would come to the rescue, and Nyerere eventually agreed to IMF conditions. Nyerere's resistance delayed donor assistance that could have prevented a bad economic situation from becoming worse. While Tanzania was better off than war-torn Uganda, the economy was in dire straits.

In 1986, Mwinyi agreed to a World Bank/IMF SAP, and the economic reform began. Tanzania, like Uganda, implemented an ERP, which was reinforced by an ESAP in 1989. Under these two programs, the Mwinyi government "worked to dismantle the system of state controls and promote private sector expansion, including liberalizing the trade and exchange system, eliminating price controls and most state monopolies, and opening the financial sector to private sector participation. Rehabilitation of key infrastructure was also made a priority, particularly roads, railways, and ports."[47] The entry of IMF and World Bank officials from 1985 onwards helped to reorient Tanzanian technocrats away from socialism and towards economic reform and market capitalism.[48]

Tanzania received more than $1 billion in aid from donors, and the economy responded with an annual growth rate of four percent from 1986 to 1994.[49] The revival of the agricultural sector was due to the IMF/World Bank package, devaluation of the Tanzanian shilling, and cheaper prices for agricultural exports. The deregulation of the market for agricultural commodities lessened urban bias and provided incentives for many farmers to produce and market their crops. As the situation improved, these farmers formed the basis for a coalition in favor of economic reform. However, many other farmers did not benefit from "getting the prices right" and still required considerable assistance in agricultural production, marketing, and infrastructure. Also, social welfare for poor farmers was cut, which increased demand for anti-poverty programs.[50]

Proportionately, Tanzania had more state-owned industries than Kenya or Uganda, and as Tanzania began privatization, the process proved to be more difficult, complex, and protracted. As in Uganda, Asian businessmen dominated the private sector, benefited from liberalization, and began to buy state-owned industries that were offered for sale. The African elite, which was composed mainly of government and party officials, could only hope to take advantage of the liberalization and privatization processes by using their positions; for instance, by accepting kickbacks from Asian businessmen.[51]

The SAPs and the introduction of market capitalism led the political elite to become engaged in business activities and to undermine the CCM leadership code, which had curbed corruption. The party experienced centrifugal forces and the rise of factions. From 1985 to 1990, Nyerere spoke out against the SAPs, the corruption and decline of the government and ruling party, and the move away from socialism. As the CCM lost its ideological moorings and began splintering, Nyerere and many other Tanzanians found that the CCM was steadily losing its moral authority to govern and called for political reform. The collapse of socialism and single-party states in Eastern Europe in 1989 and 1990 further discredited the single-party state in Tanzania. In August 1990, Nyerere stepped down as chair of CCM and pronounced that, since the CCM had moved away from socialism, the single-party state no longer suited Tanzania and that a multi-party system should be considered.[52]

From 1985 to 1991, Tanzania made large macroeconomic improvements, but the World Bank judged its macroeconomic policy stance to be poor and had a long way to go in sustaining reform. In the late 1980s and early 1990s, the rise of corruption and patronage slowed down the reform process. From 1985 to 1990, the flood of aid that Tanzania received resulted in aid dependence, doubling from 12 percent of GDP to more than 29 percent. Once aid began flowing and economic crisis no longer threatened, the government lessened its adherence to ERP/ESAP standards.[53]

In 1990, Mwinyi was reelected president but then allowed the economic reform program to deteriorate. With the ending of the CCM leadership code in 1991, elite economic activity increased, and corruption rose in both party and government. As patronage and corruption grew, Tanzania's economic progress of the late 1980s was jeopardized, as the regime's commitment to reform slackened, and external pressure increased. Western donors, the IMF, and the World Bank applied pressure for economic reform, good governance, and democratic transition. In 1991, one of Tanzania's biggest donors, Sweden, cut aid by $10 million citing a lack of accountability and the rise of corruption, especially in the civil service.[54]

External pressure helped to bring change in the political arena in 1992 and a renewed commitment to economic reform by 1996.[55] In spite of the CCM's responsibility for poor economic performance in the 1970s and 1980s and subsequent austerity measures, the party had succeeded at winning popular support from the 1960s onwards and was confident that it would continue to do so facing multi-party competition.

By 1995, the worsening macroeconomic situation led to 30 percent inflation, deferment of World Bank and IMF programs, and an interruption of balance of payment assistance from several donors.[56] However, as the 1995 elections approached, it became clear that the CCM would dominate and that the twelve weak opposition parties that formed since 1992 stood little chance against the ruling party.[57] In the November 1995 elections, the CCM won 78 percent of the seats in parliament, and the CCM leader, Benjamin Mkapa, became president.[58] In contrast, in Zanzibar, the CCM could only stay in power through voting irregularities, which helped prevent the CUF from taking power on the islands.[59]

Although President Mkapa had been a long-serving CCM official, he was more committed than Mwinyi to breaking with past practices, sustaining economic reform, and combating corruption. In spite of pressure from powerful interests in the party, Mkapa quickly reached agreement with the IMF. Subsequent adherence to an IMF fiscal program resulted in economic recovery and growth rates of five percent per year. The Mkapa government focused on improving fiscal and budgetary performance and instituting structural reforms, including privatization in a number of areas and building administrative capacity.[60]

President Mkapa campaigned to persuade the IMF and World Bank to make Tanzania a HIPC candidate and prevailed in March 2000. The government began undertaking reforms, including a poverty alleviation program, to qualify for debt relief. The revival of the economy paid political dividends, as Mkapa and the CCM won again in the 2000 elections. In November 2001, Tanzania was approved for $3 billion in debt relief under the enhanced HIPC Initiative, and the resulting savings of approximately $118 million per year were mainly allocated to priority sectors including education, health, and agriculture. It appears that the economic reform process will continue at least until 2005, when Mkapa must step down and be replaced by a new president. However, over the next decade Tanzania needs to reduce corruption and increase its growth rate from five to eight percent in order to alleviate widespread poverty. This must be done by increasing agricultural productivity, export earnings, and increase internal revenue.

Tanzania, in contrast to Uganda, possessed the ruling party dominance and political stability that enabled it to implement both economic reform and democratic transition at the same time. The long-time ruling party managed the economic reform and the democratic transition in a "top-down" manner.[61] Subsequently, economic reform was hampered by corruption and slowed to a halt, which led to renewed pressures for political change. The ruling party managed to stay in power with a change in presidential leadership that helped to reinvigorate the economic reform process.

Kenya: Struggle for Economic Reform and Democratic Transition

In the early 1990s, the Moi regime became dependent on IMF and World Bank lending, which enabled Western donors to join efforts with Kenyan democrats and successfully apply pressure to compel transition from a single-party to a multi-party constitution. Donor pressure attacked the high level of corruption in the Moi regime. By forcing periodic cutbacks in patronage, donors made the political playing field more competitive. Moi and the ruling party KANU survived two close multi-party elections in the 1990s until the opposition prevailed in 2002, and Kibaki was elected president.

The British established Kenya as the transportation hub of East Africa and as an exporter of coffee, tea, and other cash crops. After independence in 1963, Kenyatta maintained a capitalist market economy and rejected socialism. However, he did move Kenya towards a single-party state and he ensured that the Kikuyu ethnic group established political and economic dominance. In the 1970s, Kenya experienced an economic and industrial boom, while Tanzania, Uganda, and other socialist-oriented economies suffered downturns. Small-scale farmers developed through producer cooperatives and *harambee* "self help" schemes. A KANU primary system was established that enabled constituents to vote out unresponsive or corrupt members of parliament. By 1980, Kenya was one of the most promising African countries in terms of economic and political development.

In 1978, Moi became president and shifted the regime's power base towards his own Kalenjin group. In 1982, the Moi regime passed legislation making Kenya a single-party state, especially with a view to preventing the Kikuyu from forming a rival party. In order to build a new power center, Moi established extensive patronage networks to attract clients from previously disadvantaged ethnic groups. As a result, patronage and corruption snowballed and degraded a relatively effective government and contributed to economic decline and a debt crisis that began in the early 1980s.

In response to economic decline and rising debt, the Moi regime devised its own economic reform program that would cut the size of government and bring budget expenditures under control. Since Kenya was a donor favorite, the reform program was accepted. However, Moi proceeded to increase public sector employment and public construction, swelling Kenya's debt and disappointing donor expectations. The government's failure to reform began a two-decade long process of struggle between the Moi regime and donors.

As economic decline continued during the 1980s, government officials and neo-patrimonial elites increasingly sought to make money through corrupt practices, with abuses of the banking system and currency regulations and kickbacks.[62] Moi contributed to further economic decline by moving to control producer cooperatives and self-help schemes, which he perceived as centers of Kikuyu power and threats to his own power base. The result was declining agricultural marketing and quality of life in the rural areas. The introduction of "queue voting" in 1988 KANU primary elections dampened competition and lessened the power that grassroots, self-help schemes had to attract resources, which contributed to rural economic decline.

The unfree and unfair 1988 elections led donors to apply pressure for good governance and economic reform. The flawed elections, austerity measures, and changes in Eastern Europe in 1989 brought demonstrations for an end to the single-party state. From 1989 to 1991, the NCCK, the LSK, student groups, and other NGOs pressed for human rights and democracy and an end to the single-party state. These NGOs became a basis for FORD.[63]

In 1990 and 1991, the U.S. Ambassador, Smith Hempstone, as well as the governments of Germany, the Nordic countries, and other Western donors applied pressure on the Moi regime to implement political reforms. In contrast to Tanzania, where corruption was the main concern, donors in Kenya focused foremost on an end to human rights abuses and respect for civil liberties. To a lesser extent, donors were also concerned with economic reform and good governance. Moi continued to resist both political and economic reforms. In 1991, FORD pushed for a multi-party system, and Kenyan business leaders pushed for political and economic reform and funded a free press. Throughout much of 1991, Moi resisted pressures for political and economic reform, and his regime harassed reformers and the press.[64]

In November 1991, the struggle for political and economic reform culminated in the meeting of the Paris Club Consultative Group for Kenya, including the IMF and World Bank, as well as the U.S., U.K., and France. The donors suspended $350 million in quick-disbursing loans for Kenya and applied additional pressure. The donors warned that aid was dependent on political reform, respect for human rights and the rule of law, and curbs on corruption.[65]

Two weeks later, in December 1991, Moi capitulated to donor pressure and called multi-party elections, which were held in December 1992. He won with less than two million votes (one-third of the total), while the opposition compiled more than 3.4 million. The small plurality demonstrated the Moi regime's precarious political situation. In order to prepare for the 1997 elections, patronage and corruption were raised to unprecedented heights, including massive abuses of development assistance.

In 1993, economic reforms were implemented that included the deregulation of foreign exchange and agriculture and bank reform. However, donors were not satisfied. In November 1993, the Consultative Group reconvened and offered the Moi regime $170 million on condition that human rights and governance improve and KANU-provoked ethnic clashes end. The government started to meet some of the conditions.[66]

In Kenya (as in Tanzania), donor dollars helped to bring economic and political reform. However, Moi (like Mwinyi) could find ways to circumvent conditionality. Within a year, the Moi regime had already failed to live up to the November 1993 agreement. This led to a renegotiation of the 1993 agreement and a 1995 agreement with donors. However, once the donor assistance began to flow again, the Moi government reneged on the 1995 agreement, too.

In 1997, it was revealed that more than $300 million of state funds had been lost in the "Goldenberg affair." The Finance Ministry had been making payments since 1991 to Goldenberg International and its head, Kamlesh Pattni, as a premium to pay for nonexistent exports of gold and diamonds. Documents revealed that Moi and other top-level officials were aware of the transactions.[67]

As the December 1997 elections approached, Moi increased the flow of patronage to clients. Instead of cracking down on corruption, the Moi regime increased it. In July 1997, the regime cracked down on an opposition rally in Uhuru Park, which touched off demonstrations and violent repression throughout the country. Soon afterwards, the IMF suspended its $220 million ESAF, and the World Bank and donors withheld more than $180 million, which caused massive capital flight.[68] Major donors to Kenya formed an Economic Governance Group, chaired by the World Bank, with U.N. agencies and NGOs, to address issues related to governance and foreign assistance programs.[69]

In spite of economic decline and successive failed economic reform programs, the December 1997 elections were largely a rerun of the 1992 elections. The opposition was unable to come together, and Moi again was reelected by a plurality. However, internal and external pressure led to significant political reforms that reinvigorated the opposition and civil society and set the stage for struggles for constitutional change.[70]

By 1999, the economic crisis and corruption had grown so serious that the IMF, World Bank, and donors insisted that the famous opposition leader, former wildlife director, and paleontologist, Richard Leakey, be brought in to lead a team to fight corruption. Moi reluctantly agreed, and Leakey became Head of the Public Service and Secretary to the Cabinet in July 1999. Leakey initiated a number of reforms, including reducing the number of ministries from 28 to 15, the sacking of the heads of state-owned industries and top police officers, and restarting privatization. In response, the IMF considered releasing $175 million in PRGF credits to the Kenyan government. The conditions for complete release of assistance comprised of PRGF credits and $250 million in World Bank and donor funds, included progress on privatization and submitting all government-spending proposals to the IMF for approval. As a result, the Kenyan government agreed to considerable government retrenchment and fiscal audits.[71]

In August 2000, the IMF released $150 million in PRGF credits. In September 2000, Moi met with World Bank and IMF leaders in New York and agreed to adopt a Code of Conduct, whereby all top leaders, except Moi, had to declare their wealth. The reform program appeared to be going well.[72]

Once the Kenyan government began receiving donor funding, Moi and his regime reverted to form and began to renege on reform commitments. In March 2001, Moi forced Leakey to resign his positions, replaced him with a loyalist, and slowed the anti-corruption campaign. Commitments that had been made to donors were not fulfilled. Thus, it appeared that the cycle of broken reform pledges and increasing corruption would continue. However, Moi did not to stand for another term and he picked Jomo Kenyatta's son, Uhuru, to stand as the KANU candidate for president.

In the run-up to the November 2002 elections, Uhuru Kenyatta and KANU were unable to promise sufficient patronage and form the necessary alliances to ensure the regime's survival. The resounding victory by Kibaki and the NARC opposition created expectations of rapid economic reform and anti-corruption efforts that would bring a quick deal with the IMF and an influx of foreign exchange, done with World Bank and donor support. However, the fragmented coalition government decided to provide a pay increase for government employees that produced inflationary pressures. The parliament passed anti-corruption laws and established commissions, but the new government was slow to crack down on graft and corruption that appeared within its ranks. Also, the government was slow in liberalizing key sectors of the economy and opening them up to foreign investors. The government was also slow in producing a new constitution that would provide political stability. Kenya's economic recovery was also harmed by the terrorist attacks in Mombasa in November 2002, and subsequent travel warnings that seriously disrupted the tourist industry.

In spite of the slowness of economic reform and external assistance, the conditions for success are much better than under the Moi regime. In July 2003, the Managing Director of the IMF gave a positive assessment of the Kenyan situation and believed that government spending had begun to be restructured in favor of important social and economic sectors, including education and health, in spite of severe budgetary constraints. He discussed financial support for Kenya's development strategy as laid out in the Economic Recovery Strategy for Wealth Creation and Employment.[73] Furthermore, Kibaki's October 2003 state visit to the U.S. helped to make a strong case for aid and investment. Finally, in November 2003, the IMF released $250 million in aid to Kenya, which opened the way to further lending by the World Bank and donors and to foreign direct investment.

Comparative Analysis

In the 1980s, the Kenyan economy was declining but had not sunk to the depths of the Tanzanian and Ugandan economies. Therefore, donors first brought pressure to bear in response to Kenya's poor political performance, especially in the wake of the 1988 elections. Then they increased the pressure for economic reform and democratic transition together, which culminated in the 1991 Paris Club ultimatum and Moi's reluctant adoption of a multi-party system. In contrast, donors pressured Tanzania and Uganda throughout the 1980s for economic reform. In the early 1990s, when Tanzania's reform became infected by corruption, donors applied pressure for political reform and multi-party democracy. In contrast, Uganda succeeded in economic reform and was subjected to relatively little external pressure for multi-party democracy.

Kenya and Uganda have been less politically stable and have suffered from more ethnic conflict than Tanzania. The reasons include the existence of larger and more powerful ethnic groups, Buganda in Uganda and the Kikuyu in Kenya, which initially dominated post-independence politics but were then supplanted by coalitions of rival ethnic groups. In addition, Tanzania's ruling party and government were more cohesive and more successful in nation-building efforts than counterparts in Uganda and Kenya.[74]

Both Moi and Museveni had political bases in smaller ethnic groups and struggled to maintain power. While Museveni could use the no-party state to keep power, Moi was forced to accept multi-partyism, become a plurality president, and, ultimately rely on patronage to remain in power. The result was chronic corruption and running battles with the IMF and World Bank over economic reform. In contrast, as long as Museveni advanced the economic reform program, there was relatively little external pressure for a full democratic transition.

After both Kenya and Tanzania adopted economic reform packages and received flows of aid, both the Moi and Mwinyi regimes reneged on their commitments. In the Tanzanian case, the transition from socialism and the difficulty of combating high-level corruption in the late 1980s and early 1990s help to explain the declining performance of Mwinyi and his regime. Once Mkapa came to power, he broke with the old corrupt order and ensured that Tanzania adhered more faithfully to its economic reform commitments.

In the Kenyan case, the weakness of the Moi regime led to a series of struggles with the IMF and World Bank over reform. The vulnerability of the Moi regime to internal challenges meant that economic reform and democratic transition were implemented only when substantial external economic pressure was applied. Kenya's growing civil society played a secondary role until the 2002 elections, when it led the way in bringing Kibaki to power. The less vulnerable regime in Tanzania has made it possible for economic reform and democratic transition to become home grown. The problem for Tanzania is generating opposition political parties that can challenge the CCM's hold on power.

Comparative analysis demonstrates that economic reform makes an impact on political liberalization and democratic transition. Pressures for good governance that accompany reform programs have exposed the corruption of regimes and led to improvements in political rights and civil liberties, especially a freer press. In the Tanzanian case, elites have been able to manage economic and political reform without losing power, while in Kenya, the ruling elites were eventually supplanted. In Uganda, elites managed economic reform and blocked democratic transition.

As for the donors, they have verbally supported simultaneous economic reform and democratization but, in practice, have supported economic reform above all. This helps to explain the differential treatment of Uganda and Kenya by the donors. As long as Uganda put economic reform first, there were relatively few pressures for democratization against essentially a single-party state. In contrast, in Kenya, the failure to sustain economic reform led to donor pressure for both economic and political reform against a state that has had more multi-party competition than Uganda.

The *"reform first"* position appears valid in the case of Uganda, where the delay in the democratic transition and the autonomy of leaders from special interests allowed economic reforms to bring growth and socio-economic and political stability. Uganda's success in economic reform and growth led to the formation of a positive coalition in favor of economic reform. Popular participation, legislative oversight, and a relatively free press helped to expose corruption and sustain economic reform.

The Tanzanian and Kenyan cases tend to refute the *"reform first"* position and uphold the *"reform-democratization"* position. The adoption of economic reform in Tanzania led to democratic transition and, after some struggle, to relatively high levels of civil and political rights and economic growth. In the Kenyan case, the struggle for economic reform and democratic transition pressured the corrupt Moi regime to open up the political process and paved the way for a new opportunity for democracy, economic recovery, and eventual prosperity under President Kibaki.

Concluding Comments

The differential impact of economic reform on three varying regimes undergoing democratic transitions has been demonstrated and analyzed, as well as the differing tactics of the three regimes attempting to maintain power at the same time as they reform. The nation-building and mobilization efforts of Tanzania's ruling party, from the 1960s onwards, gave the leadership confidence in 1990s that it could proceed with economic reform and then democratic transition without generating major opposition from ethnic groups or political parties. When economic reform slowed, a change in leadership brought renewed commitment to the process. In contrast, Kenyan and Ugandan leaders could not escape ethnic politics, which left them unable to undertake economic reform and democratic transition simultaneously. In Kenya, the economic reform pressures led to the defeat of a corrupt government and democratic succession to one that was committed to reform.

The central themes of democratic transition in East Africa have been echoed by the preceding analysis of the impact of economic reform. The poor economic performance of all three countries in the 1980s brought growing international pressure and an increasingly vocal civil society in each country. This, in turn, led to economic reform and a slowly emerging democratic consensus on the need for accountability, cooperation among different political forces, and constitutional change. International actors throughout the 1990s helped pressure ruling elites for both economic reform and democratic transition.

As Rubongoya elucidates in his chapter, national leadership has been important in determining the trajectory of economic reform, as well as democratic transition. The comparatively cosmopolitan, technocratic leadership of Museveni helps explain Uganda's commitment to economic reform. The neo-patrimonial leadership of Moi provides an understanding of Kenya's struggles with economic reform and democratic transition. The two leadership changes in Tanzania help explain the initial commitment and subsequent recommitment to economic reform and democratic transition. In East Africa, the fragmentation of opposition political parties and the determination of the ruling parties to hang on to political and economic power caused problems with accountability and commitment to reform, as well as the difficulties of achieving regime turnover.

How will East African economic reform and democratic transition fare in an era of globalization?[75] In order to advance in the global economy, all three East African countries must develop their manufacturing and service sectors and compete with China and other large, low-cost producers. The revival of the East African Community

(EAC) will help the three states to become more competitive and will compel them to maintain economic reform programs and sound macroeconomic policies. In 2003, President Kibaki and Kenya led efforts in reviving economic cooperation within the EAC, while inspiring interest in neighbors like Burundi and Rwanda. The problem in integrating East African economies is the fact that Kenya's economy, in particular its manufacturing industry, is more developed than the other countries.

Donors and NGOs will continue to press for good governance and greater democracy, which helps to forestall corruption and foster economic reform and development. At the moment, Uganda and Tanzania appear to be on the right track, though the danger exists of sliding back into corruption and economic mismanagement. In Kenya, the specter of policy reversal will continue to linger, in spite of the new government, thus making donors and investors apprehensive, and slowing regional integration.

Notes

1 Jacques J. Polak, *The World Bank and the IMF: A Changing Relationship* (Washington, D.C.: Brookings Institution, 1994), p. 8. The IMF is a multi-lateral financial institution that provides short-term loans for economic stabilization, usually in response to a balance of payments crisis and rapid decline in the value of a country's currency. IMF loans are quick disbursing and backed by tough conditionality standards. In 1974, the IMF started the Extended Fund Facility (EFF) to finance "structural adjustment" in countries that did not stabilize. The World Bank is a multi-lateral financial institution that provides longer-term loans for economic development, with projects ranging from large-scale infrastructure to "basic needs." In the 1980s, the World Bank joined the IMF in attempting to rescue ailing economies. In March 1986, the IMF and World Bank jointly created the Structural Adjustment Facility (SAF) and the Enhanced Structural Adjustment Facility (ESAF) as vehicles for cooperation in healing ailing economies. The joint efforts of the IMF and World Bank gave rise to Structural Adjustment Programs (SAPs) that became the main type of economic reform that almost every African state adopted during the 1980s and 1990s.

2 Michael Bratton and Nicholas van de Walle, *Democratic Experiments in Africa* (Cambridge: Cambridge University Press, 1997).

3 The author wishes to thank Goran Hyden, John Harbeson, Jeffrey Herbst, and Michael Bratton for reading and commenting on a draft of this chapter and Thomas Callaghy and Nicolas van de Walle for providing specific advice.

4 World Bank, *Adjustment in Africa: Reforms, Results and the Road Ahead* (Washington, D.C.: World Bank, 1994); World Bank, *Can Africa Claim the 21st Century?* (Washington, D.C.: World Bank, 2000); World Bank, *Sub-Saharan Africa: From Crisis to Sustainable Growth* (Washington, D.C.: World Bank, 1989).

5 Robert H. Bates, *Markets and States in Tropical Africa* (Berkeley: University of California Press, 1981).

6 World Bank, *Sub-Saharan Africa.*

7 Samuel P. Huntington, *Political Order in Changing Societies* (New Haven, CT: Yale University Press, 1968); Seymour Martin Lipset, *Political Man* (Garden City, NY: Doubleday, 1960); Robert Dahl, *Polyarchy, Participation, and Opposition* (New Haven, CT: Yale University Press, 1971).

[8] World Bank, *Adjustment*; World Bank, *Can Africa?*; World Bank, *Sub-Saharan Africa.*

[9] Samuel P. Huntington, *The Third Wave: Democratization in the Late Twentieth Century* (Norman: University of Oklahoma Press, 1991); Henry Bienen and Jeffrey Herbst, "The Relationship Between Political and Economic Reform in Africa," *Comparative Politics* vol. 29, no. 1 (October 1996), pp. 23-42.

[10] Robert H. Jackson, *Personal Rule in Black Africa: Prince, Autocrat, Prophet, Tyrant* (Berkeley: University of California Press, 1982); Bratton and van de Walle, *Democratic Experiments in Africa*, pp. 61-68.

[11] Bienen and Herbst, "The Relationship," pp. 23-42.

[12] Thomas M. Callaghy, "The Challenges of Attacking Inequality: The View from Poor Country Debt," International Studies Association conference paper (February 20-24, 2001), pp. 11-14.

[13] Thandika Mkandawire, "Crisis Management and the Making of 'Choiceless Democracies,'" in Richard Joseph, ed., *State, Conflict, and Democracy in Africa* (Boulder, CO: Lynne Rienner, 1999), pp. 119-136.

[14] World Bank, *Adjustment*, pp. 58 and 141.

[15] World Bank, *Adjustment*, pp. 58 and 141. In the wake of the first wave, the World Bank, in *Adjustment in Africa*, evaluated the initiation of reform and the amount of change in macroeconomic policies in 26 countries from the 1981 to 1986 period to the 1987 to 1991 period. Between the two periods, a majority of the 26 states, including Tanzania and Uganda, initiated reform and improved their macroeconomic policies. However, no state sustained reform sufficiently to reach the "good" level. Tanzania scored a "large improvement" for moving away from *ujamaa* socialism, but its policy stance was still judged to be "poor" and, therefore, still had a long way to go in sustaining reform to reach the "good" level.

[16] Nicholas van de Walle, "Globalization and African Democracy," in Richard Joseph, ed., *State, Conflict, and Democracy in Africa* (Boulder, CO: Lynne Rienner, 1999), pp. 95-118.

[17] Bienen and Herbst, "The Relationship," pp. 23-42; Bratton and van de Walle, *Democratic Experiments in Africa*, pp. 61-68.

[18] Jeffrey Sachs, "Growth in Africa: It Can Be Done," *The Economist* (June 29, 1996), p. 19.

[19] Callaghy, "The Challenges," pp. 25-26.

[20] Thomas M. Callaghy, "North-South Relations: Reconfiguration of the Debt Regime," in Thomas M. Callaghy, Ronald Kassimir and Robert Latham, eds., *Intervention and Transnationalism in Africa: Global-Local Networks of Power* (Cambridge: Cambridge University Press, 2001), pp. 115-148. Callaghy comments that the "enhanced" version of HIPC mandates PRSPs (Poverty Reduction Strategy Papers), which must be carried out in consultation with civil society groups, is a major step forward, achieved by the NGOs, and has the long run potential to be beneficial for democracy in Africa.

[21] International Monetary Fund and International Development Association, "Heavily Indebted Poor Countries (HIPC) Initiative-Status of Implementation," Prepared by the Staffs of the IMF and World Bank, September 12, 2003, p. 15.

[22] International Monetary Fund, "Heavily Indebted Poor Countries ...", Annex II, p. 40.

[23] Yoweri Kaguta Museveni, *What is Africa's Problem?* (Kampala: NRM Publications, 1992), pp. 21-27.

[24] Joshua B. Mugyenyi, "IMF Conditionality and Structural Adjustment under the National Resistance Movement," in Holger Hansen and Michael Twaddle, eds., *Changing Uganda* (Oxford: James B. Curry, 1991), p. 70.

[25] Museveni, *What is Africa's?*, pp. 208-216; Ronald Kassimir, "Reading Museveni: Structure, Agency and Pedagogy in Ugandan Politics," *Canadian Journal of African Studies*, vol. 33, no. 2-3 (1999), pp. 649-673.
[26] Arne Bergsten and Steve Kayizzi-Mugerwa, *Crisis, Adjustment, and Growth in Uganda* (NY: St. Martin's, 1999), pp. 50-60.
[27] Brett, "Rebuilding," p. 54.
[28] Nelson Kasfir, "'No-Party Democracy' in Uganda," *Journal of Democracy* vol. 9, no. 2 (April 1998), pp. 49-63.
[29] Franz Schurmann, "Africa is Saving Itself," *Choices: The Human Development Magazine* vol. 5, no. 1 (1996), p. 5.
[30] Schurmann, "Africa," p. 7.
[31] Roy Laishley, "Uganda: Turning Growth into Prosperity," in United Nations *Africa Recovery* vol. 7, no. 2 (October 1993), pp. 16-18.
[32] Brett, "Rebuilding," p. 73.
[33] Laishley, "Uganda," p. 17.
[34] Roger Tangri and Andrew Mwenda, "Corruption and Cronyism in Uganda's Privatization in the 1990s," *African Affairs* vol. 100 (2001), p. 117.
[35] Callaghy, "The Challenges;" Bergsten and Kayizzi-Mugerwa, *Crisis Adjustment*, p. 63.
[36] Callaghy, "The Challenges."
[37] World Bank, *Can Africa?* p. 64.
[38] World Bank Group, *Uganda*, http://www.worldbank.org/afr/ug2.htm, 2000.
[39] Susan Dicklitch, "Between Stability and Anarchy: The Struggle for Democracy in Uganda," American Political Science Association conference paper (August 1999), p. 12.
[40] David E. Sahn, Paul A. Dorosh, and Stephen D. Younger, eds., *Structural Adjustment Reconsidered: Economic Policy and Poverty in Africa* (Cambridge: Cambridge University Press, 1997), p. 24.
[41] World Bank Group, *Uganda.*
[42] World Bank, *Can Africa?*, p. 76.
[43] World Bank Group, *Uganda.*
[44] Tangri and Mwenda, "Corruption and Cronyism," pp. 128-131.
[45] Philip Gourevitch, "Forsaken: Congo Seems Less a Nation than a Battlefield for Countless African Armies," *The New Yorker* (September 25, 2000), pp. 53-67.
[46] Goran Hyden, *Beyond Ujamaa in Tanzania: Underdevelopment and an Uncaptured Peasantry* (University of California Press, 1980); Andrew Coulson, *Tanzania: A Political Economy* (Oxford: Oxford University Press, 1982).
[47] World Bank Group, *Tanzania*, http://www.worldbank.org/html/extdr/offrep/afr/tz2.htm, 1998.
[48] Goran Hyden, "Top-Down Democratization in Tanzania," *Journal of Democracy* vol. 10, no. 4 (October 1999), pp. 142-155.
[49] World Bank Group, *Tanzania.*
[50] Michael F., Lofchie, "The Politics of Agricultural Policy," in Joel D. Barkan, ed., *Beyond Capitalism versus Socialism in Kenya and Tanzania* (Boulder, CO: Lynne Rienner, 1994), pp. 164-171.
[51] Joel D. Barkan, ed., *Beyond Capitalism versus Socialism in Kenya and Tanzania* (Boulder, CO: Lynne Rienner, 1994), p. 30.
[52] Julius E. Nyang'oro, "Civil Society, Democratization, and State Building in Kenya and Tanzania," in Kidane Mengisteab and Cyril Daddieh, eds., *State Building Democratization in Africa* (Westport, CT: Praeger, 1999), pp. 186-187.
[53] Barkan, *Beyond*, p. 31.

[54] Michael Chege, "The Return of Multi-party Politics," in Joel D. Barkan, ed., *Beyond Capitalism versus Socialism in Kenya and Tanzania* (Boulder, CO: Lynne Rienner, 1994), p. 55.
[55] Hyden, "Top-Down," p. 145.
[56] World Bank Group, *Tanzania.*
[57] Robert Pinkney, *Democracy and Dictatorship in Ghana and Tanzania* (New York: St. Martin's Press, 1997), pp. 197-208.
[58] Nyang'oro, "Civil Society," p. 189.
[59] Hyden, "Top-Down," pp. 145 and 153.
[60] World Bank Group, *Tanzania.*
[61] Hyden, "Top-Down," p. 142.
[62] Barkan, *Beyond*, p. 27.
[63] Nyang'oro, "Civil Society," p. 193.
[64] Nyang'oro, "Civil Society," p. 186.
[65] Barkan, *Beyond*, p. 37.
[66] Barkan, *Beyond*, p. 40.
[67] United Kingdom, "The Goldenberg Affair," (UK Home Office, Immigration and Nationality Directorate, August 1999), http://www.ind.homeoffice.gov.uk/default.asp?pageid= 569.
[68] Joel D. Barkan and Njuguna Ng'ethe, ed., "Kenya Tries Again," *Journal of Democracy* vol. 9, no. 2 (April 1998), p. 37.
[69] World Bank Group, *Kenya*, http://www.worldbank.org/afr/ke2.htm, September 2000.
[70] Barkan and Ng'ethe, p. 39.
[71] "Breakfast at the Bank," *Africa Confidential* (September 15, 2000), pp. 2-3.
[72] "Breakfast," pp. 2-3.
[73] International Monetary Fund, "Managing Director's Visit to Kenya," July 9, 2003, http://www.imf.org/external/np/sec/pr/2003/pr03107.htm.
[74] Dirk Berg-Schlosser, Dirk and Rainer Siegler. *Political Stability and Development: A Comparative Analysis of Kenya, Tanzania, and Uganda* (Boulder, CO: Lynne Rienner, 1990).
[75] Van de Walle, "Globalization," pp. 95-118.

Chapter 8

International Context

Bruce Heilman and Laurean Ndumbaro

This chapter focuses on the strategies utilized by Western donor countries and multi-lateral financial institutions (IMF, World Bank, and Paris Club[1]) to encourage the creation of more plural political systems in East Africa.[2] In trying to achieve this goal, donors employed two basic strategies: dialogue and political conditionality for aid. The exact mix of dialogue and conditionality depended on donor interests, the willingness of East African political leaders to implement political and economic reforms, and their desire to maintain cooperation in other fields. Donors were confrontational in Kenya under Moi and more accommodating in Tanzania. In Uganda, external actors quietly pushed for a more plural political order, indulging the NRM's concerns about multi-party politics leading to increased insecurity and heightened ethnic tensions. In evaluating the efficacy of donor interventions, diplomacy and economic leverage was exerted to pressure political leaders to enact reforms that fell short of establishing durable and viable democracies, especially in the area of free and fair elections to chose the president. Donor efforts to promote democratization were hindered by the following factors: counter measures taken by the ruling regimes to maintain their grip on power; a lack of agreement among donors on the best way to promote democracy; and the individual interests of donors covering a broad range of areas (economic, humanitarian, and security), which precluded democratization from being the sole defining issue in donor relations with East African governments.[3]

Historical Overview of Donor Relations with East African Governments

The important role of donors in the East African democratization processes cannot be understood separate from larger political and economic trends. The globalization of a market economy and the collapse of communism transformed donor interests in developing areas and modified the purpose, approach, and philosophy of aid provision. Prior to the 1980s, aid was tailored to fit the development plans of each East African country. Since East African governments were not completely dependent on outside funds to support their public administrations after independence, these governments were able to control, at least in part, their development agenda.[4] The radical influence of the dependency school, coupled with the lack of a generally accepted development framework among donors, facilitated bilateral relations based on priorities determined in East

Africa.[5] Reinforcing the autonomy of East African governments was a difficult moral position for Western countries to take, since their lectures on democracy and human rights were undermined by a history of colonial occupation and the support of white domination throughout southern Africa. However, the most important reason why East African countries had latitude in devising their own domestic political and economic policies was the Cold War.

The Cold War era was dominated by two superpowers trying to enhance their global strategic concerns in the region. Both the U.S (the champion of democracy) and the Soviet Union (the vanguard of the revolutionary struggle to liberate the oppressed Third World) were primarily interested in East African countries as geo-strategic allies. This enabled East African states to extract resources from both sides of the ideological divide. For example, as the Soviet Union strengthened its position in the Horn of Africa, the U.S. countered by rapidly increasing military aid to Kenya, reaching an agreement in 1980 to use its airfields and the port of Mombasa.[6] It also followed that the West tolerated autocratic single, or no-party systems until the end of the Cold War. During this period, except for the extreme case of Idi Amin, democracy and human rights were not central issues of concern for Western donors.

Although not a core feature of Western foreign policy prior to the end of the Cold War, the desire to tie foreign aid to human rights can be seen as early the 1961 Foreign Assistance Act that outlined the U.S. goal of promoting democracy in a number of developing countries. By the 1970s, the Carter administration actively promoted human rights in its foreign policy, but not at the expense of fighting communist expansion. In response to a severe crackdown on political dissidents in 1986-87, both the U.S. Congress and State Department issued strongly worded criticisms of the Kenyan government. However, no specific threats were made to curtail aid.[7] Even countries such as Sweden, that currently have democracy at the top of their agendas, did not actively promote this ideal during the Cold War. Generally speaking, most donor countries sought to separate development from politics, at least on the surface, by presenting their assistance as "apolitical." Non-interference in domestic politics was the order of the day and a country that seemed to undermine donor interests was mainly rebuked in private.[8]

By the mid 1980s it was clear that East Africa's rulers failed to keep their independence promises to promote social, economic, and political development, prompting donors to redefine their role. Donors attributed economic stagnation in East Africa to state intervention in the market, through misguided socialist policies in Tanzania, financial support for inefficient parastatal corporations in Kenya, and erratic and arbitrary dictatorship in Uganda. During the economic crisis years, or the 'lost decade' of the 1980s, multi-lateral financial institutions bartered access to desperately needed foreign capital in return for economic liberalization, leading to a major reorientation of domestic social policies in East Africa. Previously free or subsidized services, such as education and health care, were phased out through the introduction of cost-sharing (user fees).

As the 1980s economic crisis deepened, internal dissatisfaction with the status quo of single-party states grew. The existing political orders in Kenya, Tanzania, and Uganda were losing legitimacy as they failed to live up to citizen expectations and proved incapable of reversing economic decline. The downfall of the single-party communist regimes in Eastern Europe also impacted on the thinking of donors and governments in the region. One pertinent realization was that dictators, with all of their military and financial power, could not stop highly mobilized democratic forces and that repression alone was not a viable strategy for remaining in power.

The end of the Cold War made it politically prudent for donors to contend that unrestrained authoritarian regimes interfered with human rights and retarded economic growth. By 1989, the World Bank began linking political reform to development.[9] Limiting state intervention in the economy was increasingly connected in donor circles to a more general effort to encourage political reforms, such as allowing a free media and independent civil society organizations. In the United States, Herman J. Cohen, Assistant Secretary of State for African Affairs under George Bush Sr., for the first time suggested that the provision of assistance would be tied to good governance, asserting that single-party states did not allow for investment and economic growth.[10] According to President Bush Sr., with the end of the Cold War, it was time for Africa to follow other parts of the world in creating more democratic systems and the U.S. would support this process.[11]

By the early 1990s, even the more indulgent Scandinavian countries accepted the "Washington consensus," which refers to the shared belief that economic growth depends on the privatization of state-owned companies, the deregulation of economic activities, the encouragement of competition, balanced budgets, and political reforms.[12] The "Washington consensus" underpinned the coordination of individual donor activities with those of the IMF, World Bank, and Paris Club.[13] In essence, donors were now united by a common vision, which called for the adoption of multi-party politics and increased respect for human rights.

The new global environment at the end of the Cold War is a key variable that explains why donors took the lead in pressing for a more plural order and why East African leaders were willing to reengage in the often contentious dialogue of reform. As with domestic proponents of political liberalization, external actors attempted to alter the power balance inside Kenya, Tanzania, and Uganda by reducing the long enjoyed hegemony of the single-party regime. Unlike domestic activists, however, donors were ambivalent about changing the regimes in power and were more interested in reform and maintaining cordial bilateral relations.

Current Debates on the External Politics Surrounding Liberalization

While outside influence featured prominently in the domestic politics of the three East African countries, it was not decisive in creating viable democracies. Although multi-party politics was adopted in two of the region's three countries, all East African elections since 1992 were manipulated, in varying degrees, to favor the ruling parties.[14] Indeed, the first electoral transfer of power to an opposition party took place in Kenya in 2002.[15] The failure to turn political liberalization into democracy is strongly related to three factors that enhance the ability of ruling parties to manage donor demands for political reform.[16] First, given the history of colonial occupation, donor interest in transforming economic and political systems in East Africa raises concerns regarding national sovereignty. Second, unlike the economic realm, where a template exists on how to create market economies, donors have not reached a consensus on a one-size-fits-all model for building viable democracies for all three countries. Third, the desire to promote democracy in Kenya, Tanzania, and Uganda is tempered by other foreign policy goals of individual donor states, in particular security concerns.

Sovereignty

External efforts to promote democracy in East Africa are exclusively Western and take place against the historical background of imperialism, colonialism, and neo-colonialism.[17] Widespread poverty, low levels of development, and slow, sometimes stagnant, economic growth have forced East Africa's ruling parties to seek outside resources in order to shore up fragile domestic economies and unbalanced government budgets. Slightly over 50 percent of Uganda's government budget in 2002 came from external sources, while in 1996, 33 percent of Tanzania's budget came from donors.[18] From the late 1980s, Kenya's economy has been severely affected by the frequent interruptions of loan disbursements by the World Bank and IMF. By the 1990s, the donors' unprecedented influence in the region created the challenge of maintaining the tenuous balance between promoting democratic reforms and respecting sovereignty.

Donor activism in support of democracy has been the subject criticism by democracy activists, who argue that donor resources enable autocratic regimes to stay in power.[19] Cynics among the activists contend that Western demands for reform represent an attempt to co-opt the democratic struggle. Rather than equating support for reform with a commitment to democratic ideals, critics charge that donors are motivated by the fear of loosing allies should authoritarian regimes be replaced by peoples' movements that might be less supportive of short-term, Western economic and strategic interests.[20] However, while Kibaki's election in Kenya would fall short of a people's movement, it does illustrate that given the dependency of East African countries on external support, whoever controls the government will have to come to terms with Western interests. Indeed, one of the major preoccupations of Kibaki's regime has been to reopen the flows of IMF and World Bank loans in an effort to transform the moribund economy. Donor activities are also open to criticism from ruling elites, who charge that demands for internal political change is nothing short of neo-colonialism.

Donor-recipient relations can be depicted in terms of a competitive game. One player, East African leaders, have an interest in maximizing the flow of donor resources into their countries while at the same time ensuring that these economic assets are used to enhance, rather than undermine, their ability to rule. The other player, donors, have to show that aid produces results in terms of reducing poverty, promoting development, enhancing trade, increasing security, building democracy, and strengthening friendly regimes. Given that the objectives of donor and recipient countries can conflict, it is not surprising that much of the politics surrounding this relationship centers on who controls how aid is used, and whether effective 'partnerships' can be established that enable both actors to achieve their goals.

While donors speak of development partnerships with the East African countries, the local governments often have a different perspective. For CCM in Tanzania and NRM in Uganda, the partnership is based on a reluctant acceptance of externally derived policies. In the case of Kenya under Moi, government officials described conditionalities as outright ultimatums.[21] In November 2001, the Kenyan Finance Minister Chris Okemo struck a responsive chord in many African governments when he charged the IMF with forcing governments to adopt policies drawn up in Washington or risk losing millions of dollars in vital aid.[22] The donor response to charges of neo-imperialism are based on the idea that recipient states are cleverly substituting 'conditionality' for 'accountability'. In essence, donors counter that aid recipients have often misused external funds and then deflect criticisms of the lack of economic progress onto external actors.[23]

The struggle between donors and recipient governments highlights a paradox of outside efforts to build democracies. Rather than encouraging grassroots participation in the policy process, structural adjustment programs and aid conditionalities empower domestically unaccountable donor institutions to set much of the domestic agenda.[24] KANU (until 2002), CCM, and NRM have exploited this contradiction by framing their resistance to donor calls for greater democratization in terms of protecting national sovereignty, which adds legitimacy to state actions that undermine 'foreign' backed opposition groups and 'alien' democratic practices.

After the 1995 elections in Tanzania, the ruling party openly taunted the opposition presidential candidate Augustine Mrema and the opposition party CUF for running to 'foreign embassies' with grievances over electoral misconduct.[25] While clearly this is a partisan political charge, nonetheless it has some truth. In Zanzibar, Uganda, and Kenya prior to the 2002 elections, the opposition called for suspension of foreign aid. In Tanzania, it was not until January 2001 that CUF made the mobilization of mass civil disobedience, as opposed to pleading its case with donors, the cornerstone of efforts to pressure the ruling regime to enact reforms.

Ruling parties, resentful of the erosion of their autonomy over what they see as domestic political and economic affairs, angrily maintain that their governments, and not donors, represent the people of East Africa. However, government charges of foreign domination are often exaggerated. For example, the leader of a well respected, politically oriented NGO in Tanzania disputed the accusation of foreign control over civil society by noting that while donors expect strict accountability for their funds, they leave the choice of activities up to the local organizations.[26]

Lack of Consensus

A second dilemma facing donors is the lack of consensus on how to build democracies. Prior to the 2002 Kenyan elections, all three countries seemed to face a similar democratization dilemma, namely that political competition was constrained by some form of single-party rule. More specifically, the nationalist parties that guided Tanzania and Kenya to independence continued their domination of the political arena as the sole legal political parties under second generation Presidents Mwinyi and Moi. In Uganda, the no-party government struck many as being another variation of a single-party state. However, many external observers agreed that this broad regional similarity of banning political competition based on rival parties hid fundamental differences in the three countries. In contrast to the "Washington consensus" on economic liberalization, specific ways to promote successful democratic transitions, other than the basic demands for multi-party politics, the presence of a vibrant civil society, and a free press, have not been coherently articulated. Donors have not developed a universal model for building democracy and they see this process as particularistic, based on an individual country's history, culture, and political system. While the single-party regimes in Tanzania and Kenya were well institutionalized, the former was cooperating with donors to build a market economy and the later was battling them over issues of economic mismanagement and political reform. In Uganda, the military regime was younger and primarily concerned with asserting and consolidating its power. Other differences in political development included dissimilar levels of ethnic politicization, and a variation in the nature as well as the strength of both the domestic opposition and external security threats, which also shaped the responses of the three East African governments to outside pressures for reform. The ambiguity surrounding democratization allows Western governments to claim that they support political reforms while also maintaining cooperation with regimes in power, even if they are not making progress toward building democracy.

Competing Donor Foreign Policy Goals

The third problem in promoting democracy is the conflicting foreign policy objectives of Western governments. Democratization competes with other parallel goals, such as increasing trade and investment; supporting market oriented economic reform programs; fighting corruption; humanitarian concerns such as improving the status of women, increasing literacy rates, and combating infectious diseases like HIV/AIDs; protecting the environment; and promoting donor security interests.[27] These security interests include: securing support for the 1991-2 Gulf War; reducing ethnic violence in Kenya; stemming rebel attacks in western and northern Uganda and reducing Uganda's involvement in the Democratic Republic of the Congo; soliciting assistance during the Somali humanitarian crisis; coping with the 1994 genocide in Rwanda; investigating the 1998 bombings of the U.S. embassies in Nairobi and Dar es Salaam; requesting help for negotiations to end the Burundi, Somali, and Sudanese civil wars; working together on the 'war against terrorism'; and seeking support for the donor state's position regarding the 2003 U.S. coalition for the invasion of Iraq. In particular, the war on terrorism has become a major issue in the relationship between East Africa and the West. The bombings of U.S. embassies in Kenya and Tanzania were linked to Al Qaeda, an organization blamed for a number of terrorist attacks against Western targets, including the September 11, 2001, suicide airplane hijackings that destroyed the World Trade Center and damaged the Pentagon. On November 28th 2002, Kenya's port city of Mombasa was the site of a deadly car bomb attack on an Israeli-owned beach hotel, and a shoulder-launched missile that narrowly missed a large chartered jet plane filled with Israeli tourists. Early in 2004, the U.S. government charged that members of the Al Haramain Islamic Foundation, an organization with branches in Kenya and Tanzania, had links to Al Qaeda and plotted to destroy tourist hotels in Zanzibar in 2003. In response to terrorist activities in the region, some Western countries have occasionally imposed flight bans and issued travel warnings. All East African countries have co-operated closely with donors in trying to deal with terrorism, by passing anti-terrorism legislation modeled on the U.S. Patriot Act and having local police forces work closely with the FBI in monitoring and apprehending terrorist suspects.

The ruling parties in Kenya, Tanzania, and Uganda have exploited the different agendas of donors. Recipient states have cooperated with the West in terms of post-9/11 security matters and implementing limited political reforms. However, even when accounting for the December 2002 elections in Kenya, all three East African countries have steadfastly refused to hold free and fair elections. In short, by cooperating in some areas, Tanzania and Uganda were more successful than Kenya in preventing democracy from becoming the defining issue in their relationship to the West and a pretext for reducing levels of assistance.

Kenya

In the first two decades after independence, the United States and Britain had considerable influence over Kenya's development.[28] Throughout this period Britain remained Kenya's largest foreign investor and trading partner. Britain played a central role in creating the young country's armed forces, which grew out of the colonial forces created to protect British interests in East Africa. In addition to supplying weapons, equipment, and training, many British officers stayed on after independence (the Army stayed under British Command until 1969 and the Navy until 1972).[29] Kenya began receiving U.S. military aid in 1976 and has cooperated with the U.S. on numerous military activities. The Kenyan government supported the U.S.-led boycott of the 1980 Moscow Olympics and it refrained from criticizing the Western powers for their support of *apartheid* South Africa. Thus, Kenyan accommodation of Western interests was a familiar phenomenon.

With structural adjustment in the 1980s, the donors' new economic role in Kenya was not as significant for that country as was the case in Tanzania. Structural adjustment did not fundamentally alter Kenya's market oriented development trajectory, change the domestic power balance, or modify Kenya's relationship with donors. It was not until the end of the 1980s that the Kenyan regime began to feel the pressure of more interventionist donor activities designed to reduce corruption and create a more plural political system. It was at this time that donors, particularly the United States, started to publicly criticize the Kenyan government. Previously, there were no serious public donor denunciations, even when prominent national personalities were mysteriously killed.[30]

Of the three East African countries, Kenya fought the fiercest battles in the 1990s against increased external influence over political affairs. In pushing for multi-party politics, the United States and Germany took the lead and other donors followed. The nature of the new era in Kenyan-U.S. relations was outlined in President Bush's 1989 inaugural speech:

> A new breeze is blowing. Because of that wind, a world refreshed by freedom seems reborn; for in man's heart, if not in fact, the day of the dictator is over. The totalitarian era is passing. We know how to secure a more just and prosperous life for man on earth: through free markets, free speech, free elections and exercise of free will unhampered by the state.

As opposition to Moi's rule gained momentum both internally and externally, 1990 marked a turning point in the relationship between Kenya and donor countries, with the democratic transition degenerating into a confrontation between the government, on one hand, and the multi-party activists and the donor community (especially U.S., Norway, Denmark, Sweden, and Germany) on the other. Symbolic of the opposition-donor partnership was U.S. Ambassador Smith Hempstone's May 3rd speech to a Nairobi Rotary Club when he warned that Congress would cut off aid to Kenya if the government did not make progress toward building a democratic society. On the same day, multi-party activists announced the formation of FORD and demanded the legalization of multi-party politics.[31] The government steadfastly refused. President Moi declared that Kenya would not be pressured into a new system of government and that external forces would not dictate how to run domestic affairs. Faced with Moi's intransigence, FORD organized mass rallies, which the government banned and violently dispersed while also arresting high profile activists like businessman Kenneth Matiba and former Nairobi Mayor Charles Rubia.

In response to the crackdown, the international community, led by the United States, through its maverick Ambassador Smith Hempstone exerted more pressure on the Kenyan government to accept multi-party politics. Hempstone broke diplomatic precedents by openly criticizing Moi's government for its lack of democracy and human rights. He also started to openly support FORD, further encouraging the multi-party activists.[32] Congress made it clear that unless the Moi administration adopted multi-party politics; ended queue voting in the party nomination process;[33] abolished detention without trial; and restored the freedom of the judiciary;[34] the allocation of U.S. military aid to Kenya (worth $ 5 million), as well as future appropriations, would be terminated.[35] The German government supported the U.S. ultimatums.

However, not all donors agreed with the U.S.-German agenda. Other members of the international community, particularly Britain, remained silent. Perhaps because of its large commercial interests or due to the strong cultural ties (Kenya has the second largest number of British expatriates living in Africa), Britain rhetorically encouraged democracy in a general sense while at the same time taking no concrete steps to implement this stated objective.[36] However, not until after the advent of FORD did the British press and local activists begin to criticize the British government for its callous attitude toward serious human rights violations. The British government subsequently called on Kenya to end corruption, improve its human rights record, and adopt multi-partyism. Other Western governments, especially Sweden, Norway, Denmark, and Canada consistently raised complaints about human rights violations, corruption, and an unfree press. These donors began to consult with multi-party activists and threatened to withhold aid if the Moi regime did not improve. In one incident, an incensed Kenyan government broke off diplomatic relations with Norway and expelled its ambassador, who publicly protested the treatment of the political prisoner Koigi wa Wamere, who had been a resident of Norway. The confrontation cost the Kenyan government at least $31 million in canceled Norwegian aid. In a meeting with Vice President Saitoti, Western donors made it clear that they would not disburse aid to Kenya if the Moi administration failed to make satisfactory political reforms.[37] They gave the government a six-month ultimatum to improve its human rights record and governance practices.

It is important to note that while the Kenyan government was publicly denouncing international community demands, it was simultaneously implementing a reform agenda, albeit unevenly. By the end of 1990, the government implemented a number of the international community's demands, particularly those advocated by the United States, such as enhancing judicial independence by restoring the security of tenure for judges. Additionally, controversial voting methods were abandoned and a number of jailed multi-party advocates were released.

Despite these concessions, the government did not back down from its heavy-handed tactics nor did it legalize opposition political parties. As the Moi regime continued to suppress popular demands for democratization, Smith Hempstone announced that the remaining five million dollars of yet to be dispersed defense funds that Congress made conditional on reforms would be withheld, that the disbursement of $15 million in aid for 1991 would depend on fundamental steps toward creating a plural political system, and that Congress would reduce future aid.[38]

Following a public meeting called by FORD in November 1991, the Kenyan government re-arrested prominent critics of the Moi regime, including Kenneth Matiba and Charles Rubia. A number of donors reacted with a six-month suspension of aid to Kenya, subject to socio-economic and political reforms. This was the second to last nail in the coffin of government resistance to multi-party politics. The last nail was driven home shortly after a November 26, 1991, Paris Club meeting, when donor states decided to withhold new government-to-government loans worth $350 million, unless Kenya introduced multi-party politics and took steps to curb corruption.[39] On December 3, 1991, barely a week after the Paris Club meeting, the Kenyan government capitulated, launching a second era of multi-party politics through a presidential decree.

Since the creation of a multi-party political system in 1991, donor-Kenyan relations have tended to follow the general pattern of internal opposition activism, government crackdown, and donor warnings that support may be withdrawn. In the election year of 1997, countrywide disturbances provoked a harsh state response to protestors, resulting in the closure of universities and donor threats to cut aid. Despite the disturbances, Moi was re-elected on December 19th. Although donors provided funds for some aspects of the 1992 and 1997 elections (including civic and voter education programs) and support for NGOs (such as human rights organizations, women's legal aid organizations and policy advocacy groups), authoritarianism nonetheless remained an important part of the Kenyan political scene.

Donor efforts to pressure the Moi regime to accept political reforms can be explained two ways. First, Kenya was an important friend and strategic ally in the region, suggesting that Western states were concerned about the durability of bilateral ties if the opposition overthrew the Moi government. By supporting the liberalization of the political system, the U.S. and Germany hoped to build goodwill among Moi's opponents, which would pay off should they come to power. Democracy activists provocatively argued that donors enabled the Moi regime to stay in power by ignoring widespread and fundamental electoral manipulation, thus precluding any chance of the opposition taking power.[40] A strong case can be made that donor support for multi-party politics fell short of successfully pressuring for democracy, given the absence of free and fair elections. During the 1992 and 1997 contests, electoral rules were set by the KANU-controlled government to favor the ruling party. The government used intimidation against the opposition, and there was widespread manipulation of voter registration roles and vote counting. Some democracy activists further charged that donors suppressed or downplayed reports of electoral malpractice fearing a breakdown of political and economic order should aid be withheld.

Despite the charges of democracy activists, Kenya experienced a drastic reduction in Official Development Assistance (ODA) corresponding to growing donor concerns about democracy prior to the 2002 elections. Before democracy became a major concern for developed countries, the average ODA for Kenya in 1988-89 was $1,150 million.[41] By 1999 the total had dropped to $302 million, suggesting that the Kenyan government paid a price for its opposition to the political reform process.[42] In July 2001, the IMF suspended a three-year package worth $216 million and two weeks later the World Bank withdrew credits worth $71.6 million, leaving the government with a $316 million budget deficit.[43] Both institutions were upset over government backtracking on promised reforms aimed at reducing high-level corruption.

In the unprecedented 2002 election, opposition parties succeeded in doing what they failed to do in 1992 and 1997, they united to defeat KANU. Although the European Election Observer team noted that there was less violence in 2002 as compared to the 1992 and 1997, in other respects the 2002 elections closely resembled the previous ones, with charges of KANU misusing the state in an attempt to win the elections.[44] While it is impossible to completely understand the calculations behind Moi's decision not to run, it is clear that he wanted to hand over power to his handpicked successor Uhuru Kenyatta. He probably would have succeeded had the opposition not formed the NARC coalition. Unlike Tanzania and Uganda, Kenya had also fallen out of favor with the IMF, World Bank and the donor community. Cut off from IMF and World Bank loans, Kenya was registering a dismal GDP annual growth rates (1.6 percent in 1998 and 1.1 percent in 2001).[45] However, with the transfer of power to NARC, donors increased their support for the Kenya. The World Bank resumed loans to the government in July 2003, and the IMF in November 2003.[46] In the following year, German Chancellor Gerhard Shroeder announced that official assistance to Kenya would double to $30.7 million per year for the next two years.[47]

Tanzania

While the fiercest battles between the Kenyan government and the donor community did not start until the political reform era of the 1990s, in Tanzania the most heated confrontation occurred over economic policies a decade earlier. Initially, Tanzania staunchly resisted the expansion of the donors' role in the economy but eventually the government cooperated with Western countries in implementing political reforms. Unlike Kenya, which fought against the tide of political reform, the Tanzanian government accepted it and was able to determine the mode and the speed of transition. Thus, Tanzania adopted multi-party politics in July 1992, but it did not hold its first general elections under that system until 1995.

Tanzanian opposition to structural adjustment programs during the 1980s was more significant than in other East African countries because under Nyerere's leadership, the government implemented the president's vision of socialist development and it had a Pan-Africanist foreign policy agenda that included support for armed struggles against Western colonialism. Soon after gaining independence in 1961, Tanzania broke off relations with Portugal due to its colonial occupation of parts of southern and west Africa. In the early 1960s Cubans (including Che Guevara) supporting Congo's Simba rebels covertly used Tanzanian territory. By the mid-1960s, Nyerere's administration was in conflict with West Germany, United Kingdom, and the United States over Tanzanian support of nationalist movements, the establishment of an East German consulate in Zanzibar, and the refusal of Great Britain to take action against the white settlers' Unilateral Declaration of Independence (UDI) in Rhodesia.[48] In 1967 and again in 1971 a substantial amount of British-owned property in Tanzania was nationalized. In 1970 construction started on the Chinese funded TAZARA railway from Dar es Salaam to Zambia and by 1971 the People's Republic of China became Tanzania's most important donor. However, the ability of Nyerere to plot a course independent of that set by the West was weakened in the 1980s by a stagnant economy and decreasing external support. From 1979-86, the government battled against the imposition of the IMF and World Bank structural adjustment programs. However, as the economy deteriorated and donors began to unite behind a common development framework, Tanzania succumbed to the pressure by signing an agreement with the IMF in 1986. In return for assistance from the IMF and World Bank, conditionalities aimed at reducing the role of the state in the economy had to be met.

The Tanzanian government was reluctant to accept the IMF/World Bank reform package because it necessitated fundamental changes not only in economic policies but also in its relationship with donors and domestic politics. Capitulation to the World Bank/IMF meant a reversal of most, if not all, of the major policies adopted by Tanzania since independence. Through structural adjustment, the donor community wanted to set the guidelines for Tanzania's economic policy and to chart the trajectory of societal development. In the new division of labor, donors became the economic policy makers in Tanzania while the government implemented an externally formulated, market-friendly agenda. Given Tanzania's history of principled socialism, anti-colonialism, and anti-imperialism, this was a difficult decision to make. Structural adjustment undermined the credibility of the regime in power through the rollback of welfare policies that CCM presented to citizens as the "fruits of independence." Ultimately, the international community was able to force Tanzania to accept economic liberalization against its free "will." This was a turning point in the Tanzania-donor relationship, making donors a powerful actor in Tanzania's domestic socio-economic affairs. Further, by shifting economic resources from the state to the private sector, donors significantly altered the internal power balance, undermining an African middle class dependent on state employment in favor of an emerging business community, which included many non-Africans.[49]

The unsuccessful experience of resisting economic conditionalities in the 1980s made the regime in power more accommodative to donor demands for political pluralism in the 1990s. However, CCM's initial response to political reforms was negative, with Mwinyi stating that Tanzania was not ready for plural politics.[50] Mwinyi felt that Tanzania needed economic development, not competing political parties. However, the ruling party's first instinct to fight the tide of political reform was soon dropped in favor of a strategy of trying to manage change. Mwinyi used the well-known Swahili proverb "when your neighbor is being shaved, you need to get prepared" to express the government's realization that political liberalization was inevitable, if not completely desirable. In contrast to Kenya, where strong domestic political forces were at the vanguard of calls for political reforms, in Tanzania internal groups had problems mobilizing opposition to the single-party CCM regime. In 1991, the government-appointed Nyalali Commission investigated whether a single- or multi-party system was best for Tanzania and despite a vast majority of the respondents preferring a single-party system,[51] the Commission recommended the adoption of a multi-party system, which CCM proceeded to do on its own terms.

The Nordic countries that balked at forcefully pushing IMF conditionalities during the 1980s, spearheaded political reforms during the 1990s. They sponsored the first public meeting that established the National Convention for Construction and Reform (NCCR), which later grew into an opposition political party, and they supported the establishment of an independent media. In addition to limited pressure to open up the political system, the international community funded important activities to support the democratization process, such as judicial reform and the 1995 and 2000 general elections (including civic and voter education programs carried out by NGOs and the Tanzania Electoral Commission). They also assisted several human rights organizations, a research and education for democracy NGO, and policy advocacy groups. These activities were designed to have both short and long–term effects on the democratization process in Tanzania through creating a supportive political culture. Despite these activities, there was minimal donor pressure to force the government to implement Nyalali Commission recommendations aimed at establishing an even playing field for political parties or to push for meaningful electoral competition. This can be explained by the fact that the adoption of multi-party politics was the donors' primary goal.[52] While donors were united behind the goal of establishing mulit-partyism in the country, disagreements emerged on how to approach the transition after the adoption of a multi-party constitution.[53]

Despite the outward appearance of harmony between donors and the CCM government, whenever outside demands were deemed too intrusive, warnings to respect Tanzanian sovereignty were forcefully issued. During the 1995 and 2000 Tanzanian elections, CCM accused the West of engaging in a plot to remove independence era African nationalist parties from power. In late January 2001, President Mkapa again warned donors to respect Tanzanian sovereignty after their harsh criticism of the way police handled a CUF demonstration against the fundamentally flawed Zanzibar election in which at least 23 people died and 2,000 refugees fled to Kenya. Later, in April 2001, CCM once again accused donors of plotting to remove their party from power after the Dutch announced that some of their democratization program funds were to be made available to struggling opposition political parties.[54] Nonetheless, despite reservations, the Tanzanian government reluctantly accepted ownership of the political reform process advocated by its powerful development partners.

Notwithstanding arguments over the boundary line demarcating the areas for acceptable donor interventions in the political system, relations between donors and Tanzania remained cordial throughout the political reform period, except for the brief suspension of aid in 1994 over the inability of Tanzania to raise domestic revenues to fund the national budget. The close relations between donors and Tanzania are reflected in ODA statistics. Contrary to the situation in Kenya, Tanzania maintained its levels of ODA throughout the 1990s and into the new century. Before the political reform process began (1988-89), Tanzania received 2.6 percent of the total ODA from developed countries. By 1998-99 this amount remained fairly constant at 2.5 percent of the total ODA.[55] In dollar terms ODA has fluctuated during this period from around $800 million to $1 billion per year.[56] In 2002, ten donor countries ranked Tanzania among the ten most favorable destinations for their ODA, while the more troubled Kenya was not on any donor top-ten list prior to its 2002 elections.[57]

One political event that forced donors to translate their displeasure into reduced support was the disputed 1995 elections on the semi-autonomous islands of Zanzibar. In the aftermath of the Zanzibar election, most donors suspended aid to the islands while maintaining support for the Union. Interestingly, soon after the 2000 elections in Zanzibar, which were procedurally worse than in 1995, many donors expressed their interest in resuming aid to the islands.[58] Donors quietly supported direct negotiations between CCM and CUF with the aim of reducing tensions on the island. As part of an agreement reached between the two political parties, by-elections were held in Pemba in the constituencies where the CUF members of the Zanzibar House of Representatives were expelled for boycotting that legislative body's proceedings. In 2003, for the first time in Zanzibar's troubled political history, multi-party elections, closely watched by domestic and international observer groups, were conducted without any difficulties. Although the by-elections on Pemba were mainly symbolic because they did not effect who controlled the Presidency or House of Representatives (which remained in the hands of CCM), they nonetheless raised hopes that the 2005 elections, which determine who will hold power on the islands, might also be conducted in a peaceful and fair manner.[59]

Overall, Tanzania traveled a different path than Kenya, where political conditionalities on aid were invoked to make the government succumb to popular demands for political liberalization. In Tanzania, donors in dialogue with government worked to support political reforms. This was possible partly because when Tanzania reached an agreement with the IMF in 1986, it maintained amicable relations with donors by implementing cost-sharing policies and reducing the public sector labor force in return for the donors' good will in implementing political reforms.

Uganda

Uganda, more than any East African country, highlights the tradeoffs involved in donor-recipient state relations. During a period of instability following Idi Amin's rise to power in 1971, donors had limited interaction with Uganda. However, by the early 1990s donors were working closely with the Museveni government in security and economic matters, while gingerly pushing for political reform.

Immediately following its overthrow of the first UPC-Obote government, the Amin regime received short-lived support from Western countries, particularly Britain, due to hostility toward Obote's increasingly socialist orientation. However, Amin's erratic leadership style, coupled with his flagrant human rights abuses, including the expulsion of Asians[60] from Uganda in 1972, embarrassed Western governments that originally supported him. By the end of 1970s, Uganda became the first East African country to have aid suspended for political reasons, prompting Amin to present his country as an Islamic one in order to seek military and financial aid from Arab states.

After Amin was removed from power in 1979 by Tanzanian military force, the second UPC-Obote government embraced structural adjustment and a new donor role in what had previously been considered domestic socio-economic and political processes. Having come from exile, the second UPC-Obote government needed resources to consolidate its power. Moreover, donors' blamed the Amin regime for the failure of the Ugandan economy. Despite serious human rights abuses by the second UPC-Obote administration, the international community continued giving aid to Uganda as if a lingering numbness remained after Amin's human rights abuses.[61] After overthrowing Tito Okello, who ousted the collapsing Obote regime, Museveni also embraced the IMF and World Bank initiated policies, largely for the same reasons as the second UPC-Obote government.[62]

In a relatively short period, the Museveni regime convinced the IMF and World Bank that it could deliver on economic reforms and by 1990 donors acknowledged the regime's achievements in implementing structural adjustment. As a reward, bilateral aid from major Western donors increased from $179.7 million in 1989 to $342.7 million in 1994.[63] External support helped Uganda's economy to grow. GDP increased at an average annual rate of 6.4 per cent from 1991-1995, while per capita GDP growth averaged over three percent a year in real terms.[64] In 1994-95, Uganda's GDP grew at a rate of ten percent instead of the targeted five percent and inflation that year was approximately three percent. This was a remarkable achievement for Uganda as well as for donors, particularly the IMF and World Bank, because elsewhere their programs were being criticized as failures.

Although impressive economic reforms had been implemented, Museveni and his NRM government sought to convince donors that political liberalization would be destabilizing. The Ugandan government argued that political stability should be the primary goal for Uganda, given its turbulent history and continued violent conflicts in the north and west of the country. This is especially noteworthy since all of the countries surrounding Uganda, except Tanzania, were unstable. To the south, Rwanda had emerged from a genocide in 1994 and Burundi was bogged down in civil war. To the north, Sudan was in the midst of a civil war. To the west there was also civil war and a foreign occupation of parts of the Democratic Republic of Congo and there was also uncertainty to the east, as multi-party politics in Kenya seemed to inflame ethnic tensions. Museveni insisted that the political situation in Uganda was so fragile that a pluralist political system would be a recipe for endemic political upheaval.[65] According to the NRM, a no-party regime was the best way to maintain unity, peace and progress. Domestic and regional insecurity bolstered Museveni's claims that what Uganda needed was limited political liberalization that precluded multi-party politics. The fear that multi-party politics would damage the limited economic progress achieved under Museveni made the international community reconsider their push for political reform.

Furthermore, the new NRM system was seemingly different (more participatory and inclusive) from the previous authoritarian governments, and Museveni convinced donors that a no-party state based on local level Resistance Councils should be given a chance.[66] Museveni's NRM maintained that the RC system was an inclusive and democratic way of nation building. It argued that after years of exclusion, RCs provided a platform where Ugandans could gain political experience and participate in the management of local affairs. The RC system was also presented as a gender sensitive way to ensure women's political representation.

The Uganda situation contrasts sharply with Kenya, where donors froze or suspended aid in an attempt to force political reform. The case of Uganda clearly shows that donors' demands for democratization were blurred by the desire to achieve other objectives, such as presenting Uganda as a structural adjustment success story and finding a dependable Western ally in an unstable region.[67] Instead of invoking political conditionality, donors opted for the tactic of dialogue to convince the government to move toward multi-partyism. However, since external actors continued to try to convince the Museveni government to adopt multi-party politics, this indicates that donors did not fully accept the movement's political system as democratic. Western donors pressured Museveni to allow competing political parties during the 1994 Constituent Assembly elections but they were conducted according to no-party movement principles. During the 1996 presidential and parliamentary elections, the police and other state machinery harassed politicians who organized themselves independent of the NRM, prompting donors to intervene. Donor influence helped to allow candidates who opposed the movement system to have better access to the media. Outside pressure also helped to suspend the *mchaka mchaka* pro-NRM political education courses held during the campaign period.[68] During the 1998 local government elections, campaigns on party platforms were again forbidden, but donors also supported the elections by backing civil organizations as opposed to directly funding the government's electoral commission. Donor indulgence of the movement system in Uganda was again tested during the general elections in 2001 by widespread reports of intimidation and electoral irregularities that featured a heated presidential campaign between Museveni and Besigye.[69]

In addition to dialogue with the Ugandan government, the international community supported important activities to strengthen the democratization process. Donors provided funding for the constitutional reform process (which led to the adoption of the new Uganda constitution), judicial reform, and some aspects of the 1994 Constituent Assembly elections. Resources were also provided for civic and voter education, human rights organizations, women's legal aid organizations, and human rights training for police. Donors hoped that these activities and groups would have both short and long-term positive impacts on the democratization process. It is important to recognize that the lack of political conditionality covering the provision of aid to the Ugandan government did not mean that donors stopped demanding the introduction of multi-party democracy. But largely for reasons explained above, they opted for tactics of persuasion and dialogue and not political conditionality. That donor displeasure with the lack of progress in political reforms was mitigated by other concerns can be seen in the levels of bilateral ODA extended to Uganda. Since the mid 1990s, the amount has remained fairly constant, with a slight decline.[70]

For Uganda, the new international environment associated with the 9/11 terrorist attacks on the United States heralded an emphasis on maintaining the *status quo*. On March 21, 2002, the Ugandan parliament passed an anti-terrorism act, which former presidential candidate Besigye claimed would be used to silence NRM opponents and block political reform. While donors understood the concerns of Besigye, their lack of forceful criticism of the act illustrated other priorities, especially the desire to maintain Uganda's cooperation in the areas of security, economic affairs, and health (with a particular emphasis on fighting AIDS).[71] However, by 2004 there were indications that the donor's honeymoon with Museveni was ending. Museveni's rumored desire to seek another presidential term in 2006 prompted U.S. Under-Secretary for Africa Charles Snyder to state that his government would do its best to convince Museveni to relinquish power. Museveni's colorful response was made in a symbolically rich, January 27th, 2004, speech in Kololo to celebrate 18 years of NRM rule. Invited guests included the Vice President of North Korea, a representative of one of the countries the U.S. claimed was part of an axis of evil. In the speech Museveni castigated donors for using aid as way to meddle in the internal affairs of African countries and he warned them to steer clear of Uganda's domestic politics.[72]

Concluding Comments

The rise of neo-liberalism in the 1980s and the subsequent collapse of the Communist block reinvigorated the values of good governance and democratization in East Africa. By the 1990s, the international community believed that it had a duty to promote democratization processes and to recognize and protect basic human rights. Donors were increasingly prepared to use their resources to encourage political reforms, if not outright democratization. By the end of the century Kenya, Tanzania, and Uganda had reached a conditional transition phase to a more plural political order in which the state's power to interrupt, delay, or even abort democratization remained strong.[73]

The introduction of multi-party politics in the region did not translate immediately into free, fair, and competitive elections. Both internal and external observers of Kenya's 1992, 1997, and 2002 elections; Tanzania's 1995 and 2000 elections; and Uganda's 1996 and 2001 elections noted their manipulation in favor of the ruling party.[74] It was not until the December 2002 Kenyan elections that political power was actually transferred from one political party to another in the region. Despite systematic bias in favor of the ruling parties, donors were critical but not forceful in pushing for free and fair elections. Western countries attenuated their urge to push for reforms with the realization that overzealous pressure for democratization could harm bilateral relations. Also, donor countries recognized that democratization in East Africa was taking place in three similar yet ultimately different economic, social, and political environments, with each of the three countries providing a unique case study of the impact of Western countries, and the multi-lateral institutions they dominate, on democratization.

Kenya most fiercely opposed political reform and was a case where donor pressure tipped the scales in favor of the multi-party system. The government's overt resistance to donor pressure to open up the political system abruptly ended when KANU decided to hold multi-party elections barely one week after the

Paris Club placed political conditionalities on the release of aid. The importance of Kenya to the West for both economic and military purposes declined considerably following the end of the Cold War. Regional changes, such as a growing Western friendship with Tanzania and Uganda also reduced Kenya's strategic importance. Counter-intuitively, another explanation for outside pressure for political reform was that Kenya was an important friend to Western countries and that this relationship could be jeopardized if the new democratic forces were less supportive of Western interests. According to this view, donor intervention in Kenya's democratization process was largely to safeguard Western interests by building friendly relations with a possible successor regime. Indeed, since taking power, Kibaki's government has looked to repair strained relations with the West and tap into donor resources to support populist domestic policies.

Tanzania, on the other hand, instituted multi-party politics peacefully with minimal donor pressure. By the end of the 1980s, Tanzania recognized the growing power of donors. It opted for a course of action aimed at managing rather than resisting change, implying a wish to avoid repeating the bitter experience of futilely resisting donor structural adjustment policies. Thus, though Tanzania adopted a system of multi-party politics relatively late, it did so in the absence of significant international and domestic pressure. This supports the impression that the decisive impetus for change came from within the ruling party itself. CCM's opening up of the political system was calculated to preempt opposition demands and make donor pressure less necessary.[75] However, by taking the lead in the democratization process, CCM was able to set the rules of the game and avert the emergence of a powerful domestic movement demanding a say in national affairs.[76] In terms of macro-economic policy, especially under Mkapa, the Tanzanian government worked hard to please donors. Consequently, Tanzania received supportive signals at a time when donors were shouting orders in Kenya.

In Uganda, despite its reluctance to adopt multi-party politics, the Museveni regime continued to enjoy a high level of donor support. Instead of pressuring Uganda to introduce plural politics, donors opted for dialogue for three main reasons: fear of continued domestic instability in Uganda; increased donors' confidence in the government's ability to manage the economy; and President Museveni's leadership style. Museveni emerged in the 1990s as a strong regional leader willing to cooperate with the West. However, with indications that he wants another term in 2006, coupled with widespread reports of corruption and war profiteering in the DRC, tensions are emerging between Uganda and the West.

This chapter demonstrates that one of the major aims of donor foreign policies is to support political liberalization. However, questions can be raised as to whether donor interventions are leading to long-term sustainable democracy. While they share a consensus about the desirability of political and economic liberalization, there is disagreement about what concrete steps need to be taken to bring about democratization. This is especially manifested when pressure for reforms, such as free and fair elections, undermines donor and recipient state economic interests, security, or bilateral relations.

The real test of democracy lies within the ruling regimes and societies in East Africa. The positive impact of outside support for political reform is limited when the ruling parties themselves are not fully committed to liberal democracy.[77] While attaching conditions to the provision of aid gains the attention of the recipient state, it is no guarantee that donor preferences will be incorporated into the political system. Likewise, while donors' financial assistance and programs have helped to expand and strengthen pro-democratic forces in all the East African countries, there is also the danger that both opposition parties and civil society organizations see donors, and not the people of East Africa, as guardians of democratic transitions.

Notes

1 The Paris Club has 19 members representing major creditor countries.

2 Donor countries active in East Africa include Belgium, Canada, Denmark, Finland, France, Germany, Ireland, Italy, Japan, Netherlands, Norway, Sweden, Switzerland, U.K. and the U.S.

3 In preparing this chapter, the following people were interviewed: Rwekaza Mukandala, Chair, Tanzania Election Monitoring Committee, Chair, Research and Education for Democracy in Tanzania (REDET), November 8, 2001; Sean Hall, Democracy and Governance Officer, USAID, Dar es Salaam, November 6, 2001; Professor A. Liviga, Program Officer, Politics, Royal Netherlands Embassy, Dar es Salaam, November 1, 2001; Vincent J. Kibwana, Principal Foreign Service Officer, Ministry of Foreign Affairs, United Republic of Tanzania, Dar es Salaam, October 22, 2001; Members of Parliament, Dodoma, Tanzania, June 2000 (as part of a REDET study on Parliament); and officials from the Swedish International Development Agency (SIDA), Stockholm, Sweden, 1997 (as part of doctoral dissertation field research on SIDA).

4 Goran Hyden and Rwekaza Mukandala, *Agencies in Foreign Aid: Comparing China, Sweden, and the United States in Tanzania* (London: Macmillan Press, 1999); Maria Nzomo, "A Derailed Democratic Transition: Election in a Multi-party Context in Kenya" in J. Oloka-Onyango, J. Kibwana, and C. Peter, eds., *Laws and the Struggle for Democracy in East Africa* (Nairobi: Claripress, 1996).

5 In the 1960s and 1970s free market capitalism had not yet defeated the notion of state-led industrialization in donor thinking about development. For more information on this subject see Laurean Ndumbaro, "The Relative Shift of Power Centre in Tanzania Public Policy Making in the 1980s," MA. thesis., University of Dar es Salaam (1993); and Dirk Berg-Schlosser and Rainer Siegler, *Political Stability and Development: A Comparative Analysis of Kenya, Tanzania, and Uganda* (Boulder CO: Lynne Rienner Publishers, 1990).

6 Africa Watch Report, *Kenya: Taking Liberties* (New York: Africa Watch, 1991), pp. 372-373.

7 Africa Watch Report, *Kenya*, pp. 373-375; Oda van Cranenburgh, "International Policies to Promote African Democratization," in Jean Grugel, ed., *Democracy without Borders: Transnationalism and Conditionalities in New Democracies* (London: Routledge, 1999), p. 94.

8 Hyden and Mukandala, *Agencies in Foreign Aid.*

9 World Bank, *Sub-Saharan Africa: From Crisis to Sustainable Growth, a Long-Term Perspective Study* (Washington D.C.: The World Bank, 1989).

[10] G. Anyona, "The One-party Debate in Kenya," *Nairobi Law Monthly*, vol. 22 (1990).
[11] Anyona, "The One-party Debate in Kenya."
[12] Michael Cox, "International History Since 1989" in John Bayliss and Steve Smith, eds., *Globalization of World Politics* (Oxford: Oxford University Press, 2001).
[13] Cranenburgh, "International Policies to Promote African Democratization," p. 92.
[14] Stephen Brown, "Authoritarian Leaders and Multi-party Elections in Africa: How Foreign Donors Help to Keep Kenya's Daniel arap Moi in Power" *Third World Quarterly* vol. 22, no. 5 (2001), pp. 725-741; *East African* "Tanzania Returning to One-Party Rule, Report" (April 9 – 15, 2001), pp. 1 and 32; *East African* "Besigye Court Loss a 'Victory for Democracy'" (April 23 – 29, 2001), p. 2.
[15] K. Musambayi, "Internationalization of Democracy: External Actors in Kenya Elections" in Ludeki Chweya, ed., *Electoral Politics in Kenya* (Nairobi: Claripress, 2002).
[16] Oda van Cranenburgh, "International Policies to Promote African Democratization."
[17] Smith Hempstone notes that only a few Western countries were interested in promoting democracy and human rights in Kenya. See Smith Hempstone's *Rogue Ambassador: An African Memoir* (Sawanee, TN: University of the South Press, 1998), p. 95.
[18] Mutumba-Lule, "Force Pluralism on Uganda," *East African* (May 13 – 19, 2002), p. 2.; World Bank, *Tanzania at the Turn of the Century* (Washington D.C.: World Bank, 2001), p. 24.; Gould, Jeremy and Julia Ojanen, "Merging in the Circle: The Politics of Tanzania's Poverty Reduction Strategy," Institute of Development Studies, University of Helsinki Policy Papers (2003), p. 41.
[19] Musambayi, "Internationalization of Democracy: External Actors in Kenya Elections"; and Stephen Brown, "Authoritarian Leaders and Multi-party Elections in Africa."
[20] Barya, "Internal and External Pressure in the Struggle for Pluralism" in J. Oloka-Onyanga, K. Kibwana, and C. Peter, eds., *Law and Struggle for Democracy in East Africa* (Nairobi: Claripress, 1996).
[21] *Daily News,* "IMF denies forcing Kenya into Reforms" (Dar-es-Salaam, November 1, 2001).
[22] *Daily News*, "IMF denies ..." (Dar-es-Salaam, November 1, 2001).
[23] *Daily News*, "IMF denies ..." (Dar-es-Salaam, November 1, 2001).
[24] Cranenburgh, "International Policies to Promote African Democratization," p. 95; Tim Dunne, "Liberalism" in John Bayliss and Steve Smith, eds., *The Globalization of World Politics* (Oxford: Oxford University Press, 2001), pp. 172-173.
[25] Interviews with Tanzanian MPs, June 2000.
[26] Interview with Chair of TEMCO and REDET, Dar es Salaam, November 8, 2001.
[27] Cranenburgh, "International Policies to Promote African Democratization," p. 95; Dunne, "Liberalism," pp. 172-173.
[28] Berg-Schlosser and Siegler, *Political Stability and Development*; Nzomo, "A Derailed Democratic Transition: Election in a Multi-party Context in Kenya."
[29] Africa Watch Report, *Kenya: Taking Liberties*, pp. 369-370.
[30] Ndumbaro, "The Relative Shift of Power Centre in Tanzania Public Policy Making in the 1980s."
[31] Smith Hempstone, *Rogue Ambassador: An African Memoir,* p. 91.
[32] See Smith Hempstone, *Rogue Ambassador: An African Memoir.*
[33] Queue voting in the KANU primary elections entailed supporters standing in line behind a candidate or his/her portrait.
[34] *Daily Nation* (Nairobi, 1990) various issues.
[35] K. Kelley, "Now U.S. Has No Time for Africa," *Daily Nation* (January 20, 1991); *The Weekly Review* (Nairobi, November 16, 1990), pp. 14-16.
[36] Africa Watch Report, *Kenya: Taking Liberties*, pp. 362-371.
[37] *Society Weekly* (Nairobi, 1991), various issues.

[38] *The Weekly Review* (Nairobi, 1990), various issues.

[39] Brown, "Authoritarian Leaders and Multi-party Elections in Africa."

[40] Brown, "Authoritarian Leaders and Multi-party elections in Africa."

[41] Official Development Assistance (ODA) is used as a proxy indicator of the level of cooperation between donors and East African countries. This indicator is imprecise, as it does not include military assistance, and ODA flows can also be influenced by a number of factors, such as level of economic development or strategic importance. One would expect a correlation between ODA and level of development. For example, Tanzania receives the largest amount of ODA in East Africa, and it is also the most impoverished of the three countries. Likewise Kenya receives the least and it has the highest GNP per capita. However, while ODA can be related to levels of economic development, this is not the only consideration. In 1996 Israel and Egypt were the two leading destinations for U.S. ODA, even though they were far from being the poorest countries in the world. The statistics for ODA are from the OECD and are found in the *DAC Journal* vol. 2, no. 1 (2001).

[42] This is based on bilateral ODA using 1998 exchange rates and prices. Information and OECD figures found in the *DAC Journal*, vol. 2, no. 1 (2001).

[43] Vitalis Omondi, "Kenya's Budget Deficit Balloons by $101 million," *East African* (July 29 – August 4, 2002), p.1.

[44] Polity IV County Report 2002 Kenya, http://www.cidcm.umd.edu/inscr/polity/Ken1.htm; European Union Election Observation Mission Report: Kenya General Elections 27 December 2002; Fred Oluoch, "KANU's $40 million Plan to 'Buy' House Majority," *East African* (December 9th, 2002) [online].

[45] World Bank figures.

[46] BBC, "World Bank Pledges Kenya Aid" (July 23 2003), http://news.bbc.co.uk; BBC, "IMF Unfreezes Key Funds for Kenya" (November 22, 2003), http://news.bbc.co.uk.

[47] Fred Oluoch, "German Investors Wary of Kenya's Insecurity," *East African* (January 26-February 1, 2004), p. 36.

[48] S. S. Mushi, "The Making of Foreign Policy in Tanzania" in S. S. Mushi and K. Mathews, eds., *Foreign Policy of Tanzania: 1961-1981* (Dar es Salaam: Tanzania Publishing House, 1981); Hyden and Mukandala, *Agencies in Foreign Aid: Comparing China, Sweden, and the United States in Tanzania.*

[49] Bruce Heilman, "Who are the Indigenous Tanzanians? Competing Conceptions of Tanzanian Citizenship in the Business Community," *Africa Today* vol. 45, no. 3-4 (1998), pp. 369-388.

[50] M. Baregu, "The Economic Origins of Political Liberalization and Future Prospects," in Bagachwa and Mbelle, eds., *Economic Policy Under a Multi-party System in Tanzania* (Dar es Salaam: Dar es Salaam University Press, 1993).

[51] A scientific opinion poll taken in 1994 by REDET verified the assertion that Tanzanians did not favor switching to a multi-party system.

[52] Interviews with Swedish International Development Agency Officials, Stockholm Sweden, 1997.

[53] Laurean Ndumbaro, "Learning and Policy Change: The Case of Swedish International Development Cooperation Agency (SIDA): 1980-1995," Ph.D. diss., University of Florida, 1998.

[54] Faustine Rwambali, "CCM Queries Dutch Aid to Tanzanian Opposition," *East African* (May 14-20, 2001), pp. 1 and 36.

[55] From OECD figures found in the *DAC Journal* vol. 2, no. 1 (2001).

[56] From OECD figures found in the *DAC Journal* vol. 2, no. 1 (2001).

[57] From OECD figures found in the *DAC Journal* vol. 2, no. 1 (2001).

[58] See various TEMCO reports on the 2000 Zanzibar election.

[59] Various TEMCO reports on the 2003 by-elections.

[60] Asian is used to describe East African residents of Indian and Pakistani origin.

[61] Berg-Schlosser and Siegler, *Political Stability and Development: A Comparative Analysis of Kenya, Tanzania, and Uganda.*

[62] J. Barya, "Internal and External Pressure in the Struggle for Pluralism."

[63] OECD, *Geographical Distribution of Financial Flows to Aid Recipient: Disbursements, Commitments, Country Indicators 1990-1994* (Paris: OECD, 1996).

[64] UNDP, *Development Cooperation: Uganda, 1993-1994 Report* (Kampala: Business Services Ltd, 1995).

[65] Barya, "Internal and External Pressure in the Struggle for Pluralism."

[66] Barya, "Internal and External Pressure in the Struggle for Pluralism."

[67] Paul Redfern, "Report Criticizes World Bank over Privatization in Uganda," *East African* (April 9 – 15, 2001), p. 3.

[68] *Mchaka mchaka* were political propaganda courses used by the Museveni government to persuade people to vote for the NRM candidates.

[69] *East African,* "Besigye Court Loss a 'Victory for Democracy'" (April 23 – 29, 2001), p. 2.

[70] From OECD figures found in the *DAC Journal*, vol. 2, no. 1 (2001).

[71] See *Monitor* (Uganda) and *New Vision* (Uganda) newspapers for the year 2002.

[72] BBC, "Museveni Azinonya Nchi Wahisani," *Majira* (Dar es Salaam: January 28, 2004), p. 2.

[73] This observation borrows from Richard Joseph's models of political transitions in Africa in Richard Joseph's "Africa: The Rebirth of Political Freedom," *Journal of Democracy* vol. 1, no. 4 (1991).

[74] For information on the Kenyan elections, see Brown, "Authoritarian Leaders and Multi-party Elections in Africa." For information on the Tanzanian elections from the perspective of local election observers consult the TEMCO final reports on the 1995 and 2000 elections. The International Foundation for Electoral Services organized external monitoring of the 1995 Tanzanian General Elections and the 2000 Zanzibar elections and also issued reports. In a court case initiated by the opposition presidential candidate, the Uganda Supreme Court noted widespread electoral malpractices in the March 13, 2001, presidential elections. In evaluating the conduct of elections in East Africa for the Tanzanian mainland a strong case could be made that flaws did not alter the electoral outcome. This argument is more difficult to make for Kenya and Uganda, and cannot be made for Zanzibar.

[75] M. Okema, *Political Culture of Tanzania* (New York: The Edwin Mellen Press, 1996).

[76] G. Sundet, ed., *Democracy in Transition: The 1995 Elections in Tanzania* (Oslo: Norwegian Institute of Human Rights, 1996).

[77] Cranenburgh, "International Policies to Promote African Democratization."

Chapter 9

The Crisis of Legitimacy, Representation, and State Hegemony

Earl Conteh-Morgan

Democratization as one aspect of globalization is characterized by both integrative and disintegrative outcomes. In many instances, as democratic values spread, existing peaceful patterns of interaction between state and society and within civil society, are undermined. The increasing pervasiveness of norms of egalitarianism and freedom continue to delegitimize previous *modus operandi*. In particular, as old structures and modes of behavior disappear, challenges to state hegemony and legitimacy intensify. Similarly, individual and group insecurity develop as past structures that cemented the community and bound it together are also eliminated. This creates further challenges to state legitimacy, hegemony, and political representation that are often underlined by inter-ethnic disputes and violence.

Democratization in East Africa, as in other sub-regions of the continent, is better understood in the context of the interactive effects of pre-colonial, colonial, and post-colonial disjunctures. These "artificial" transitions from one era to another are also integral to the anomalies and dilemmas of politics in the East Africa region. The democratic electoral process has helped to mobilize groups that were previously passive and weak, as leaders have tended to polarize sensitive issues in order to attract followers. This chapter will focus on the following questions: what is the nature of power in all three territories and how was it historically shared in ways that impact the current democratization process?; what has been the impact of ethnicity on the democratization process involving ruling elite and the ruled?; and what are the internal and external factors that impinge on issues of legitimacy, representation, and state hegemony (leadership and dominance) in East Africa's democratization process?

Conceptual and Theoretical Grounding

Legitimacy is the right a government has to influence the behavior of its citizens because they accept its authority. When the government's acceptance (legitimacy) is, however, contested, it resorts to authoritarianism, intimidation, or manipulation, and exercises power rather than seek authority.[1] In East Africa's political struggles, claims for legitimacy have often been contested, except during the immediate post-independence years.[2] For example, the lack of widespread legitimacy for the Moi regime in Kenya led to its use of varied strategies designed to ensure its hold on power, including the co-optation of the opposition, regional isolation, ethno-political violence, and imprisonment.

In particular, African regimes are prone to use a combination of distributional and coercive (carrot and stick) political strategies to weaken the opposition and thereby ensure their hold on power. In Kenya, the establishment of junior ministries with attendant perquisites, appointments to parastatals, and a liberal delivery of resources to specific constituencies has been used to ensure majority status and thereby legitimacy.[3]

However, a ruling and/or single party can be considered as legitimate only if there is widespread acceptance that the party is widely representative, or is dedicated to realizing a set of overriding common goals that adequately benefit the entire populace. In Kenya, Tanzania, and Uganda the perception and/or reality is that government is not adequately representative of all segments of society. This is because ethno-regional resentments and rivalries perennially undermine a sense of national unity and block the process of nation-building. Besides, the perception and/or reality of a government based on patron-client relations, nepotism, and corruption excludes many from the resources distributed by party and state.[4] The excluded segments of society thus tend to conclude that government does not represent their interests. Representation is thus the belief by citizens, or a segment of society, that government genuinely seeks their interests and is therefore dedicated to realizing a set of general, and more specific, goals that adequately benefit them as a group.

Democratization in East Africa has been characterized by electoral manipulation, intimidation of opposition candidates, co-opting members of the opposition, and occasionally detaining, harassing, and even killing those that threaten the hegemony of the state or incumbent regime. State hegemony is a particular power structure within a *modus vivendi* characterized by government and/or ruling power domination of society and its sectors. In state hegemony, there is an implicit as well as explicit configuration of factors that make the state (government or ruling party) dominant in the political system.[5] In the areas of political control, economic resources, influence, and domination, the hegemonic authoritarian state surpasses others. This translates into a situation where it is capable of perpetuating itself in power, subverting democratization through electoral manipulation, and intimidation of the opposition. The consolidation of state hegemony over the opposition involves the interactive and reinforcing influence of condign power (threats and punitive actions), compensatory power (use of resources to buy influence and votes), and conditioned power (persuasion, appeal to the ruling party's ideology).[6] In East Africa, state capacity to mobilize human and material resources for national development has been in marked contrast to its growing capacity to coerce and condition groups to desist from challenging or criticizing its policies or engaging in collective political violence. The state's preoccupation with containing internal cleavages (ethnic, class, religious, and regional) and with challenges to its own authority has become an end in itself rather than a means to mobilize national resources for development.

East African governments have limited access to the material resources necessary for effective governance due to the diversion of tax revenues and foreign aid to patronage systems, and the relative autonomy of local strongmen who exercise local power and control resources that should be administered transparently by the central government. The dominance of the informal economy also deprives the government and its bureaucracies of funds essential to development. This woeful lack of compensatory power capabilities can be substantiated by World Bank data on the plight of their economies since the 1980s, economies that were largely dominated by a large public sector.[7] In contrast, the condign and conditioned power capabilities of the East African state has achieved more political and decisional efficacy in the pursuit of objectives of internal security and power consolidation.

The state's perennial struggle to maintain hegemony results in extreme executive centralization as well as the weakening of formal institutions. The overall consequence is a deepening of neo-patrimonial relationships that tend to encourage regional and ethnic insecurity, as well as conflicts over state resources. The interrelated factors of hegemonial rule, deinstitutionalization, and personalization of the state's distributional function inevitably lead to a serious loss in legitimacy by the incumbent regime.[8] Widespread perception of state illegitimacy translates into the belief that the government is only representing those who are firmly connected to the mechanisms of distributing the state's "booty." The consequence is frustration, anger, and even aggression on the part of those permanently locked out of available societal opportunities.

Power Politics in the Immediate Post-Independence Era

Since independence, politics in Kenya, Tanzania, and Uganda have been characterized by the competitive interactions of active cleavages, resulting in power consolidation behavior after the immediate post-independence euphoria evaporated. In most of their nearly four decades of independence, these countries have had a checkered political history, with Uganda oscillating between military rule and single-party authoritarian regimes, with brief interludes of multi-party competition. Kenya and Tanzania were characterized by civilian single-party regimes underlined by sharp cleavages.[9] In socio-historical and structural terms, the authoritarian tendencies of these post-colonial regimes are a reflection of the colonial state, which dominated society in the areas of legitimacy, representation, leadership, and overall authority. The post-colonial regimes of these countries have not been able to completely legitimize their rule because of the inherited disjuncture in state-society relations. This disjuncture is largely responsible for the woeful lack of legitimate, efficient, and well-developed institutions that can transcend and weld together parochial ethno-regional and class interests. The consequence is that the three countries have experienced multi-party democracy for only a brief period, and longer periods of either civilian single-party or military, authoritarian rule.

In general, the politics in East Africa can be characterized as a perennial struggle by the state to ensure its legitimacy and hegemony over varied groups whose loyalties were primarily directed towards their ethno-regional origins. Accordingly, not long after independence, the immediate and critical question was how would power be effectively shared so that peace and stability are ensured. The problem of regime legitimacy and power would loom larger as internal economic dislocation, external pressures for political-economic liberalization, and inter-ethnic competition, intensified.

The issues of legitimacy, representation, and state hegemony are problematic in Kenya, Uganda, and Tanzania because of the persistent effects of the contradictions between colonial and post-colonial conceptions of power, and the equally disruptive contradictions between *de jure* statehood (*pays légal*) and *de facto* statehood (*pays réel*).[10] The colonial state did not require the elements of government legitimacy such as consent and collaboration in order to be effective since its authority emanated from the reality of military hegemony and control. The state in post-colonial or post-Cold War Kenya, Uganda, and Tanzania was based on the constitutional requirements of legitimacy and representation that experienced serious challenges after the euphoria of nationalist success evaporated. Juridical statehood was not historically rooted in empirical statehood.[11]

Political legitimacy during the immediate independence era (roughly 1965-1970) was guaranteed by the emotional resource of nationalism and the call for national unity in the face of nation-building and economic development challenges. However, by the early to mid-1970s, the euphoria of nationalism and the legitimacy conferred on nationalist leaders had subsided, giving way to constant demands for greater representation, and increased challenges from below against state integrity. The consequence was increased power consolidation measures and authoritarian rule. Before these developments, the overall legitimacy of the nationalist claim, whether expressed as African socialism, or African cooperation and unity, was a result of the erosion (domestic and international) of the legitimacy of colonialism rather than the representativeness of KANU, TANU, or UPC. This is because the democratic tradition that the three countries inherited is itself in many ways an elite process. According to Scholte "in the present-day globalizing world, the construction and implementation of rules occurs mainly through elite competition rather than through representative, let alone participatory, democracy."[12] The democratization process across the continent is a far cry from China's people's democracy, or from the original Greek idea of democracy–rule by and in the interests of the *demos*, the common people. It is more inclined to "bourgeois liberalization." In all three states, the legitimacy of the nationalist parties derived more from their nationalist quality than from their representativeness as political organizations. Similarly, calls for democratization in the early 1990s were equally the result of the national and international erosion of the legitimacy of KANU, CCM, and the NRM.

The ethnic cleansing episodes in Kenya's Rift Valley and Western provinces, the disjuncture between political rhetoric and reality in Uganda, and the increasing salience of popular religious identities in Tanzania have combined to create a sense of profound democratization-related disorders in the sub-region.

Kenya: Turbulent Democratization

During the 1960s and 1970s, while many states in Africa were undergoing political upheaval, Kenya was a model of stability, experiencing a smooth transfer of presidential power from Kenyatta to Moi in 1978.[13] It was a lesson on peaceful transfer of power for numerous African states. However, with the charisma of its first president gone and the euphoria of anti-colonial nationalism and independence long diminished, Moi had to resort to questionable policies and maneuvers in order to maintain his rule and ensure the hegemony of his regime. The severely diminished legitimacy of the regime resulted in its use of coercion (paramilitary forces, police, and prisons) to ensure continued state hegemony over all challenges emanating from civil society and the opposition.[14] The regime's resort to authoritarian measures ensured that by the end of the 1980s, Moi' power consolidation was complete with his ethnic and non-ethnic allies dominating key political positions.

However, far more serious internal and external opposition to the regime's authoritarian tendencies began to surface as the African continent entered the decade of the 1990s, which was characterized by the end of the Cold War and intensified calls for democratization. Even though Kenya emerged as one of the more prosperous African countries, it did not escape the widespread economic malaise that gripped the continent during the 1980s. Economic discontent coupled with authoritarian rule soon resulted in strong internal pressures for the regime to reform and liberalize.[15] A broad cross-section of Kenyan society – university students and intellectuals, labor unions, women's movements, and other civil society groups – actively opposed the corrupt and authoritarian rule of the Moi regime. Added to these internal challenges were the international pressures from the major Western donor nations and international financial institutions that indexed the continued provision of aid to progress in efforts at political liberalization.

In Kenya, several events precipitated the democratic transition process. It was alleged that in February 1990, the country's Foreign Minister, Dr. Robert Ouko, was murdered while preparing a report that disclosed massive cases of corruption within the Kenyan government.[16] In 1997, Kenneth Matiba, a businessman and leader of FORD, published a book that detailed how $1.6 billion had been stolen from state coffers between 1990 and 1997. According to John Msafari, the Director-General of the Kenya Revenue Authority, up to a third of tax and other levies accrued to the government disappeared before it was deposited in the state coffers.[17] Transparency International's Global Corruption Report also underscores the fact that between 1991-97 Kenya lost more than $6 billion through corruption. The problem of corruption became so serious that in the late 1990s, the IMF and the World Bank successfully pushed for the establishment of the Kenya Anti-Corruption Authority (KACA), an independent body that would investigate and prosecute corrupt practices without hindrance from threatened politicians. However, in December 2000, the Kenyan High Court ruled that the KACA was unconstitutional, forcing donors to promptly freeze all lending to Kenya until an effective anti-corruption agency is established.[18]

Opposition activism against the Moi regime intensified in the form of street demonstrations, and appeals by Kenya's religious leaders and other civil society groups for President Moi to resign.[19] The regime responded by equally intensifying its crackdown on opposition groups. The intransigence of the regime forced the donor nations and agencies to announce suspensions of aid to Kenya towards the end of 1991. The combined internal and external pressures finally convinced the Moi regime to capitulate to the new political environment of democratization. Immediate democratization reforms took the form of abandoning the "queue-voting" system that required voters to publicly line up in open support of a certain candidate instead of using a secret ballot. A second reform was the repeal of Section 2A of the constitution that ended the single-party system in December 1991. Thus in 1992 Kenya finally experienced its first multi-party elections since 1966.

Multi-partyism did not resolve the crisis of legitimacy and effective representation that Kenya was experiencing. Instead, the transition intensified the Moi regime's determination to hold on to power with tenacity. Accordingly, the introduction of democratic reforms coincided with, and aggravated ethno-political violence underlined by disputes over land and high rates of unemployment. Multi-party competition therefore unleashed severe inter-ethnic competition due in large part to the politicization of ethnic identities by the Moi regime. According to Human Rights Watch, the government was involved in inciting Kalenjin and pro-KANU elements against members of the opposition and those ethnic groups that were not supporters of Moi.[20]

In 1992, elections did not confer legitimacy on the Moi regime despite its defeat of the opposition. On the issue of representation, the government remained as parochial as it had been before the advent of the democratization process. According to Haberson, parliamentary seats were significantly malapportioned, under-representing areas of opposition strength, including Nairobi.[21] The Moi regime also frustrated the opposition through the tight control of election rules. The opposition itself was so divided that it failed to confer any aura of legitimacy on itself. The consequence was that KANU won the elections and the Moi regime continued its old policy of widespread corruption and abuse of human rights. The 1997 elections were, in large part, a repeat performance of the 1992 elections: ethnic violence instigated by the government; refusal to change election rules that openly favored the ruling party; and detention of political activists, among many others.[22] Once again, the disunity among the opposition meant that Kenya's democratization process would still be plagued by problems of illegitimacy, under-representation, and continued authoritarian hegemony of the Moi regime.

The December 2002 general elections and subsequent peaceful transition of presidential power to NARC candidate Kibaki is positively significant for democratization in Kenya. This development might even have a ripple effect on the pace and nature of democratization in Uganda and Tanzania. The decision on the part of the fragmented opposition to close ranks and work toward the defeat of Moi and his KANU party paid dividends in the end.

In order for the Kibaki regime to maintain its legitimacy, it needs to change the current image of Kenya as one of the world's most corrupt countries. The regime also needs to continue with its politics of inclusion – the fair and equal treatment of all, including minority groups and/or those previously marginalized. A review of cabinet appointments demonstrates that the Kibaki regime has been, for the most part, largely inclusive. For example, women have become an increasingly integral part of the Kenyan political process, something that did not occur during the Moi's rule.

At the heart of Kenya's democratization problematic as it relates to legitimacy, representation, and state rigidity, is the deepening social inequality and fragmentation aggravated by the introduction of structural adjustment programs, with their implications for reduced state capacity. The instrumental use of ethno-politics in political competition in Kenya intensified in response to the simultaneous introduction of liberal political and economic reforms. The former KANU regime had been able to exploit ethnic cleavages because of overt group tensions associated with the economic dislocation of the 1980s, manifested in the adverse balance of payments position and burdensome debt servicing experienced by the country. The checkered democratization process in Kenya is as much problematic of politics and institutions as it is problematic of the economy and society. The sustainability of the process is, in part, a function of whether the senior NARC officials who were once part of the KANU old guard are genuine reformers.

Uganda: Rhetoric versus Reality

The NRM has, for the past twelve years, prohibited organized political activity, forcibly halted political rallies, frequently harassed political opponents, and at times resorted to arbitrary arrests.[23] The government has worked to discredit the democratization process by arguing that political parties are to blame for past abuses in Uganda, although the NRM behaves in many ways like a political party. While the constitution adopted in 1995 theoretically allowed the formation of political parties, the normal activities associated with them, such as public rallies, delegates' conferences, and grassroots activities by branch offices, were outlawed. However, the NRM exempted itself from all these regulations. The NRM ensured its hegemony and contained all challenges to its legitimacy by fusing its structures with both state and society. However, the recent challenge has called into question this political order.

The NRM's influence has permeated Ugandan society via local, regional, and national institutions. According to Human Rights Watch:

> The NRM has effectively excluded itself from regulation by characterizing itself not as a political party but as a "movement," fusing its structures with those of the Ugandan state, and creating a pyramid of "movement" structures from the village level to the national level. All Ugandans belong to the "movement," even those who oppose it: compulsory membership that is itself inconsistent with the right to be forced to belong to an association.[24]

Such coerced membership into a single party or movement has effectively neutralized any serious attempts at democratic reforms based on multi-party politics. Both the political elite within the NRM, including Museveni, and officials of local government such as the local councils, and the resident district commissioners, have often viewed advocates of pluralism as enemies of the state. As a result, even seminars on the topics of human rights and democracy by NGOs have often been prohibited and at times dispersed violently.[25] In June and July of 1998, four such seminars sponsored by the Foundation for African Development (FAD) and the Uganda Young Democrats (UYD) were disrupted, some violently.

The pressures for democratic reforms originate almost entirely within Ugandan society. The society is accordingly characterized by partial openness in the form of the existence of a number of independent newspapers, radio, and television stations, which are not as politically effective because of frequent arrests and the harassment of journalists by the government. While the international community has been vigorous in its call for democratization in Kenya, it has adopted a remarkably quiet policy posture in the case of Uganda, ignoring abuses of civil rights and political liberties. Calls for a more pluralistic democratic system by the United States and other Western donors have rarely been backed up by actions, and as a result have had minimal impact on the progress towards a more democratic society. Forging a more amicable relationship with Museveni and the Ugandan government has been more of a priority for the international community than any serious efforts to dismantle the many abuses and restrictions of political rights in the country.

The international community has not been vigorous in its push for democratization in Uganda for the following reasons: (1) Museveni is considered a critical figure to the resolution of the ongoing crisis in the Great Lakes region, and he was especially crucial in ending the 1994 Rwandan genocide; (2) he is also viewed as a strong ally in the containment of radical Islamism in Sudan through his support of the Sudan Peoples Liberation Army (SPLA); (3) compared to the regimes of his predecessors, Museveni has so far more respect for human rights and has managed to maintain greater stability; and (4) his slogan of "African solutions to African problems" is in accord with the policy objectives of some Western leaders who are reluctant to get directly involved in Africa's crisis situations.[26]

However, in terms of legitimacy, Museveni and the NRM command a great deal of support within Ugandan society. The NRM has largely succeeded in preventing "the politics of religion, sectarianism, rivalry, and hatred" that characterized the Obote and Amin regimes.[27] Its prohibition of political party activities could in fact be considered a more effective implementation of former President Godfrey Binaisa's August 1979 government-imposed ban on political parties.

The NRM has succeeded in fostering a more accountable and representative government. Compared to past regimes, the human rights climate in the country has improved significantly because of institutional changes introduced by the NRM administration. It is in the area of political activities that the NRM seems to maintain a rigid and uncompromising attitude. To a large extent, the Ugandan parliament can be characterized as very representative. For example, during the 1996 elections some opposition politicians were allowed to contest elections as independents, and were successfully elected.[28] These opposition politicians were in fact closely associated with groups such as the Acholi parliamentary group, or the Gulu and Kitgum representatives. They often criticize government policy, thereby indicating that the Museveni regime tolerates some level of organized opposition.

During the pre-Museveni era, the civilian role in politics was minimal, mostly revolving around a small elite group. In 1995, Uganda implemented a far-reaching political decentralization program whose objective is to increase citizen participation and empower them in the crucial areas of taxation and development. This policy of decentralization intensified as a result of the 1997 Local Government Act based on Resistance Councils.[29] The council system encourages extensive civilian participation in the areas of local government. The NRM has especially made substantial progress in the empowerment of women through affirmative action programs aimed at increased representation of women at both the local and national levels. However, despite the increased scope of citizen political participation, the Ugandan national government, and especially the executive, is still far more dominant in the areas of overall policy for the country. In return for such inclusion into the political process, women are expected to be loyal to the movement system.

Similar to Kenya, Uganda's level of, and response to, democratization has been shaped by its post-independence experience. However, despite what appears to be substantial progress in the areas of participation and representation in the no-party model, the Ugandan political system is still lacking in many of the ingredients of democratic pluralism. For instance, while there is substantial citizen participation at the local grassroots level, there is no such participation at the national level. According to Mamdani, appointed by the NRM in 1987 to study local government, "the NRM was unable to link its participatory reform at the higher levels ..."[30] State authoritarianism, which persisted at the higher levels of government, was reflected in the lack of participation at the national level. Besides, local government structures undermine multi-party politics by subjecting political opponents and their supporters to abuse during elections. Only NRM candidates can become effective political candidates because local councils openly express their preference for a movement candidate.[31] During the 1996 presidential and parliamentary elections, both the National Organization for Civic Education and Elections Monitoring (NOCEM) and the International Foundation for Election Systems (IFES) confirmed the partisan role of local council officials in favor of movement candidates. Activities of these local council officials ranged from mobilization of pro-NRM support to paramilitary coercion or intimidation, and the use of what critics refer to as a disguised political indoctrination course emphasizing the belief that political parties are the root cause of Uganda's instability. Uganda's democratization process, similar to the Kenyan experience, is characterized by coerced legitimacy, limited representation, and continued authoritarianism, especially at the national level.

Tanzania: Transition from Socialism to Liberalization

Tanzania's democratization process, although turbulent on the islands of Zanzibar, seems to be gradually taking root within the society. The rural populace is now able to openly challenge the corrupt practices of district officials as reflected in the tax revolt against officials of Ameru District during the first half of 1998, when approximately 15,000 people marched on the regional headquarters in Arusha.[32] The tax uprising is significant because it indicates that the rural population has changed its attitudes from an acceptance of corrupt and illegitimate officials to open challenges against officials no longer viewed as legitimate and as genuinely representing the interests of the people.

In the pre-democratization Cold War era, Tanzanians rarely explicitly revolted against policy measures detrimental to their interests. Concrete examples of such detrimental policy measures were the abolition in 1972 of district councils, the 1975 abolition of primary co-operative societies, the coerced transfer of about five million people into nucleated *ujamaa* villages between 1973 and 1975, and the extensive and deliberate governmental erosion of producer prices for export crops throughout the 1970s.[33] Despite the unpopularity of these measures, they did not elicit any popular revolts against the government's legitimacy. Recent rural mobilization efforts and protests such as the Ameru tax revolt is a consequence of the effects the democratization ethos is having on the populace. Embedded in the democratization process is the need for regimes and their officials to be more representative and accountable by involving the population in the development process. Multi-party politics, a relatively free press, the separation of party and state, and a wider scope for civil society, among others, seem to be enhancing good governance in Tanzania.

The Tanzanian state's level of legitimacy has been affected by the continuing effect of economic stagnation and dislocation during the early 1980s. While the era of post-independence authoritarianism may have been tolerated because of the euphoria of newly-won independence, the era of post-Cold War democratization is one of reduced legitimacy. In economic terms, the position of Tanzania changed drastically in the 1980s when it dropped from the 14th poorest country in 1982, with a GNP per capita of $280, to the second poorest in 1990, with a GNP per capita of $110.[34] It was at this time that the Tanzanian government began negotiations with the IMF and the World Bank leading to the adoption of economic austerity programs. The consequence of the reduction in government spending, devaluation of the local currency, the liberalization of the national economy, and the promotion of international trade, resulted in ideologically undermining the accustomed post-war consensus over the role of the state in society, and especially the role of the Tanzanian state and its socialist program. The overall effect was a new economic environment for both groups and classes in society.[35]

Under the *ancien régime* of President Nyerere, the state was unequivocally dominant as reflected in its direct administration over all commercial banks, insurance companies, grain mills, and the main import-export firms.[36] Tanzania's economy was a distant cry from an open economy or a liberal democracy, as five-year plans were used to allocate resources and control patterns of development. The state extended its policies over the rural sector and the peasantry because political power and economic control were centralized in the president, TANU, and the bureaucracy.

However, since the 1980s, Tanzania has undergone a series of adjustment programs that have reduced the state's hegemony, impacted its capacity to perform social welfare functions, and thereby undermined its legitimacy. The combined impact of internal socio-economic developments, and external pressures from donors, forced Tanzania to endure a series of adjustment programs described in the Stephen Burgess chapter. The economic reform process has produced some positive results in the Tanzanian economy, such as 4 percent GDP growth by the end of the 1980s. However, this positive growth has not neutralized the effect of adverse earnings and rising unemployment.

The economic malaise of the 1980s was mainly caused by a decline in the terms of trade, a four-fold rise in oil prices, the rise in food grain prices, the war with Uganda, the breakup of East African Community, and the severe droughts of 1973-74 and 1981-82.[37] These factors undermined the administrative capacity of the Tanzanian state to perform its economic functions, dependent on its ability to extract sufficient resources from society, utilize a professional, competent, and cohesive bureaucracy for national development, and command the consent (legitimacy) of most of its citizens. While the Tanzanian state is weakest in performing the first two functions, it has, at the same time, lost a great deal of legitimacy, or the sense of citizens' obligations to obey state directives.

The current controversies and weaknesses surrounding Tanzania's democratization process thus largely stem from economic malaise, and the decrease in the state's capacity to perform its normal duties. The consequence has been an increase in the predatory (corrupt) behavior of state officials, who use public office for private gain because of the adverse effects of economic decline and economic austerity measures. This in turn translates to the diversion of funds earmarked for national development into private hands, and it reinforces the feeling that the incumbent regime does not adequately represent society.

Tanzania's road to democratization has been far from stable. The issues of regime legitimacy, representation, and state integrity are in fact being threatened by two inter-related factors: the resurgence of religious activism in politics, and election-related political violence. In the recent past, religion has resurfaced as a major issue in Tanzanian national politics.[38] This is true of both politics on the mainland and on the islands of Zanzibar. During the early post-independence years, it was the church that was urging the state to cooperate with and maintain close ties with representatives of the many religious groups in Tanzania. "Secular religiosity" was a major instrument utilized by the church to combat Marxism, which was then viewed as the only viable threat to the church. However, by the late 1960s, Islam emerged as a threat to the hegemony of the church over the secular Tanzanian state. The consequence was political insecurity on the part of the church, which viewed Islam as a threat to its long-held hegemony over Tanzanian national politics. Sivalon underscored this political anxiety on the part of the church:

> Islam [became] more and more of a problem. The Muslims succeeded to have a very big influence in policy making in Tanzania, trying to supplant our influence with their own and to profit to the utmost from our social services without accepting the principles of collaboration in a pluralist way laid down by a state.[39]

In particular, the Roman Catholic elite viewed the Muslims as simply intent on displacing the church from its dominance in Tanzanian society.

With this underlying religious struggle and tensions, it is therefore not surprising that democratization in Tanzania in the early 1990s was impacted by Muslim/Christian relations. In February 1993, Mwinyi admitted that "religious (Islamic) fanaticism is now vivid. This we must admit."[40] On the one hand, the church was worried about losing its dominant position and influential access to the Tanzanian state, and on the other hand, Muslims complained that they were systematically marginalized and largely excluded from the political hierarchy of the Tanzanian state.

The tensions between the two religions and their struggle for political control of the secular Tanzanian state have been responsible, along with the introduction of economic liberalization, for declining legitimacy and credibility for the Tanzanian state. The tensions and eroding state legitimacy intensified with the ideological vacuum that ushered in the 1990s. Besides, the opposition groups that emerged as a result of the democratization process could not articulate a broad policy posture that would enhance the state's decreasing legitimacy and foster unity among the different groups struggling for political hegemony. Similar to Kenya and Uganda, the combined effect of the end of political ideology that came with the Cold War's demise and the introduction of economic and political liberalization, produced the resurgence of ethno-political tensions, regional parochialism, sub-nationalistic and religious tensions.

The catalyst for the reaction of the church hierarchy to Muslim political activism was the unilateral decision by Zanzibar to join the Organization of Islamic Conference (OIC). This decision was interpreted as a challenge to the unitary secular state, and as a deliberate move towards the Islamicization of Tanzania. However, the Zanzibar political elite argued that their decision to join the organization was based solely on economic reasons.[41] While many Muslims applauded the move, many Christians condemned it as a dangerous trend. Muslim leaders responded that CCM tended to marginalize and under-represent them in the institutions of government. By the 1990s, the continued expectations of a genuine secular unitary Tanzania had been challenged. Many articulated the view that the supposed secularity of the unitary nation-state was a myth. Aboud Jumbe, a former president of Zanzibar, pointed to the gross imbalance between Muslim and Christian representation in the organs of power.[42]

In 1993, churches directed their attacks at both the state and the CCM. In a May 1993 pastoral letter by Catholic bishops, the country's political elite was described as "... full of hypocrisy, lies, tricks and laxity. As a result, leadership is unstable, the nation has lost political direction and gets easily swayed by external forces."[43] In particular, the churches accused the state of gross corruption, mismanagement of public funds and natural resources. The scope and intensity of Christian attacks against the state were such that by 1994 they had assumed the proportions of an opposition party. While the Muslims emphasized their marginalization and under-representation, the Christians demanded more democratic rule in the form of greater transparency, human rights, and constitutionality.

Apart from the potential instability from the Christian-Muslim divide, electoral competition in Tanzania has also been a problem. In the 1995 presidential elections, CUF refused to accept the outcome partly because of a four-day delay in the announcement of the results. Violence erupted on the islands following opposition claims of massive electoral fraud by the incumbent CCM, which had been in power since independence. Similarly, in October 2000 opposition supporters clashed with police in Zanzibar following a day of chaotic elections in which thousands of people failed to vote because ballot papers either arrived late or did not arrive at all. The police had to use teargas and live ammunition to disperse hundreds of CUF supporters. In the view of the Commonwealth Observer Group, the elections of October 29, 2000 were "a shambles."[44]

The fact that the 1995 and 2000 general elections in Zanzibar were widely believed to have been rigged by the ruling party demonstrates that Tanzania is still plagued by the legacy of decades of authoritarian rule. Intimidation of the largely Muslim opposition during the October 2000 Zanzibar elections took the form of denying the opposition permits to hold rallies, bureaucratic sabotage of the opposition by preventing it from registering, and the movement of unregistered CCM supporters from the mainland to opposition strongholds on the islands.[45] In Tanzania, Kenya, and Uganda, the issue of the legitimacy of power has not ceased to be a problem, even with the post-Cold War democratization process.

The Impact of Institutional-Structural Constraints

The democratization process in Kenya, Uganda, and Tanzania should be viewed within the context of structural-institutional constraints that severely restrict political elite's room for autonomous decision-making. State structures and institutional constraints, coupled with external pressures, undermine a regime's legitimacy, as well as elites' perceptions of, and the possibilities for, more egalitarian policies. Reduced state capacity and inept rule are often the result of the inherent incompatibilities between informal (pre-colonial) and formal institutional (colonial and postcolonial globalization) values that manifest themselves in patronage, corruption, mal-representation, coercive state hegemony, and external impositions.

These past and current structural constraints make the issues of legitimacy, balanced representation, and regime integrity irreconcilable goals. Instead of helping to control the worst impulses of ethno-nationalism, the freedom of action and expression inherent in democratization often exacerbates inter-communal and state-society tensions. Thus, in East Africa, the success modalities of a democratization process that enhances ethnic and religious harmony have yet to be worked out. Besides, the necessary resources and institutional means necessary to achieve greater inter-communal inclusion and cohesion are woefully lacking.

Legitimacy and responsible governance are challenged even more by economic liberalization, which has been tied to the process of democratization by the international donors. Economic liberalization in weak states has undermined the twentieth-century ethos of the state as the responsible advocate for facilitating the economic well-being of its citizens. The state bears responsibility for functions ranging from the maintenance of domestic tranquility and protection of the territory against external attacks to contributions to the material security of the members of society.[46] In general, however, political liberalization devoid of societal cohesion and a high level of economic development is often plagued by electoral conflict and intense political rivalry. The recent past in Kenya and Uganda support this assertion. The indexing of economic liberalization to political liberalization has also served as a stumbling block to the realization of democratic stability in many African states, including Kenya, Uganda, and Tanzania.

The developmental success of advanced industrial states is generally a strong argument that economic liberalization and political liberalization are interconnected and mutually supportive processes.[47] Evidence from developing countries, however, suggests that there is no consensus regarding the real dynamics between them. To a large extent, the general relationship between the two is one of a dialectical tension with economic liberalization acting as a constraint on political liberalization because of the limits it can put on the extent of political reforms. The consequence of this dialectical tension is an oscillation between progress and regression within a context of lingering authoritarianism erroneously labeled democratization.

The interaction of economic liberalization and political liberalization presents serious dilemmas for African states because of its contradictory consequences. The government is often confronted with the choice of when and how much to liberalize the economy or how to prioritize the various adjustment programs that constitute economic liberalization and reform. Often the state, concerned with the negative consequences of economic liberalization, can deliberately stall in its implementation of the required measures. It is forced to waver between strict control and restricted elections. In the final analysis, political liberalization can act as a brake on economic liberalization, and the latter can in turn severely undermine democratization. The fear of political instabilities caused by severe distributional inequities often keeps the state heavily involved in the economy.

African governments operating in a context of fragile legitimacy and a legacy of structural-institutional constraints are often faced with the dilemma of whether to shield the military or other groups from the austerity measures inherent in structural adjustments. If certain groups are privileged by economic liberalization, the government is invariably confronted with resistance from the economically deprived and politically excluded groups in society whose interests are not protected by the new political economy. Generally, political liberalization without visible economic improvement is likely to cause enough deprivation to delegitimize the incumbent regime, awaken nostalgia for a more authoritarian regime, intensify ethnic divisions, or instigate a military intervention in politics, or even civil war.[48] This is why in East Africa, corruption maintains legitimacy and is an integral aspect of neo-patrimonial politics characterized by the allocation of patronage favors by politicians to their clients. In return, the recipient of the benefactor's largess provides political allegiance and influence peddling throughout the general population. The politics of patronage is also used to provide government jobs and certain types of gifts as a means of securing support from various individuals and groups.

In order to make the appropriate transition from authoritarian to neoliberal systems, the institutional frameworks need to be developed. Where well-established and supportive economic institutions are absent, far-reaching political reforms are likely to generate a barrage of demands and problems that increasingly undermine regime legitimacy.

The international donors and other foreign actors are involved in efforts to legitimize the regimes in these countries by: (1) urging the observation of civil rights and political liberties; (2) targeting the corrupt practices of politicians and top government officials through the establishment of anti-corruption agencies; (3) ensuring that, at least, procedural democracy (regular, free, and fair elections) is observed; and (4) using economic aid to strengthen the new institutions of liberalization. The IMF and World Bank, in particular, have often frozen lending when a country refuses to comply with all or some of these requirements.

In all three states, the overwhelming success of the incumbent parties have, to a large extent, produced a situation akin to single-party rule as the opposition becomes increasingly marginalized and ineffective. The tendency of "absolute" power continues to generate corrupt practices that practically undermine democratization. Recent advances in Kenya provide evidence that this is not inevitable, but sufficient energy and resources need to be devoted to the democratic gains achieved to assure for sustainability. One consequence of overwhelming incumbent party dominance is that the military becomes politicized in favor of the regime. The ruling party therefore stifles the growth of a pluralistic and democratic political culture by ensuring a symbiotic relationship with the government and the military. A regime-party-military symbiotic relationship can be defined as a process and condition whereby the boundary line between the military, the democratically elected civilian government, and its political party is hardly distinguishable.[49]

Finally, democratization in East Africa also tends to be diluted by "old guard" politicians devoid of any innovative ideas and still plagued by corrupting tendencies.[50] The Kenyan and Tanzanian political systems are no doubt full of old timers who have been active in politics since the 1960s. There remains the risk that throughout the democratization process these politicians will simply recycle and reinvent themselves but remain devoid of genuine democratic pluralist values and new ideas necessary for genuine democracy to flourish.

Concluding Comments

Issues of legitimacy, representation, and state hegemony constitute a problematic in the democratization process and the overall nation-building effort in East Africa. At the heart of this transitional problematic is the negative competitive relationship among groups reflected in either ethno-political, ethno-religious, or state-society conflicts. The internal and external issues of deepening social inequality, reduced state capacity impacting on societal welfare, coupled with other negative effects of globalization processes seemed to have slowed down the progress of political pluralism in the sub-region. While civil society and popular identities mobilized in response to the introduction of political liberalization, the state decided to reassert its political hegemony by frustrating many attempts at genuine democratic pluralism.

In all three countries, the state of democratization can be characterized as one of partial openness where regime legitimacy is constantly challenged. Representation is also unbalanced in favor of areas of incumbent party support, with the state ensuring its hegemony through systematic government interference with the work of human rights groups and the media, as well as by timely state-sponsored internal terror.

In the final analysis, democratization in East Africa is bound to suffer a checkered course because of the lack of any profound changes in political and economic values both within society and in terms of state-society interactions. Any changes in political and economic practice seem to be occurring together in a mutually destructive fashion as manifested in the intensification of ethno-political tensions and conflicts. Democratization has been underlined by widespread misery and socio-political conflicts in which ethnic, regional, religious, class, group, and other struggles play a key role. Responsible and progressive leadership, constructive criticism, and an active and equally responsible civil society are essential to overcoming the myriad obstacles to the democratization process in the region.

Notes

[1] The literature on the issue of legitimacy is abundant. For example, see Paul M. Sniderman, Joseph F. Fletcher, Peter H. Russell, and Philip E. Tetlock, eds., *The Clash of Rights: Liberty, Equality, and Legitimacy in Pluralist Democracy* (New Haven, CT: Yale University Press, 1996); Matteí Dogan, ed., *Comparing Pluralist Democracies: Strains on Legitimacy* (Boulder, CO: Westview Press, 1988); and Pippa Norris, ed., *Critical Citizens: Global Support for Democratic Government* (New York: Oxford University Press, 1999).

[2] For details, see Patrick Chabal, *Power in Africa: an Essay in Political Interpretation* (Hampshire: Macmillan, 1992).

[3] See for example, James S. Wunsch, and Dele Olowu, eds., *The Failure of the Centralized State: Institutions and Self-governance in Africa* (Boulder, CO: Westview Press, 1990).

[4] On neo-patrimonialism, see Jean-François Medard, "The Underdeveloped State in Tropical Africa: Political Clientelism or Neo-Patrimonialism," in Christopher Clapham, ed., *Private Patronage and Public Power* (London: Frances Pinter, 1982).

[5] For further details, see Earl Conteh-Morgan, *Democratization in Africa - The Theory and Dynamic of Political Transitions* (Westport: Praeger, 1997).

[6] For a detailed analysis of the concept of power, see John K. Galbraith, *The Anatomy of Power* (Boston, MA: Houghton Mifflin, 1983); and Peter Morriss, *Power: A Philosophical Analysis* (New York: St. Martin's Press, 1987).

[7] See for example: World Bank data from *Poverty Assessments* and *World Development Reports, 1991-1993* (Washington, D.C.: 1991-1993).

[8] For details see, James S. Wunsch, "Centralization and Development in Post-Independence Africa," in James S. Wunsch and Dele Olowu, eds., *The Failure of the Centralized State* (Boulder, CO: Westview, 1990).

[9] For more details on Kenya, Uganda, and Tanzania, see Mario Azevedo, ed., *Kenya: the Land, the People, and the Nation* (Durham, NC: Carolina Academic Press, 1993); Thomas R. Ofcansky, *Uganda: Tarnished Pearl of Africa* (Boulder, CO.: Westview Press, 1996); and Rodger Yeager, *Tanzania: An African Experiment* (Boulder, CO.: Westview, 1982).

[10] For an elaboration, see Patrick Chabal, *Power in Africa: an Essay in Political Interpretation* (Houndsmill: Macmillan, 1992).

[11] See for example, Robert H. Jackson, and Carl G. Rosberg, *Personal Rule in Black Africa: Prince, Autocrat, Prophet, Tyrant* (Berkeley: University of California Press, 1982).

[12] Jan Aart Scholte, "The Globalization of World Politics," in John Baylis and Steve Smith, eds., *The Globalization of World Politics: An Introduction to International Relations* (Oxford: Oxford University Press, 1997), p. 28.

[13] For details see Akbarali Thobhani, "Political Developments During the 1990s" in Mary Ann Watson, ed., *Modern Kenya* (Lanham: University Press of America, 2000), pp. 1-21.

[14] For evidence on the use of state terror in Kenya, see Human Rights Watch, *State Sponsored Ethnic Violence in Kenya* (New York: Human Rights Watch, 1993).

[15] See, *New People* (April 1, 2001); and *the Daily Nation* (April 23, 2001).

[16] See, Boniface Kaona, "Moi Sues Hempstone over Ouko," *East African Standard* [Online Edition] (Tuesday, July 31, 2001); and *Sunday Nation* (May 9, 1999).

[17] See for details, Jonah Anguka, *Absolute Power* (London: Penn Press, 1998); and *West Africa* (July 1998), p. 578.

[18] For details, see Transparency International, *Global Corruption Report 2001* (Berlin: Transparency International, 2001), East and Central Africa, pp. 68-80.

[19] See Akbarali Thobani, "Political Developments During the 1990s," in Mary Ann Watson, ed., *Modern Kenya*.

[20] Human Rights Watch, *State-Sponsored Ethnic Violence in Kenya*.

[21] John W. Harbeson, "Political Crisis and Renewal in Kenya–Prospects for Democratic Consolidation," *Africa Today* (April-June 1998), p. 169.

[22] For details on violence during the 1997 elections see: Amnesty International, *Kenya: Political Violence Spirals* (June 10, 1998).

[23] For further details see Human Rights Watch, *Hostile to Democracy: The Movement System and Political Repression in Uganda* (New York: Human Rights Watch, 1999).

[24] Human Rights Watch, *Hostile to Democracy*, p. 3.

[25] See for example, Sylvia Tamale, *When Hens Begin to Crow: Gender and Parliamentary Politics in Uganda* (Boulder, CO: Westview Press, 1999).

[26] For details, see: Human Rights Watch, *Hostile to Democracy*, pp. 7-8.

[27] Phares Mutibwa, *Uganda Since Independence: A story of Unfulfilled Hope* (Trenton, NJ: Africa World Press, 1992), p. 134.

[28] See for example John M. Waliggo, "Constitution-Making and the Politics of Democratization in Uganda," in Holder B. Hansen and Michael Twaddle, *From Chaos to Order: The Politics of Constitution-Making in Uganda* (Kampala: Fountain Publishers, 1995).

[29] For details on the decentralization process in Uganda, see Apolo Nsibambi, ed., *Decentralization and Civil Society in Uganda: The Quest for Good Governance* (Kampala: Fountain Publishers, 1998).

[30] Mahmood Mamdani, *Citizen and Subject: Contemporary Africa and the Legacy of Late Colonialism* (Princeton, NJ: Princeton University Press, 1996), p. 216.

[31] Human Rights Watch, *Hostile to Democracy*, p. 55.

[32] For details on the revolt, see Tim Kelsall, "Governance, Local Politics and Districtization in Tanzania: The 1988 Arumeru Tax Revolt," *Africa Affairs* (2000), pp. 533-551.

[33] See Goran Hyden, *Beyond Ujamaa in Tanzania: Underdevelopment and an Uncaptured Peasantry* (University of California Press, 1980).

[34] See World Bank, *World Development Report 1992* (Oxford: Oxford University Press, 1992); and Mahmood Messkoub, "The Social Impact of Adjustment in Tanzania in the 1980s: Economic Crisis and Household Survival Strategies" (University of Leeds: School of Business and Economic Studies, 2001).

[35] See World Bank, *World Development Report 1994* (Oxford: Oxford University Press, 1994); B.C. Nindi, "Compulsion in the Implementation of Ujamaa," in Norman O'Neill and Kemal Mustafa, eds., *Capitalism, Socialism and the Development Crisis in Tanzania* (Aldershot: Avebury, 1990).

[36] For details see: Mahmood Messkoub, "The Social Impact of Adjustment in Tanzania in the 1980s: Economic Crisis and Household Survival Strategies."

[37] See for example: Aili Mari Tripp, *Changing the Rules: the Politics of Liberalization and the UrbanIinformalEconomy in Tanzania* (Berkeley: University of California Press, 1997).

[38] See Nestor N. Luanda, "Christianity and Islam Contending for the Throne on the Tanzanian Mainland," in Adebayo O. Olukoshi and Liisa Laakso, *Challenges to the Nation-State in Africa* (Uppsala: Nordic Institute of African Studies, 1996).

[39] J.C. Sivalon, as quoted in Nestor Luanda, "Christianity and Islam Contending for the Throne on the Tanzanian Mainland," p. 170.

[40] *The Express* (February 3, 1993).

[41] *Mfanyakazi* (January 28-February 3, 1993).

[42] *Mwananchi* (March 22-28, 1993).

[43] *Heko* (June 24-30, 1993).

[44] Inter Press Service, "Post Election Violence Erupts in Zanzibar" (October 30, 2000).

[45] For details see Nathalie Arnold and Bruce Kim, "Zanzibar is Besieged by Tanzanian Security Forces," *Media Monitors Network* (Feb. 3, 2001), pp. 1-6.

[46] For details, see Peter Gibbon, Yusuf Bangura, and Arve Ofstad, *Authoritarianism, Democracy, and Adjustment: The Politics of Economic Reform in Africa* (Uppsala, Sweden: Scandinavian Institute of African Studies, 1992).

[47] See World Bank, *World Development Report (1991): The Challenge of Development* (New York: Oxford University Press, 1991).

[48] See Lual Deng, Markus Kostner, and Crawford Young, eds., *Democratization and Structural Adjustment in Africa in the 1990s* (Madison: African Studies Program, University of Wisconsin-Madison, 1991).

[49] For details on this relationship see Earl Conteh-Morgan, *Democratization in Africa: The Theory and Dynamics of Political Transitions* (Westport, CT: Praeger, 1997).

[50] For an elaboration, see Julius E. Nyang'oro, "Critical Notes on Political Liberalization in Africa," *Journal of Asian and African Studies* vol. 31, nos. 1-2 (June 1996), p. 117.

Timeline of Key Historical Events

Kenya

1895	Kenya, known as British East Africa, becomes a British colony.
July 1923	"White Paper" issued, determining that Kenya colony would ultimately be developed in the interests of the African majority.
October 1944	Eliud Mathu becomes first African representative on Kenya's Legislative Council.
	Kenya African Union (KAU) is formed to agitate for inclusion of Africans in ownership of land. Jomo Kenyatta assumes the leadership of KAU three years later.
October 1952	Mau Mau insurgency begins in Kenya; Jomo Kenyatta is arrested and tried for leading the insurgency.
February 1956	Dedan Kimathi, the military head of Mau Mau, is captured; Mau Mau insurgency is suppressed.
January 1960	KAU is reorganized as Kenya African National Union (KANU).
August 1961	Kenyatta is released from detention and assumes KANU leadership.
May 1963	KANU wins elections in Kenya.
June 1963	Kenya gains self-rule.
December 1963	Kenya gains independence from Britain under the KANU with Jomo Kenyatta as the Prime Minister.
December 1964	Kenyatta becomes President following the adoption of a republican constitution and establishes KANU as the

	dominant political party in Kenya after the dissolution of the Kenya African Democratic Union (KADU), the main opposition party of which Daniel arap Moi was Chair.
March 1966	Oginga Odinga resigns from the vice-presidency and KANU, and forms the Kenya People's Union (KPU).
	Pio Gama Pinto, a radical political of Goan descent and close ally of Oginga Odinga, is assassinated.
April 1966	Odinga and his KPU emerge as a major opposition party to KANU.
	"Mini-elections" held to weed out Kenyatta opponents.
July 1969	Tom Mboya, ambitious KANU Secretary General and Minister of Economic Planning, is assassinated. Riots break out in Nairobi and Kisumu leading Kenyatta to proscribe KPU and detain its leaders.
October 1969	KPU is banned.
March 1975	Josiah Mwangi (JM) Kariuki, a populist politician and vocal critic of the Kenyatta regime, is assassinated.
June 1976	In response to Soviet military support for Uganda and Somalia, the U.S. extends for the first time military assistance to Kenya.
August 1978	Jomo Kenyatta dies and is succeeded by Vice President Daniel arap Moi in a smooth transfer of power.
November 1979	Moi is elected to a full five-year term in a general election, which runs concurrently with legislative elections.
June 1980	U.S. signs a military facilities access agreement with Kenya. U.S. gains over flight rights, access to airfields, and port of call permission at Mombasa.
June 1982	Constitution amended to establish a *de jure* single-party state.
August 1982	Elements of the Kenya Air Force stages a coup to overthrow Moi's government. The *coup* is crushed, but

	the event marks a steady rise in repressive policies by the Moi regime.
May 1983	The so-called "traitor affair" leads to the dismissal of Constitutional Affairs Minister Charles Njonjo, the dissolution of the National Assembly and a snap election.
September 1983	Moi is elected to another five-year term. Political opposition is harshly quelled following elections.
February 1988	KANU abandons the secret ballot and introduces the "queue voting" electoral system, which required voters to line up in open support of a certain candidate. Those who garner over 70 percent of the votes were also declared winners of the general elections.
August 1988	National Assembly grants the president the power to dismiss judges at will, and to detain people for 14 days without charges.
November 1989	Smith Hempstone is appointed U.S. ambassador to Kenya by the George Bush Sr. administration. Hempstone later turns out to a staunch supporter of the multi-party campaign, drawing the ire of the Moi Administration.
February 1990	Robert Ouko, the Foreign Minister, is mysteriously murdered by political opponents for investigating government corruption. The public's suspicion of a government cover-up sparks off mass demonstrations and riots.
May 1990	Ambassador Hempstone tells Kenya that U.S. Congress is not likely to reward countries with aid that are not making progress in creating democratic systems of government. This warning coincides with the announcement by two former cabinet ministers, Kenneth Matiba and Charles Rubia, of plans to push for political reforms and then remove Moi from power. KANU unleashes harsh criticism of Hempstone for interfering with internal affairs.
June 1990	Catholic Bishops' Conference issues a pastoral letter questioning a single-party system.

July 1990 Anti-government riots, dubbed Saba Saba, leave 28 killed and 1,400 arrested after police use strong arm tactics to break up a political rally.

October 1990 U.S. Senator Patrick Leahy visits Kenya and promises that next year's military aid will not be dispersed unless meaningful progress is made toward building democracy.

Political activist Koigi wa Wamwere is arrested. When the Norwegian Ambassador complains about how Koigi is treated at the hands of the state, he is expelled from the country, Kenya severs diplomatic relations, and Norway retaliates by suspending $31million in aid.

December 1990 A KANU conference reconfirms its support for a single-party system.

February 1991 Doyen of Kenyan opposition politics, Oginga Odinga, challenges the Moi government and KANU by launching the National Democratic Party.

August 1991 Forum for the Restoration of Democracy in Kenya (FORD) is formed, but it is outlawed and its members are arrested.

November 1991 President Moi's closest ally, Nicholas Biwott, is implicated in the assassination of Robert Ouko and dismissed from the cabinet.

"Paris Club" of international lenders postpones a decision on $350 million in quick-disbursing loans to Kenya, calling for progress on political reform. U.S. suspends assistance worth $28m.

December 1991 Special Conference of KANU endorses Moi plan for a multi-party system and abandons the system of "queue-voting." A number of KANU prominent members join the opposition. The former vice president and the health minister Mwai Kibaki resigns from the cabinet to form the Democratic Party of Kenya.

Section 2A of the constitution is repealed ending the single-party system.

Moi repeatedly warns that multi-party politics would lead to ethnic violence.

October 1992 FORD splits into FORD-Asili, led by Kenneth Matiba, and FORD-Kenya, led by Oginga Odinga.

Government set date for national elections to be held on December 7, but High Court rules against the short notice and sets the date at December 29.

December 1992 Moi wins presidential elections with 37 percent of the total vote, while KANU wins majority seats in legislative elections with less than 50 percent of the vote. The first multi-party elections since 1966 are considered tainted by fraud, rigging and government voter intimidation by international observers.

February 1993 Citizens' Coalition for Constitutional Change launched to mobilize civil society to pressure for reforms.

November 1993 Consultative Group reconvenes and offers the Moi regime $170 million with conditions, including improved human rights, better governance, and an end to the KANU-provoked ethnic clashes.

February 1994 Oginga Odinga dies and Michael Wamalwa Kijana takes over leadership of FORD-Kenya and official opposition.

October 1996 IMF and World Bank launch the Highly Indebted Poor Countries (HIPC) program.

July 1995 The U.K. withholds financial assistance pending an improvement in the Moi Administration's human rights policies and financial management.

February 1997 Moi signs into law the Preservation of National Security Act, which grants sweeping powers to the government including the suppression of political party activities.

June 1997 Moi accedes to opposition demands for constitutional reforms, which would remove archaic and repressive laws.

July 1997	Moi regime cracks down on an opposition rally in Uhuru Park, touching off countrywide demonstrations and repression.
	IMF suspends its $220 million Enhanced Structural Adjustment Facility (ESAF), and World Bank and donors withholds more than $180 million, causing massive capital flight.
August 1997	Violence targeting non-coastal people breaks out in the Coast Province, severely damaging the tourist industry – a mainstay of the Kenyan economy.
November 1997	Inter-Parties Parliamentary Group (IPPG) negotiates minimal constitutional and legal changes to allow 1997 elections to proceed.
	Moi signs into law the constitutional amendments that aim at ensuring future free and democratic elections.
December 1997	Moi is re-elected with a 39 percent of the votes. KANU retains control of parliament with a razor thin majority.
January 1998	Moi declared winner and sworn in for a fifth five-year term as President.
	Moi enters into a cooperative agreement with Raila Odinga and his National Development Party (NDP).
	Implementation of Constitution of Kenya Review Act (1997), part of IPPG package of reforms, begins but stalls amid controversies.
August 1998	U.S. Embassy in Nairobi is attacked by a terrorist car bomb, leaving 254 dead and over 5,000 injured. Osama bin Laden and his Al Queda organization are linked to the attack.
July 1999	Moi appoints paleontologist and conservationist Richard Leakey to head the Kenya civil service and lead a "dream team" in the fight against government corruption and inefficiency.
July 2000	Kenya and the IMF reach an agreement for a three-year aid package worth $198 million.

August 2000	IMF releases $150 million in "poverty reduction and growth facilities" PRGF credits to Kenya.
September 2000	Moi meets with IMF and World Bank leaders in New York and agrees to adopt a Code of Conduct, whereby all top leaders, except Moi, must declare their wealth.
November 2000	Yash Pal Ghai appointed to chair the Constitution of Kenya Review Commission (CKRC).
December 2000	Kenya Anti-Corruption Authority (KACA) is effectively dismantled after a Constitutional Court rules that it had no powers to prosecute corruption cases.
January 2001	IMF withholds funds after the reform process suffers serious setbacks, particularly the disbandment of KACA.
	Moi and Raila Odinga sign a MOU that later leads to the formation of a coalition government between KANU and NDP.
March 2001	Moi fires Leakey's "dream team" that was appointed to cut corruption, please donors, and lead the anti-corruption campaign.
May 2001	Parliament amends Constitution of Kenya Review Act to allow the merger of civil society and religious group with the parliament sanctioned Review Commission. Formal review begins.
June 2001	Reshuffling his cabinet, Moi appoints Raila Odinga energy minister, creating Kenya's first coalition government.
July 2001	President files libel lawsuit in Kenya accusing Smith Hempstone of speculating in his memoirs, the *Rogue Ambassador*, that Moi was involved in the murder of Robert Ouko.
	IMF suspends three-year $216 million loan package to Kenya.
August 2001	Kenyan parliament votes down a bill that would have created an anti-corruption body to investigate official graft in the country.

	World Bank and IMF suspend loans and credits worth $71.6 million.
February 2002	DP, Ford-Kenya, the National Party of Kenya and opposition parties sign MOU to form the National Alliance for Change (NAC).
March 2002	NDP dissolves and merges into KANU to form the New KANU. The NDP leader, Raila Odinga is "elected" secretary-general of New KANU in a stage-managed election.
June 2002	Government sends signals that it intends to delay elections scheduled in December by one year on the pretext that the constitutional review process must first be completed. The plan is abandoned and Moi announces he would retire after the elections following fierce international and domestic opposition.
	NAC becomes National Alliance Party of Kenya (NAK)
July 2002	Twelve opposition parties, among them DP and FORD Kenya, form an electoral alliance, the National Alliance Party of Kenya (NAK).
August 2002	Moi's anointment of Uhuru Kenyatta, the son of his predecessor, as his successor leads to divisions within the ruling party. This dissension leads to the formation of a Rainbow Coalition within KANU comprising Odinga, George Saitoti, Musalia Mudavadi, Kalonzo Musyoka and Joseph Kamotho, all ministers in the Moi government.
September 2002	CKRC produces a draft constitution despite attempts through the High Court to derail its work.
October 2002	Members of the Rainbow Alliance defects from KANU to Liberal Democratic Party (LDP).
	LDP enters into a series of talk with other opposition parties that lead to signing of two MOUs on power sharing after Moi and the formation of the National Rainbow Coalition (NARC) with Kibaki as its Presidential candidate and Michael Wamalwa as his running mate.

December 2002	NARC ousts KANU from power with a landslide victory. Moi peacefully hands over power to Mwai Kibaki, who becomes the third president of the Republic of Kenya.
January 2003	Kibaki forms a new government but immediately faces criticisms for not following the MOU that called for "equal" distribution of government positions.
April 2003	Implementation of the MOU becomes acrimonious issue threatening the newly installed government. LDP emerges as the main opposition to the government although it is a partner. This leads alliance formations between the parties and within the ruling coalition.
June 2003	President Kibaki and Kenya lead Tanzania and Uganda in reviving economic cooperation within the East African Community (EAC), while neighbors like Burundi and Rwanda become interested.
July 2003	World Bank resumes loans to Kenya.
September 2003	National Constitutional Conference is threatened with collapse over contentious issues such as creation of the office of an executive prime minister.
October 2003	Release of a judicial report by a team headed by Justice Aaron Ringera culminates in the suspension of 23 judges of the Court of Appeal and High Court for corruption and incompetence. Seventeen of the judges opt to retire/resign rather than go before a judicial tribunal.
November 2003	Paris Club resumes aid.
December 2003	KANU and FORD-People form the Coalition for National Unity (CNU) with Simeon Nyachae as its head and Uhuru Kenyatta as his deputy.
January 2004	Last phase of the National Constitutional Conference (Bomas III) convenes.
	Expanded NARC Summit meets amid controversies over the power sharing and implementation of the MOU.

Tanzania

1885	Tanganyika declared a German protectorate.
1920	Great Britain assumes a League of Nations Mandate over Tanganyika.
1946	Tanganyika becomes a U.N. trust territory under British Administration.
1954	Tanganyika African Association (TAA) is formed under the leadership of Julius Nyerere.
August 1960	TANU wins elections decisively in Tanganyika under leadership of Julius Nyerere, who becomes the Chief Minister.
May 1961	Tanganyika granted self-rule.
December 1961	Tanganyika gains independence from Britain under TANU as the ruling party and Julius Nyerere as the Prime Minister.
December 1961	Tanganika breaks diplomatic relations with Portugal over its colonial occupation of African territories.
January 1962	Nyerere resigns as Prime Minister and is succeeded by Rashidi Kawawa.
November 1962	Nyerere is elected President.
December 1962	Tanganika becomes a republic with Nyerere's return to power as the first president.
December 1963	Zanzibar becomes an independent sultanate under the Zanzibar Nationalist Party (ZNP).
January 1964	Zanzibar Revolution takes place; ZNP and the Sultan are overthrown and Afro-Shirazi Party (ASP) is installed as ruling party. West warns that Zanzibar is the 'Cuba of Africa'.
	Tanganyika army troops go on a mutiny and are put down by British troops.

	Tanzania for the first time accepts military assistance from a non-Western power, China.
April 1964	Tanganyika signs an Act of Union with Zanzibar to form Union of the United Republic of Tanzania.
October 1964	Mainland Tanganyika and the islands of Zanzibar and Pemba become a new country named Tanzania with Nyerere as its president and Abeid Karume, the leader of ASP, as the first vice-president.
January 1965	Two U.S. diplomats are expelled from Tanzania on the suspicion of plotting a counter-revolution in Zanzibar. The U.S. responds by recalling its ambassador and expelling a Tanzanian diplomat from Washington.
February 1965	West Germany suspends military assistance to Tanzania because an East German consulate is opened in Zanzibar.
July 1965	A new constitution that provides for a single-party state is introduced.
December 1965	Tanzania breaks diplomatic relations with U.K. over Rhodesian white settlers' unilateral declaration of independence (UDI). In response U.K. suspends aid.
February 1967	The Arusha Declaration announced to launch Tanzania on a socialist path of development. Considerable British property is nationalized.
September 1965	Nyerere is returned to power through the first single-party election.
April 1970	Construction of Chinese financed Tanzania-Zambia railway (TAZARA) line from Dar es Salaam to Zambia begins.
April 1971	Another round of nationalizations in Tanzania results in transfer of ownership of 2 million pounds of British property.
December 1971	Peoples Republic of China takes over from U.K. as Tanzania's most important external donor.

April 1972	President Karume in Zanzibar is assassinated; Aboud Jumbe succeeds him.
July 1972	District Councils are abolished.
September 1972	Tanzania supports an invasion of Uganda by pro-Obote forces. Ugandan Air Force bombs target in northwestern Tanzania and wades off invasion.
November 1973	Beginning of coerced relocation of about five million people into nucleated villages (*vijiji*), and governmental erosion of producer prices for export crops through the 1970s.
June 1975	National Assembly votes to incorporate the fundamental principles of African Socialism and self-reliance into the constitution.
February 1977	TANU and Afro-Shirazi Party (ASP) merge to form the Chama Cha Mapinduzi (CCM) or the Revolutionary Party of Tanzania. Nyerere is elected CCM Chairman and Jumbe his deputy.
April 1977	National Assembly adopts a permanent constitution for the Union with a clause making CCM the only legal political party in Tanzania.
July 1977	East African Community acrimoniously breaks up.
October 1977	A new Constitution makes CCM the only political party.
January 1979	Tanzania invades Uganda and Amin is forced to flee the country in April heading first to Libya and then to Saudi Arabia where he is granted political asylum.
October 1979	Supreme Revolutionary Council of Zanzibar adopts a separate constitution for the islands and calls for popular elections of the president and members of the House of Representatives by CCM delegates.
January 1984	Jumbe resigns.
April 1984	Ali Hassan Mwinyi is elected president of Zanzibar and becomes Tanzanian vice-president.

October 1984	Forty of 153 articles of the Union constitution are amended to liberalize politics, allowing Zanzibar some autonomy, limiting presidential terms to two but retaining a single party.
January 1985	Mwinyi introduces a new constitution in Zanzibar that provides for direct election of House of Representatives delegates and a Commonwealth legal system.
November 1985	Nyerere retires as president of the republic and is succeeded by Ali Hassan Mwinyi. Nyerere retains his portfolio as CCM leader.
August 1986	Tanzanian President Mwinyi agrees to a World Bank/IMF SAP, and Economic Recovery Program (ERP) begins.
October 1987	Nyerere is re-elected CCM chair for another 5-year term. Cleopa Msuya, finance minister who had been holding talks with the IMF, is dropped from the party central committee.
January 1988	Seif Shariff Hamad is removed as Zanzibar's chief minister.
	Zanzibari President Wakil suspends the Supreme Revolutionary Council on the grounds that some of its members were planning to overthrow his government.
May 1988	Hamad and associates are expelled from CCM.
May 1989	Hamad is arrested in Zanzibar.
July 1989	Tanzania's ERP is reinforced by an Economic and Social Action Program (ESAP).
December 1989	1,000 troops are dispatched from the mainland to Zanzibar in response to reports that a *coup* is being planned.
February 1990	Nyerere opens multi-party debate in Tanzania.
	CCM initiates a campaign against corruption among government officials.

March 1990	Mwinyi dismisses 7 cabinet ministers allegedly opposed to his economic reform program and for corrupt and irresponsible practices.
August 1990	Former President Nyerere steps down as chair of CCM and pronounces that, since the CCM had moved away from socialism, the single-party state no longer suited Tanzania and that a multi-party system should be considered. Mwinyi succeeds Nyerere as head of the CCM.
October 1990	Mwinyi is re-elected for a second and last five-year term with a 96 percent vote, while Salmin Amour is elected president of Zanzibar with 98 percent of the vote. CCM wins 216 of the 291 seats in the National Assembly.
February 1991	The NEC relaxes Leadership Code with proclamation of Zanzibar Declaration.
March 1991	Nyalali Commission is appointed to examine multi-party issue.
November 1991	Nyalali Commission publishes its recommendations on the establishment of a plural political system.
February 1992	Extraordinary national conference of CCM agrees to the Nyalali Commission's recommendation of multi-party system.
May 1992	CCM approves the de-linking of party and government and the switch to multi-partyism in Tanzania.
	Tanzania's and Zanzibar's Constitutions are amended to reflect the political changes.
June 1992	Mwinyi signs a bill legalizing opposition parties. National and local elections to follow.
July 1992	Tanzania officially adopts multi-party system. Several political parties are registered, but the government continues to impose restrictions on opposition activities.
December 1992	Separate office and secretariat of the CCM vice president for Zanzibar was established.

February 1993	National Assembly Parliamentary Constitutional and Legal Affairs Committee (Marmo Committee) rules that Zanzibar's membership in Islamic Conference Organization (OIC) violates the 1964 Articles of Union and the 1977 Union Constitution; both denied Zanzibar an independent foreign policy and made it an exclusive responsibility of the Union government.
August 1993	National Assembly votes unanimously to move toward establishment of a separate government for mainland.
	Zanzibar formally withdraws from OIC.
	A group of 55 mainland MPs (dubbed G55) successfully sponsors legislation in the National Assembly that calls for the establishment of a third level of government within the Union to administer the mainland separately from Zanzibar. This motion was eventually rescinded in August 1994 after Nyerere's strenuous intervention.
October 1993	CCM's National Executive Council calls for a presidential commission to assess popular feelings about the form of Union.
November 1994	Nyerere, in a publication, accuses the Prime Minister and CCM Secretary General of "poor leadership."
	Foreign donors suspend aid disbursements in protest at official connivance in widespread corruption.
February 1995	Augustine Mrema, the Home Affairs minister, is dismissed from the Cabinet and joins the opposition National Convention for Construction and Reform (NCCR-Mageuzi).
July 1995	Nyerere influences a special CCM national conference to nominate Benjamin Mkapa as the party presidential candidate in the October elections.
October 1995	First multi-party elections in thirty years are held, but logistical problems cause the electoral commission to schedule a new round of elections in some districts for November. Benjamin Mkapa is elected as President of United Republic of Tanzania and Salmin Amour the President of Zanzibar. CCM wins 186 out of 232 elective seats in the national assembly.

	CUF, despite winning 49.8 percent of the seats on the Islands, refuses to take seats in the House of Representatives.
November 1995	Benjamin Mkapa assumes office of President of the Republic of Tanzania. Mkapa enacts sweeping economic and political reforms the following year.
February 1996	Zanzibari government bans demonstrations by CUF in Southern Pemba.
October 1996	IMF and World Bank launch the Highly Indebted Poor Countries (HIPC) program.
December 1996	Warioba Commission issues report asserting corruption was widespread in the public sector.
January 1998	Commonwealth Secretary General, Chief Emeka Anyaoku, visits Zanzibar and offers to mediate between CCM and CUF. Both sides coldly receive his peace proposal.
April 1998	Religious violence in Dar-es-Salaam kills three people.
May 1998	U.N. Secretary General, Kofi Annan, lends support to Commonwealth on-going peace mediation efforts.
August 1998	A terrorist bomb outside U.S. embassy in Dar-es-Salaam kills 11 people and injures 86.
July 1998	Government appoints committee to assess public opinion on constitutional reforms.
April 1999	Mrema defects from NCCR-Mageuzi to Tanzania Labour Party (TLP).
May 1999	Mrema is banned by court from leading TLP.
June 1999	A mutual agreement, witnessed by Chief Anyaoku, is reached between CCM and CUF in Zanzibar. CCM later reneged on implementing the mutual agreement claiming that political reforms will have to wait until October 2000 elections.
September 1999	IMF and World Bank lower HIPC standards enabling Tanzania to join.

October 1999 Former President Julius Nyerere dies.

Committee assessing public opinion on constitutional reform finds 96 percent of Zanzibaris and 85 percent of mainlanders favored a "two-tier" government for the United Republic, but the committee recommended a "three-tier system."

February 2000 NEC announces various measures aimed at guaranteeing free and fair elections.

National Assembly approves draft legislation to amend Constitution in accordance with the citizens' recommendations.

March 2000 IMF and World Bank name Tanzania and 12 others as HIPC candidates.

May 2000 Zanzibari government charges CUF with 114 criminal offences, including terrorism.

July 2000 Media agrees to new guidelines, among them being objective reporting during elections.

Seven parties agrees on a code of conduct on electoral behavior; CUF, CHADEMA, TLP, and UDP refuses to sign code.

August 2000 CCM removes 40 incumbent deputies (five of them ministers) for election malpractices during the primaries.

Army troops deployed to Zanzibar to improve security during the elections. CUF claims the deployment is aimed at suppressing the opposition.

October 2000 Ben Mkapa and CCM win an overwhelming victory in national elections. Although Mkapa secured 71 percent of the votes cast, and CCM secures 244 seats in the National Assembly, claims of electoral fraud and malpractice continue to mar political transition on the island of Zanzibar.

November 2000	Political violence in Zanzibar breaks out in response to election irregularities affecting CUF. Amani Abeid Karume is declared President of Zanzibar.
January 2001	Many CUF members killed in protests in Zanzibar and hundreds flee to Kenya.
	East African Community officially launched.
April 2001	Mass protests by opposition in Dar-es-Salaam.
October 2001	*Muafaka* peace accord signed between CCM and CUF in Zanzibar, ending political violence.
November 2001	Tanzania approved for $3 billion in debt relief under the enhanced HIPC Initiative, and the resulting savings of approximately $118 million per year were mainly allocated to priority sectors including education, health, and agriculture.
January 2002	CCM and CUF agree to implement *Muafaka* to be monitored by a Joint Presidential Commission.
April 2002	House of Representatives approves amendments to the Zanzibari Constitution that relate to electoral reform.

Uganda

1894	Kingdoms of Buganda, Bunyoro, Toro, Ankole, and Busoga are declared British Protectorates.
November 1953	Kabaka of Buganda sent into exile.
October 1955	Buganda Agreement returns the Kabaka to power.
1956	Democratic Party (DP) is formed to promote a unitary independent state of Uganda.
1958	Uganda People's Congress (UPC) is formed and led by Milton Obote.
1961	DP wins majority seats in first country-wide legislative elections. DP leader, Benedict Kiwanuka, is appointed Chief Minister but is rejected by the Baganda ruling

	elite who instead form Kabaka Yekka (KY, or King Alone) to champion the Baganda interests.
April 1962	UPC wins majority seats in National Assembly.
October 1962	Uganda gains independence from Britain; under UPC-KY coalition and a federal constitution with Kabaka Mutesa II as the President and Milton Obote as the Prime Minister.
November 1964	Inhabitants of the "lost counties," two districts in Buganda, vote in a referendum to return to Bunyoro. The Kabaka refuses to endorse the results.
February 1966	National Assembly approves a motion demanding an investigation into gold smuggling in which Obote, the Defense Minister, and the Deputy Army commander, Col. Idi Amin, were implicated.
April 1966	Milton Obote suspends the 1962 Constitution and introduces an interim constitution, which withdraws regional autonomy and introduces an executive president.
	Obote becomes executive head of state.
May 1966	Army under the command of Idi Amin seizes Kabaka's palace after the Buganda Lukiiko (legislature) demanded restoration of regional autonomy.
	Kabaka flees into exile and state of emergency is declared in Buganda.
September 1967	New constitution establishing a unitary republic and abolishing traditional rulers and legislatures is adopted.
December 1969	Obote launches "Common Man's Charter" which contains a program to nationalize foreign-owed enterprises.
	Obote is wounded in assassination attempt.
January 1970	Brig. Pierino Okoye, Amin's most vocal critic, is murdered.

January 1971	Idi Amin overthrows Obote's government and imposes a brutal rule that lasts 8 years. Britain is first country to recognize Amin's government.
August 1972	Idi Amin expels Asians from Uganda. Most seek refuge in U.K., which suspends aid to Uganda. U.S. overtake Britain as Uganda's main trading partner.
September 1972	A group of pro-Obote guerrillas, led by former Chief of Staff David Oyite and Yoweri Museveni, invade Uganda from Tanzania in a bid to oust Amin from power but are repulsed with military assistance of the Soviets and Libyans.
July 1976	Amin allows Palestinian terrorists to use old Entebbe Airport after they hijack an Air France plane. In retaliation for Israeli hostages' rescue, Amin's government kills a British-Israeli passport holder who was left behind. Britain responds by breaking diplomatic relations with Uganda.
February 1977	Anglican Archbishop Luwum and two cabinet ministers are murdered in mysterious circumstances.
July 1978	U.S. announces a trade embargo of Uganda.
October 1978	Tanzania acts in defense of its territory in the Kagera salient, which had been annexed by Amin.
April 1979	Amin is overthrown by a combination of Tanzanian soldiers and Ugandan exiles. Professor Yusuf Lule becomes president of a Uganda National Liberation Front (UNLF) coalition government.
June 1979	UNLF replaces President Lule with Godfrey Binaisa, a former Attorney General.
May 1980	A Military Commission headed by Paulo Muwanga and Museveni as vice-chair overthrows Binaisa.
December 1980	Milton Obote and Uganda People's Congress (UPC) returns to power through rigged general elections. Losing candidate Yoweri Moseveni decides to wage a guerrilla war against the Obote government.

July 1985	Brigadier Basilio Olara Okello overthrows Obote and names General Tito Okello Lutwa the head of ruling Military Council and head of state.
December 1985	Uganda National Liberation Army and Yoweri Museveni's National Resistance Army (NRA) signs a peace agreement, which is not implemented.
January 1986	NRA overthrows the Military Council and Museveni is sworn in as president for a four-year interim term.
March 1986	Party activities are suspended in Uganda; but Uganda People's Democratic Movement (UPDM) is formed to challenge Museveni's leadership. Other rebel groups, the Holy Spirit Movement of Alice Lakwena and Lord's Resistance Army of Joseph Kony, are also formed.
May 1987	IMF shock treatment applied to Ugandan economy as Economic Recovery Program (ERP) begins.
May 1988	NRC passes legislation that prohibits the practice and promotion of sectarianism and introduces press censorship.
September 1988	IMF, World Bank, and Western donors make an Enhanced Structural Adjustment Facility (ESAF) available to Uganda.
February 1989	Elections are held to expand to National Resistance Councils (NRC) held – giving partial democracy.
October 1989	NRC extends the NRM interim period of rule by five years from January 1990.
March 1990	Ban on party activities extended for a further five years.
July 1990	Otema Allimadi, leader of UPDM, signs a peace accord with government.
May 1991	Museveni formally invites all emigre Ugandan Asians, who had been expelled by Amin, to return.
May 1992	Paris Club Consultative Group meeting of donors commits $800 million to Uganda.

October 1992	Uganda launches a far-reaching political decentralization program whose objective is to increase citizen participation and political empowerment.
	Government bows to pressure from the international donors and reduces the size of NRA by half.
December 1992	Constitutional Commission presents draft constitution to government.
March 1993	A draft constitution prescribing party political activities for seven years is published.
July 1993	NRC passes legislation approving restoration of traditional monarchies, which are given cultural but not political powers.
	Ronald Mutebi crowned the Kabaka of Buganda.
January 1994	Uganda Democratic Alliance (UDA) and Uganda Federal Army (UFA) suspend guerrilla activities.
March 1994	Elections held for a constituent assembly to legislate for a new constitution.
	Constituent Assembly adopts a new constitution entrenching the no-party Movement system for five years. Constitution comes in force in October 1995.
May 1994	A Constituent Assembly (CA) is elected to debate and enact a new constitution.
February 1995	IMF and World Bank establish the Ugandan Multilateral Debt Fund (UMDF).
June 1995	CA rejects the restoration of multi-party democracy.
August 1995	The CA promulgates a new constitution.
October 1995	New Uganda constitution legalizing political parties but banning their activities is adopted.
May 1996	Museveni is formally elected president in a direct presidential election under a new constitution and declares that he would not restore multi-party democracy for at least five years.

June 1996	Local and national legislative "no-party" elections are held. Local councils replace Resistance Committees, and a 276-member Parliament replaces the NRC.
October 1996	IMF and World Bank launch the Highly Indebted Poor Countries (HIPC) program.
April 1997	World Bank designates Uganda as the first country to receive HIPC debt relief.
March 1997	Local Government Act is established to guide "Local Councils." The council system encourages extensive civilian participation in the areas of local government.
November 1997	Nationwide local elections are held.
March 1998	Uganda becomes the first country to benefit from a new World Bank grant-credit initiative by receiving $185 million to improve education.
April 1998	IMF certifies Uganda's HIPC qualification.
August 1998	President Museveni orders the Ugandan army to intervene in the Democratic Republic of the Congo (DRC) to combat rebel insurgencies. The army occupies the northwest DRC for the next three years.
May 1999	Museveni offers Kony a carrot, appointment to the cabinet if he is democratically elected.
	IMF suspends $18 million loan to protest Uganda's military involvement is the DRC.
December 1999	Parliament passes bill granting general amnesty to all rebels.
January 2000	Ugandan government presents a Poverty Reduction Strategy Paper in qualifying for the Enhanced HIPC initiative.
February 2000	IMF and IDA agree to increase Uganda's HIPC relief; bringing the total to $2 billion.
March 2000	Uganda's economic reform progresses and reaches the completion point of the "enhanced HIPC framework."

June 2000	National Referendum on the restoration of a multi-party political system is held; 91 percent vote for the extending the "Movement" system for another five years.
August 2000	Supreme Court declares illegal the Referendum Act that had been passed by parliament to entrench the January 2000 referendum results into law. This decision is reversed by passage of new legislation validating the referendum.
September 2000	"Paris Club" cancels $145 million of Uganda's debt under the HIPC initiative.
March 2001	Museveni is elected to another five-year term as president.
	"No-party" presidential and parliamentary elections are held; Museveni and NRM win decisively once again.
	IMF allows Uganda to withdraw $11 million under the PRG strategies.
June 2001	Legislative elections are held.
August 2001	Kiiza Besigye, Museveni's main presidential challenger, flees to the U.S.
January 2002	Local elections are held.
May 2002	Uganda's anti-terrorism law take effect. Museveni opponents say the law will be used to curb domestic political reforms and constrain opposition politicians.
	Political Parties and Organizations Act is passed.
March 2003	Constitutional Court rules that the Movement was a political organization.
September 2003	Movement (Amendment) Bill is passed.
October 2003	National Political Commissar Crispus Kiyonga is appointed to head talks with the opposition regarding the transition to a multi-party system.

January 2004 Ugandan Supreme Court rules that the Constitutional Amendment Act 13 of 2000 was unconstitutional. Talks with opposition parties regarding the transition to a multi-party system begin.

Select Journals and Periodicals

Africa Confidential
Africa Report
Africa Today
African Affairs
African Journal of Political Science
African Studies Review
American Political Science Review
Canadian Journal of African Studies
Christian Science Monitor
Comparative Politics
The Economist
International Studies Quarterly
Issue: A Journal of Opinion
Journal of Asian and African Studies
Journal of Democracy
The Journal of Developing Areas
Journal of International Affairs
Journal of Modern African Studies
New York Times
Peace Review
Political Science Quarterly
Third World Quarterly
Washington Post
World Affairs
World Development
World Politics

Select East African Newspapers

Kenya

Daily Nation
The East African
Nairobi Law Monthly
The Standard
Weekly Review

Tanzania

African
Business Times
Daily News
The Express
Financial Times
Guardian
Majira
Mtanzania
Mwananchi
Nipashe
Rai
Uhuru

Uganda

Monitor
New Vision

Major Works Cited

Abrahamsen, R. *Disciplining Democracy: Development Discourse and Good Governance in Africa.* London: Zed Books, 2000.

Andrews, William G., ed. *Constitutions and Constitutionalism.* Princeton: Van Nostrand, 1961.

Aseka, Eric Masinde, J.S. Nabende and Martha Wangari, eds. *Political Economy of Transition in Kenya.* Nairobi: Eight Publishers, 1999.

Assefa, Hizkias and George Wachira, eds. *Peacemaking and Democratization in Africa.* Nairobi: East African Educational Publishers, 1996.

Austin, Dennis, ed. *Liberal Democracy in Non-Western States.* New York: Paragon House, 1995.

Avirgan, Tony and Martha Honey. *War in Uganda: The Legacy of Idi Amin.* Westport: Lawrence Hill & Company, 1982.

Ayittey, George B.N. *Indigenous African Institutions.* Ardsley-on-Hudson, New York: Transnational, 1991.

Barkan, Joel D., ed. *Beyond Capitalism vs. Socialism in Kenya and Tanzania.* Boulder, CO: Lynne Reinner, 1994.

Barkan, Joel D. with John J. Okumu. *Politics and Public Policy in Kenya and Tanzania.* Westport: Praeger, 1979.

Bates, Robert H. *Markets and States in Tropical Africa.* Berkeley: University of California Press, 1981.

Bayart, Francois. *The State in Africa – The Politics of the Belly.* London: Longman, 1993.

Bennett, Norman. *Kenya: A Political History: The Colonial Period.* London: Oxford University Press, 1963.

Berg-Schlosser, Dirk and Rainer Siegler. *Political Stability and Development: A Comparative Analysis of Kenya, Tanzania, and Uganda.* Boulder, CO: Lynne Rienner, 1990.

Bergsten, Arne and Steve Kayizzi-Mugerwa. *Crisis, Adjustment, and Growth in Uganda.* New York: St. Martin's Press, 1999.

Bratton, Michael and Nicolas Van de Walle. *Democratic Experiments in Africa: Regime Transitions in Comparative Perspective.* Cambridge: Cambridge University Press, 1997.

Butler, David and Austin Ranney. *Referendums Around the World: the Growing Use of Direct Democracy.* American Enterprise Institute, 1994.

Campbell, Horace and Howard Stein, eds. *Tanzania and the IMF.* Boulder, CO: Westview, 1992.

Chabal, Patrick. *Political Domination in Africa: Reflections on the Limits of Power.* Cambridge: Cambridge University Press, 1986.

Chabal, Patrick. *Power in Africa: An Essay in Political Interpretation.* New York: St. Martin's Press, 1992.

Chabal, Patrick and Jean-Pascal. *Africa Works: Disorders as Political Instrument.* Oxford: James Currey, 1999.

Clark, J.F. and David E. Gardinier. *Political Reform in Francophone Africa.* Boulder, CO: Westview, 1996.

Coulson, Andrew. *Tanzania: A Political Economy.* Oxford: Oxford University Press, 1982.

Dahl, Robert. *Polyarchy: Participation and Opposition*. New Haven: Yale University Press, 1971.

Decalo, Samuel. *Pyschoses of Power: African Personal Dictatorships*. Boulder, CO: Westview Press, 1989.

Diamond, L. *Developing Democracy: Toward Consolidation*. Baltimore: Johns Hopkins University Press, 1999.

Diamond, Larry and Marc F. Plattner, eds. *Democratization in Africa*. Baltimore: John Hopkins University Press, 1999.

Diamond, L., J. Linz and S. Lipset, eds. *Politics in Developing Countries: Comparing Experiences with Democracy*. Boulder, CO: Lynne Rienner, 1995.

Diamond, L. and M.F. Plattner, eds. *Democratization in Africa*. Baltimore: Johns Hopkins University Press, 1999.

Dicklitch, Susan. *Elusive Promise of NGOs in Africa: Lessons from Uganda*. New York: St. Martin's Press, 1998.

Doro, Marion and Newell E. Stultz, eds. *Governing Black Africa*. New York: Africana Publishing, 1970.

Engel, Ulf, Gero Erdmong and Andrew Mehler, eds. *Tanzania Revisited: Political Stability, Aid Dependency and Development Constraints*. Hamburg: Institute of African Affairs, 2000.

Feierman, Steven. *Peasant Intellectuals: Anthropology and History in Tanzania*. Madison: University of Wisconsin Press, 1990.

Franklin, Daniel P. and Michael J. Baun. *Political Culture and Constitutionalism*. Armonk: M.E. Sharpe, 1994.

Gillies, D. and M. Mutua. *A Long Road to Uhuru: Human Rights and Political Participation in Kenya*. London: West Minister Foundation, 1993.

Gordon, David F. *Decolonization and the State in Kenya*. London: Westview Press, 1986.

Gros, Jean Germain, ed. *Democratization in Late Twentieth-Century Africa: Coping with Uncertainty*. Westport: Greenwood Press, 1998.

Grugel, Jean, ed. *Democracy without Borders: Transnationalism and Conditionalities in New Democracies*. London: Routledge, 1999.

Gukiina, Peter. *Uganda: A Case Study in African Political Development*. London: University of Notre Dame Press, 1972.

Hansen, Holger, Bernt and Michael Twaddle. *From Chaos to Order: The Politics of Constitution-Making in Uganda*. Kampala: Fountain Publishers, 1995.

Hansen, Holger, Bernt and Michael Twaddle, eds. *Changing Uganda*. London: James Currey, 1991.

Hansen, Holger, Bernt and Michael Twaddle, eds. *Developing Uganda*. Oxford: James Currey, 1998.

Hansen, Holger, Bernt and Michael Twaddle, eds. *Uganda Now: Between Decay and Development*. London: James Currey, 1988.

Harbeson, John W., Donald Rothchild and Naomi Chazan. *Civil Society and the State in Africa*. Boulder, CO: Lynne Rienner, 1994.

Harbeson, John W. and Donald Rothchild, eds. *Africa in World Politics: the African State System in Flux*. Boulder, CO: Westview Press, 2000.

Harden, Blaine. *Africa: Dispatches from a Fragile Continent*. New York: W.W. Norton, 1990.

Hempstone, Smith. *Rogue Ambassador: An African Memoir*. Sawanee, TN: University of the South Press, 1997.

Hippler, Jochen, ed. *The Democratization of Disempowerment: The Problem of Democracy in the Third World*. Boulder: Pluto Press with Transnational Institute, 1995.

Human Rights Watch. *Hostile to Democracy: The Movement System and Political Repression in Uganda*. New York: Human Rights Watch, 1999.

Human Rights Watch. *State Sponsored Ethnic Violence in Kenya*. New York: Human Rights Watch, 1993.

Huntington, Samuel P. *Political Order in Changing Societies*. New Haven: Yale University Press, 1968.

Huntington, Samuel P. *The Third Wave: Democratization in the Late Twentieth Century*. Norman: University of Oklahoma Press, 1991.

Husain, Ishrat and Rashid Faruqee, eds. *Adjustment in Africa: Lessons from Country Case Studies*. Washington, D.C.: World Bank, 1994.

Hyden, Goran. *Beyond Ujamaa in Tanzania: Underdevelopment and an Uncaptured Peasantry*. Berkeley: University of California Press, 1980.

Hyden, Goran and Micheal Bratton, eds. *Governance and Politics in Africa*. Boulder, CO: Lynne Rienner, 1992.

Hyden, Goran and Rwekaza Mukandala. *Agencies in Foreign Aid: Comparing China, Sweden, and the United States in Tanzania*. London: Macmillan Press, 1999.

Ibingira, G.S.K. *The Forging of an African Nation: The Political and Constitutional Evolution of Uganda From Colonial Rule to Independence, 1894-1962*. New York: Viking Press, 1973.

Iliffe, John. *A Modern History of Tanganyika*. Cambridge: Cambridge University Press, 1979.

Jackson, Robert H. and Carl G. Rosberg. *Personal Rule in Black Africa*. Berkeley: University of California Press, 1982.

Joseph, Richard, ed. *State, Conflict, and Democracy in Africa*. Boulder, CO: Lynne Rienner, 1999.

Karugire, Samwiri. *A Political History of Uganda*. London: Heinemann Educational Books, 1980.

Kimambo, Isariah. *Penetration and Protest in Tanzania: The Impact of the World Economy on the Pare, 1860-1960*. London: James Currey, 1991.

Kpundeh, Sahr John, ed. *Democratization in Africa: African Views, African Voices: Summary of Three Workshops*. Washington, D.C.: National Academy Press, 1992.

Kuria, Gibson Kamau. *Majimboism, Ethnic Cleansing and Constitutionalism in Kenya*. Nairobi: Kenya Human Rights Commission, 1994.

Kyarimpa, G.E. *Civil Society and Political Participation in Uganda: Prospects for Consolidating Democracy*. Kampala: Makerere University, 2001.

Lipset, Seymour Martin. *Political Man*. Garden City, NY: Doubleday, 1960.

Linz, Juan and Alfred Stepan. *Problems of Democratic Transition and Consolidation*. Baltimore, MD: John Hopkins University Press, 1996.

Lofchie, Michael. *Zanzibar: Background to Revolution*. Princeton, New Jersey: Princeton University Press, 1965.

Maddox, Gregory, James Giblin and Y.Q. Lawi eds. *Nation and Nationalism in Tanzania: Essays in Honor of I.M. Kimambo*. Forthcoming, 2002.

Maghimbi, F. *Women Participation in National Affairs: The case of Tanzania*. Dar-es-Salaam: Tema Publishers Company, 1996.

Mainwaring, Scott, Guillermo O'Donnell and J. Samuel Valenzuela, eds. *Issues in Democratic Consolidation*. Notre Dame, IN: University of Notre Dame Press, 1992.

Mamdani, Mahmood. *Citizen and Subject: Contemporary Africa and the Legacy of Late Colonialism*. Princeton, NJ: Princeton University Press, 1996.

Marshall, Monty G. and Keith Jaggers. *Polity IV Project, Political Regime Characteristics and Transitions, 1800-2000*. Up-dated version available at http://www.cidcm.umd.edu/inscr/polity/index.htm.

Mbaku, John Mukum. *Multi-party Democracy and Political Change: Constraints to Democratization in Africa*. Brookfield: Ashgate, 1998.

McHenry, Dean. *Limited Choices, The Political Struggle for Socialism in Tanzania.* Boulder, CO: Lynne Rienner, 1994.

Mengisteab, Kidane and Cyril Daddieh. *State Building and Democratization in Africa, Faith, Hope, and Realities.* Westport: Praeger, 1999.

Meyns, Peter and Dani Wadada Nabudere. *Democracy and the One-Party-State in Africa.* Neuer Jungfernstieg: Institut fuer Afrika-Kunde, 1989.

Mmuya, M. *Towards Multi-party Politics in Tanzania.* Dar-es-Salaam: Dar-es-Salaam University Press, 1991.

Mmuya, Max and Amon Chaligha. *Political Parties and Democracy in Tanzania.* Dar es Salaam: Dar es Salaam University Press, 1994.

Monga, C. The Anthropology of Anger: Civil Society and Democracy in Africa. Boulder, CO: Lynne Rienner, 1996.

Monshipouri, M. *Democratization, Liberalization and Human Rights in the Third World.* Boulder, CO: Lynne Rienner, 1995.

Mugaju, Justus and J. Oloka-Onyango, eds. *No-Party Democracy in Uganda: Myths and Realities.* Kampala: Fountain Publishers, 2000.

Muriithi, Samuel M. *African Crisis: Is There Hope?* University Press of America, 1996.

Museveni, Yoweri Kaguta. *What is Africa's Problem?* Kampala: NRM Publications, 1992.

Mushi, Samuel S. and K. Mathews, eds. *Foreign Policy of Tanzania: 1961-1981.* Dar es Salaam: Tanzania Publishing House, 1981.

Mushi, Samuel S. and Rwekaza S. Mukandala, eds. *Multiparty Democracy in Transition, Tanzania's 1995 General Elections.* Dar es Salaam: Tanzania Election Monitoring Committee (TEMCO), Department of Political Science and Public Administration, University of Dar es Salaam, 1997.

Mutibwa, Phares. *Uganda Since Independence: A Story of Unfulfilled Hope.* Trenton, NJ: Africa World Press, 1992.

Mwansasu, Bismarck and Cranford Pratt, eds. *Towards Socialism in Tanzania.* Toronto: University of Toronto Press, 1979.

Ndegwa, Stephen N. *The Two Faces of Civil Society: NGOs and Politics in Africa.* Bloomfield, CT: Kumarian Press, 1996.

Nelson, J.M. and S.J. Eglinton. *Encouraging Democracy: What Role for Conditioned Aid*? Washington D.C.: Overseas Development Council, 1992.

Nelson, P.J. *The World Bank and Non-Governmental Organizations: The Limits of Apolitical Development.* New York: St. Martin's Press, 1995.

Nohlen, Dieter, Michael Krennerich and Bernhard Thibaut, eds. *Elections in Africa, A Data Handbook.* Oxford: Oxford University Press, 1999.

Nsibambi, Apolo, ed. *Decentralization and Civil Society in Uganda: The Quest for Good Governance.* Kampala: Fountain Publishers, 1998.

Nwokedi, Emeka. *Politics of Democratization, Changing Authoritarian Regimes in Sub-Saharan Africa.* Munster: LIT Verlag, 1995.

Nyang'oro, Julius E. *Discourses on Democracy: Africa in Comparative Perspective.* Dar es Salaam: Dar es Saalam University Press, 1996.

Obote, Milton A. *The Common Man's Charter.* Entebbe: Government Printer, 1970.

Ochieng', William R., ed. *Themes in Kenyan History.* Oxford: James Currey, 1991.

O'Donnell, Guillermo and Philippe C. Schmitter. *Transitions from Authoritarian Rule: Tentative Conclusions about Uncertain Democracies.* Baltimore, MD: John Hopkins University Press, 1986.

Ofcansky, Thomas R. *Uganda: Tarnished Pearl of Africa.* Boulder, CO: Westview Press, 1996.

Ogot, B.A. and W.R. Ochieng', eds. *Decolonization and Independence in Kenya, 1940-93.* London: James Currey, 1995.

Ojo, Bamidele A., ed. *Contemporary African Politics, A Comparative Study of Political Transition to Democratic Legitimacy*. Lanham, NJ: University Press of America, 1999.

Okema, M. *Political Culture of Tanzania*. New York: The Edwin Mellen Press, 1996.

Oloka-Onyango, Joseph, Kivutha Kibwana and Peter Chris Maina, eds. *Law and the Struggle for Democracy in East Africa*. Nairobi: Clari Press Ltd, 1996.

Olukoshi, Adebayo O. and Liisa Laakso, eds. *Challenges to the Nation-State in Africa*. Upsala; Nordic Institute of African Studies, 1996.

O'Neill, Norman and Kemal Mustafa, eds. *Capitalism, Socialism, and the Development Crisis in Tanzania*. Aldershot: Avery, 1990.

Othman, Haroub, et al., eds. *Tanzania: Democracy in Transition*. DUP: Dar es Salaam, 1990.

Ottaway, Marina. *Africa's New Leaders: Democracy or State Reconstruction?* Washington, D.C.: Carnegie Endowment for International Peace, 1999.

Ottaway, Marina. *Democracy in Africa: The Hard Road Ahead*. Boulder, CO: Lynne Rienner, 1997.

Oyugi, Walter, et al., eds. *Democratic Theory and Practice in Africa*. Portsmouth, NH: Heinemann, 1988.

Parenti, Michael. *Democracy for the Few*. New York: St. Martin's Press, 1995.

Pinkney, Robert. *Democracy and Dictatorship in Ghana and Tanzania*. New York: St. Martin's Press, 1997.

Pinkney, Robert. *The International Politics of East Africa*. Manchester University Press, 2001.

Polak, Jacques J. *The World Bank and the IMF: A Changing Relationship*. Washington, D.C.: Brookings Institution, 1994.

Przeworski, Adam. *Democracy and the Market*. Cambridge: Cambridge University Press, 1991.

Ronen, Dov. *Democracy and Pluralism in Africa*. Boulder, CO: Lynne Rienner, 1986.

Sahn, David E., Paul A. Dorosh and Stephen D. Younger, eds. *Structural Adjustment Reconsidered: Economic Policy and Poverty in Africa*. Cambridge: Cambridge University Press, 1997.

Sartori, Giovanni. *Parties and Party Systems, A Framework for Analysis*. Cambridge: Cambridge University Press, 1976.

Schatzberg, Michael, ed. *The Political Economy of Kenya*. New York: Praeger, 1987.

Schmitz, G.J. and E. Hutchful. *Democratization and Popular Participation in Africa*. Ottawa: The North South Institute, 1992.

Sheriff, Abdul. *Slaves, Spices and Ivory in Zanzibar*. London: James Currey, 1987.

Shivji, Issa. *Class Struggles in Tanzania*. Dar es Salaam: Tanzania Publishing House, 1976.

Siegan, Bernard. *Drafting A Constitution for A Nation or Republic Emerging into Freedom*. George Mason University Press, 1994.

Sklar, Richard L. and C.S. Whitaker. *African Politics and Problems in Development*. Boulder, CO: Lynne Rienner, 1991.

Sundet, Geir, ed. *Democracy in Transition, The 1995 Elections in Tanzania*. Oslo: Norwegian Institute of Human Rights, Human Rights Report No. 8, June 1996.

Tamale, Sylvia. *When Hens Begin to Crow: Gender and Parliamentary Politics in Uganda*. Boulder, CO: Westview Press, 1999.

Tanzania Elections Monitoring Committee. *The 2000 General Elections in Tanzania: Report of the Tanzania Election Monitoring Committee*. Dar es Salaam: TEMCO, 2001.

Tanzania Elections Monitoring Committee. *The 1995 General Elections in Tanzania: Report of the Tanzania Election Monitoring Committee*. Dar es Salaam, 1997.

Thompson, Kenneth W., ed. *The U.S. Constitution and Constitutionalism in Africa*. Lanham: University Press America, 1990.

Throup, David and Charles Hornsby. *Multi-party Politics in Kenya*. Oxford: James Currey, 1998.

Tripp, Aili Mari. *Changing the Rules: the Politics of Liberalization and the Urban Informal Economy in Tanzania*. Berkeley: University of California Press, 1997.

Udogu, E.I., ed. *Democracy and Democratization in Africa: Toward the 21st Century*. Leiden, The Netherlands: E. J. Brill, 1997.

Vanhanen, Tatu, ed. *Strategies of Democratization*. Washington: Crane Russack, 1992.

Watson, Ann, ed. *Modern Kenya*. Lanham: University Press of America, 2000.

Wekkin, Gary D. *Building Democracy in One-Party Systems: Theoretical Problems and Cross-Nation Experiences*. Westport: Praeger Publishers, 1993.

Widner, Jennifer. *Building The Rule of Law*. New York: W. W. Norton, 2001.

Widner, Jennifer. *The Rise of a Party State in Kenya: From "Harambee!" to "Nyayo!"*. Berkeley: University of California Press, 1992.

Widner, Jennifer, ed. *Economic Change and Political Liberalization in Sub-Saharan Africa*. Baltimore: Johns Hopkins University, 1994.

Wiseman, John A. *Democracy in Black Africa: Survival and Revival*. New York: Paragon House Publishers, 1990.

Wiseman, John A. *The New Struggle for Democracy in Africa*. Aldershot: Avebury, 1996.

Wiseman, John A., ed. *Democracy and Political Change in Sub-Saharan Africa*. London: Routledge, 1995.

World Bank. *Adjustment in Africa: Reforms, Results and the Road Ahead*. Washington, D.C.: World Bank, 1994.

World Bank. *Can Africa Claim the 21st Century?* Washington, D.C.: World Bank, 2000.

World Bank. *Sub-Saharan Africa: From Crisis to Sustainable Growth*. Washington, D.C.: World Bank, 1989.

Wunsch, James S. and Dele Olowu, eds. *The Failure of the Centralized State: Institutions and Self-Governance in Africa*. Boulder, CO: Westview Press, 1990.

Yeager, Rodger. *Tanzania: An African Experiment*. Boulder, CO: Westview, 1982.

Young, Crawford. *The Colonial State in Comparative Perspective*. New Haven: Yale University Press, 1994.

Young, Crawford. *Ideology and Development in Africa*. New Haven: Yale University Press, 1982.

Index